Fooled by Technical Analysis

MICHAEL HARRIS

Published by MICHAEL HARRIS, 2025.

FOOLED BY TECHNICAL ANALYSIS

First edition. October 31, 2025.

ISBN: 979-8232430917

Written by MICHAEL HARRIS.

To my wife, Natalia: This one is for you. Thank you!

The most important facts are those which can be used several times, those which have a chance of recurring... Which, then, are the facts that have a chance of recurring? In the first place, simple facts. Jules Henri Poincaré, 1908

DISCLAIMER

CFTC RULE 4.41 – HYPOTHETICAL OR SIMULATED PERFORMANCE RESULTS HAVE CERTAIN LIMITATIONS. UNLIKE AN ACTUAL PERFORMANCE RECORD, SIMULATED RESULTS DO NOT REPRESENT ACTUAL TRADING. ALSO, SINCE THE TRADES HAVE NOT BEEN EXECUTED, THE RESULTS MAY HAVE UNDER-OR-OVER COMPENSATED FOR THE IMPACT, IF ANY, OF CERTAIN MARKET FACTORS, SUCH AS LACK OF LIQUIDITY. SIMULATED TRADING PROGRAMS IN GENERAL ARE ALSO SUBJECT TO THE FACT THAT THEY ARE DESIGNED WITH THE BENEFIT OF HINDSIGHT. NO REPRESENTATION IS BEING MADE THAT ANY ACCOUNT WILL OR IS LIKELY TO ACHIEVE PROFIT OR LOSSES SIMILAR TO THOSE SHOWN.

The trading methods, systems, and patterns included in this book are for informational purposes only, and none are recommended. Past results do not guarantee future results, so using any of the methods or techniques shown may not yield trading profits. This material is not a solicitation for any order to buy or sell. Trading stocks, futures, options on stocks or futures, exchange traded funds, or forex involves substantial financial risks and may result in a total loss of capital.

PREFACE

Most traders use technical analysis because of its wide acceptance but are not aware of its pitfalls. Trading the markets profitably and doing it consistently for an extended period requires an understanding of the myths, traps, and limitations of technical analysis. Although most books focus on the methods of technical analysis, there is a definite lack of publications that concentrate on its limitations. This book primarily aims to address this gap, and I believe we have successfully done so.

When I started trading in the late 1980s, my quantitative background helped me understand and avoid some pitfalls. My objective in writing this book is to convey the knowledge I have accumulated in the past 25 years and to help readers avoid getting fooled by technical trading methods that have no chance of ever being profitable.

Technical analysis is a broad body of knowledge based on the study of price and volume time series to trade the markets. There are several different levels of technical analysis, but in this book, I focus on four of them that I think are fundamental in the sense of the pitfalls involved and the effectiveness of the methods used: Level I refers to naive technical analysis, Level II to expert technical analysis, Level III to naive quantitative analysis, and Level IV to expert quantitative analysis. The second part of this book is structured around these four basic levels of technical analysis.

Most technical analysis books that were available when I started as a trader were based on principles and techniques developed in the early twentieth century. I soon realized that one of the fundamental problems of classical chart patterns was that the books included mostly profitable formations and few unprofitable ones, indicating significant selection bias. More importantly, there was no mention of the statistical distribution of the returns of such patterns. After doing some detailed studies, I determined that the selection bias was large, and there was no way of knowing in advance, or even after its confirmation, whether some classical chart pattern would behave as a reversal or continuation formation. This conclusion was true irrespective of market conditions, i.e., regardless of whether the pattern was formed at the top or bottom of an uptrend or downtrend. I further realized that any claims that a head and shoulders pattern, for example, formed at the top of an uptrend would signal a trend reversal were in most cases based on wishful thinking, and there was no rigorous justification behind such claims.

Thus, in the late 1980s, I concluded that technical analysis based on chart patterns without detailed statistics differed little in the way it made its claims from the practice of astrology. I also tried to avoid falling victim to the fallacy of reversing the burden of proof; if classical chart patterns could facilitate profitable trading, then those who promoted these techniques, not their users, bore the responsibility to provide evidence for that claim. Such proof was impossible because these patterns, despite occasional symmetrical formations, are mostly artifacts of random price motion. I discovered that by generating random price series, these patterns naturally emerge as they do in actual price data. I then decided to abandon this part of the technical analysis, and I started developing trading systems based on well-defined indicators, including moving averages, oscillators, relative strength, etc., an area of technical analysis that was becoming popular while I began trading.

I started developing mechanical trading systems in the late 1980s for trading commodities, fixed income, and currency futures. Developing trading systems was fun, especially when one is young and energetic, but it is a process that is time-consuming and full of pitfalls, as it turned out. I was a user of early backtesting programs and technical analysis software. I soon found out that, in addition to the difficulties inherent in trading, some of the software that offered backtesting capabilities had flaws and limitations that were probably unknown to the majority of users. More important was the fact that, in some cases, such programs generated false results. I then decided to develop my software for analyzing price action and backtesting systems to ensure that I would not become a victim of retail software limitations and bugs. That was a decisive step that helped me win third and fourth place in a prestigious, year-long futures trading contest with real account money. It was also the first step into the uncharted territory of quantitative trading, which led to a long journey.

One definition of quantitative trading is that this type of trading involves the use of mathematics and computers to identify profitable sequences of entries and exits in a market and timeframe of choice. This approach to trading became feasible in the past 40 years due to the rapid progress in information technology. Before that, traders found it tedious to calculate a few moving averages of the closing price, and only those with access to expensive and bulky mainframe computers could accomplish real-time calculations of indicators. The advent of the microcomputer changed everything, and quantitative trading started becoming popular in the mid-1980s. Many traders abandoned the "old way" of dealing with the markets that involved visual inspection of charts for patterns and turned to computers for help in analyzing price action.

One of the main advantages of quantitative trading is that it is based on results obtained from historical analysis of performance, a process known as backtesting. Most trading methods that can be described mathematically can be backtested, and as a result, quantitative trading gained popularity when backtesting software programs were developed for public use in the mid-1980s. However, when abused, backtesting can work against a trader rather than in their favor. Another advantage of quantitative trading is that it facilitates automated trading. Medium- and high-frequency trading became possible only because of quantitative analysis, coupled with technological progress.

The quantitative approach to trading has many pitfalls, and even though technology has allowed an increase in the speed of developing trading systems and analyzing them, the generation rate of unprofitable systems has also increased. The main cause of the generation of unprofitable systems is data-mining bias, which is the result of the dangerous practice of reusing data and testing many trading models to identify profitable ones. When one finds an edge that seems to be validated on out-of-sample data, it may be due to curve-fitting in the in-sample and good performance in the out-of-sample by chance. This condition often occurs because accepting a good result ignores many other results that were bad or not as good. Another fundamental problem of quantitative trading is the optimization of system parameters, a process that can result in curve-fitting performance to historical data. In general, curve-fitted systems are not robust because they fail as soon as market conditions change from those that were encountered during the backtesting process. It is effortless for trading system developers, especially novice ones, to fall victim to data-mining bias and curve-fitting, a process that facilitates data fishing. Traders must become aware of the importance of minimizing the negative impact of such practices and avoid ending up using trading systems that are not robust to changing market conditions with known results.

Developing robust trading systems that can deliver consistent profits is a complex but potentially rewarding task that requires an understanding of what distinguishes an edge from a fluke. Getting fooled by data-mining bias and spurious correlations through the constant reuse of historical data is probably the most important obstacle to overcome. Minimizing the negative effects of curve-fitting is another challenge trading system developers constantly face. Equally important is the proper application of risk and money management. Based on my 25 years of experience in this field, most technical traders are fooled by randomness and employ market timing methods that reflect spurious correlations. Even worse, some elect to trade in timeframes and markets that do not allow consistent profits due to their microstructure. In this book, I discuss some key factors that impact the profitability of quantitative trading systems and provide a set of rules for maximizing their robustness. Before that, I discuss some basic concepts and market realities that all technical traders must know and understand in depth.

Structure of the book

This book is divided into two parts. Part I is called "Basic Concepts" and includes basic notions that every trader, systematic or discretionary, should understand in some depth. Chapter One lists the four levels of technical analysis, which are part of the foundation for Part II of the book. Chapter Two introduces the notion of trading expectation and the solution to the paradox of trading system inversion. This charter aims to clarify the issues with trading expectation, a misunderstood concept. Chapter Three focuses on the notion of the risk of ruin and its importance, as well as the need to realize a high win rate. This chapter also includes specific methods for determining initial capital requirements. Chapter Four examines the impact of trading friction, such as commissions and slippage, and choice of timeframe on capital requirements. Specific examples and detailed analysis show that some trading timeframes cause technical traders with insufficient capital to lose money, even when the trading cost is low.

Part II is called "Fooled by Technical Analysis" and it is based on the classification of the basic levels of the technical analysis presented in Chapter One as the foundation for demonstrating why naïve chartists and quants are being fooled by random price action and have a low chance of ever profiting from the markets. Then, there is a discussion of the methods expert chartists and quants use to confront the perils of technical analysis and profit from the markets. Chapter Five specifically debunks the myths and issues with charting and shows how random patterns can deceive chartists. We also present major cognitive biases that contribute to the high failure rate among chartists. Next, we introduce the concept of expert charting and discuss its application in maintaining a competitive advantage. Chapter Six begins with an introduction to backtesting, which is the main tool of quant traders, with special emphasis placed on its pitfalls. The two main methods of developing trading systems are then introduced: analysis and synthesis, along with a discussion of the three main factors that contribute to data mining bias and ways of dealing with them. At the end of Chapter Six, a set of rules for increasing the effectiveness of trading system development is presented. Chapter Seven discusses practical methods of determining position size and controlling risk. Chapter Eight briefly discusses a few alternatives to technical analysis, some of which suffer from the same issues, such as data-mining bias and the creation of erroneous correlations.

Why you should read this book

You should read this book because it was not written to promote technical analysis; instead, it represents an effort to help traders understand and deal with its flaws and pitfalls. I decided to write this book after receiving requests for it from my blog readers; they are the main motivation behind this work.

I am grateful for the emails I have received, providing support for my efforts in educating traders about the risks involved when using technical analysis without a proper understanding of its limitations. The three trading books I wrote in the past were introductory and did not deal with some of the more important but also more inherently complex problems of technical analysis that are discussed in this book, such as curve-fitting, data-mining bias, and validation. This book goes beyond my earlier works, exploring the myths and traps of technical analysis as well as the factors influencing trading profitability, including strategies for addressing these issues. Anyone who has attempted to trade using a system or a technical method, in automated or discretionary mode, will find the material invaluable. More importantly, traders who continue using naïve technical analysis methods may get valuable hints as to why their approach to trading the markets fails or even the reasons that temporary positive results can be mostly attributed to luck. In this book, I also deal with some widely held misconceptions about trading system development; for example, one of them is that out-of-sample testing validation suffices for developing robust systems or that statistical hypothesis testing can be applied to trading system development. I believe that such misconceptions have contributed to trader failures, and I present specific alternatives for dealing with their limitations.

I strongly recommend reading Part I thoroughly, starting with Chapter One and the four levels of technical trading. Next, I suggest focusing on Chapter Two, which introduces the concept of expectation. It is important to understand the impact of small trade samples on the chances of discovering a true edge, and this chapter provides the foundation for that. The risk of ruin is an important notion that is related to the win rate, and it is the subject of Chapter Three. This chapter also provides useful methods for determining initial capital requirements. Going through the examples in Chapter Four will assist the reader in understanding how capitalization and trading friction impact profitability when trading in different markets and timeframes. Some markets and timeframes are not suitable for technical low- to medium-frequency retail trading because they are too expensive or efficient to provide any profit opportunities.

I also strongly recommend going through Chapter Five, where the reasons are discussed as to why trading based on chart patterns and indicators is not profitable. Chapter Six is a must-read for quants that rely on backtesting. I invite all quantitative trading system developers to use the methods presented in this chapter to test their systems against randomness and curve-fitting.

Most traders fail because they have no clear concept of risk and money management and use spurious correlations for generating entry signals. The profits of the winners come from the losses of the losers, who outnumber them significantly due to a lack of skill and knowledge. This book intends to provide the knowledge necessary for developing the skill to join the winner group while avoiding the pitfalls of technical analysis.

What this book is not about

This book assumes that the reader is familiar with the basic principles of logic, mathematics, and the scientific method. This book will not serve as an introduction to this important body of knowledge. It is easy to write a book that is filled with an elementary discussion of the principles of science. Instead, the objective of this book is to first expose some of the problems and limitations of technical analysis and then set the foundations of trading system development at a more advanced level. This book does not make promises of an effortless path to wealth by trading the markets but it shows traders how to avoid making mistakes by exposing the traps and fundamental mistakes of technical trading. No one can become a successful trader without first understanding how to avoid the obstacles in achieving this goal.

PART I

Basic Concepts

CHAPTER ONE
Levels of Technical Analysis

Technical analysis is a diverse method of trading the markets. In this chapter, I present a classification of technical analysis levels that are then used throughout this book as a guide to exposing its myths and various pitfalls, as well as in developing a path towards profitability. Each level of technical analysis uses a different methodology and requires different knowledge, skills, and experience.

Level I Naïve chart analysis

Retail traders, some authors of well-known trading books, and even some analysts working for banks and funds perform this kind of analysis the most. This type of analysis is usually based on facts about price action, such as "Yesterday, the S&P 500 index tested its 30-day moving average support and then rebounded." This method is an after-the-fact analysis that mostly relies on looking at charts or having software automatically look at charts based on certain criteria to detect different price and volume patterns. In addition, this type of analysis is often used as the starting point in attempts to forecast future price direction or establish price targets. This kind of analysis is rather limited because it rarely estimates the mathematical expectation or the likelihood of pattern success. Confirmation bias is another problem with this kind of analysis; for example, a Level I technical analyst will only look at the patterns on a chart that support his bias, even though there may be several others that reveal a different story about market direction. Even without confirmation bias, this analysis cannot prevent it. Confirmation bias can affect statements about the market that are not backed up by quantitative analysis. Such an effect makes this type of analysis problematic to begin with and almost useless for long-term profit, unless the person making the statement has a unique skill and a strong track record.

Scanning for chart pattern formations, such as head and shoulders or triangles, without knowing their success rate, i.e., the percentage of winners, and also the associated payoff ratio, which is the ratio of the average winning to average losing trade, is an ambiguous practice, as we will see with specific examples in Chapter Five, unless one qualifies as a Level II expert chartist. Specifically, trendlines and resistance/support levels, including the simple use of technical indicators, are not useful unless one knows the profit expectation, the associated win rate, and the payoff ratio. A Level I technical analyst typically recalls only the instances when his method was successful, reinforcing a self-enhancing cognitive bias, while often overlooking the occasions when it did not succeed. This level of analysis has a negative profit expectation because of trading friction effects (commission and spread cost), as will be discussed in more detail in Chapter Five. Simultaneously, this method serves as a widely promoted approach to trading in the financial media, leading to the growth of an entire industry that awards degrees and titles to its students. Some individuals in that industry exhibit the cognitive bias known as the backfire effect, attacking critics by selectively presenting examples of their visual method's past successes while ignoring, undermining, or avoiding discussion of more recent failures. Even worse, some of the promoters of the visual charting methods, when confronted, make an *appeal to authority*, which is an informal logical fallacy, by claiming that the method was invented by an indisputable authority in this area many years ago and was documented in a book he wrote, which they then do not hesitate to call the "Bible of technical analysis."

Level I technical analysis methods in the form of books or courses are widely available to retail traders, even through brokerages, with vague warnings about limitations and pitfalls. Users of online technical analysis services can scan thousands of stock charts to identify a few where a head-and-shoulders pattern has formed or a trendline has been violated, while ignoring many other charts where the same conditions occurred and the result was against expectations. These tools are available to anyone with Internet access, but they can't make money because most scanner results show patterns from random price action that Level I traders can't profitably exploit.

Level II Expert chart analysis

Type II technical analysis differs significantly from the naïve Level I type because it is performed by those who are experts in evaluating price action due to their experience with the markets. One use of technical analysis at this level is as a risk management tool rather than a market timing method. Often, a Level II trader has a good feel for market direction and uses technical analysis to assist her in adding to positions, reducing exposure, or exiting an open position. The proportion of traders who succeed with this type of analysis is small, and these traders often struggle to convey their knowledge to others because navigating the market at this level requires eliminating cognitive biases and managing emotions, which relates more to psychology than to technical trading. More importantly, a Level II experienced trader may not always interpret classical chart patterns and indicator signals along the same lines as a Level I technical trader. For example, in the early 1990s, I met some people who were developing software to identify classical chart patterns, but not for trading them in the usual way described in books or taught in courses, but instead for fading them because they believed that there was more profit potential in doing that than in applying technical analysis the classical way.

Level II technical traders understand that when some major pattern is about to be formed, there will be some reaction from Level I traders, who thus attempt to establish positions in advance and make the bulk of the profit before the crowd jumps in. Chapter Five presents specific examples along these lines. This phase is probably the most intriguing, but also the hardest, aspect of mastering Level II technical analysis. The majority of those who attempt to operate at this level fail because they do not have enough experience with price action dynamics. This level of technical analysis is suitable for people with many years of "screen time" experience. One cannot just buy software tools and try to compete with this group of traders because it would be like an average driver buying a race car and trying to beat experienced race car drivers in their game.

Level III Naïve quant analysis

A group of traders that first appeared in the late 1980s used this type of analysis. The popularity of the method is still growing due to the proliferation of strategy-backtesting tools in the form of standalone software or online services. However, in reality, this group faces the same fate as the Level I group, despite doing significantly more work crunching numbers. A naïve quant uses software, standalone or web-based, to program and backtest trading algorithms on historical data, and this process often involves optimizing a few parameters to maximize performance objectives. One issue is that the performance of trading algorithms changes with market conditions, and most of the time, algorithms that pass profitability tests on historical data exhibit false correlations due to curve-fitting. As a result, randomness frequently succeeds in fooling the naïve quant. Even "loose fits" can cause the algos to fail; overfitting isn't necessary. Chapter Six provides more details and examples.

There are a lot of new online services that let you do backtesting, and you can obtain free software that even uses neural networks or genetic algorithms. This approach has given technical traders a false sense of progress in this area. However, most users of this technology are doomed to fail because of the bias inherent in any number-crunching process that utilizes data in a repeated fashion. Backtesting can only reject a trading system if it fails on historical data. Backtesting cannot predict whether a system that worked in the past will continue to do so, as that depends on future market conditions. If one includes several indicators in a system and optimizes their parameters, then the chances of this system performing well in the future are, for all practical purposes, zero. The system will fail if the parameters' value, based on past market conditions, changes. Even worse, some of the spurious systems pass all of the validation tests and even statistical hypothesis testing, as discussed in more detail in Chapter Six. Naïve use of quant analysis leads to trading that is indistinguishable from gambling, i.e., Level III technical traders are essentially gamblers but in a game with unknown odds and payoffs, unlike those of casinos, where both the odds and payoffs are well-known in advance.

Level IV Expert quant analysis

Expert quants know the limitations of quantitative methods based on backtesting and also understand the impact of data-mining bias on the chances of finding a true edge. They attempt to develop techniques to address these realities of quantitative trading that increase the probability of future profitability of the systems they develop. This task is time-consuming and requires diverse skills, including programming knowledge, applying statistical methods, and performing system simulations. Many hedge funds operate at this level, and for this purpose, they employ well-qualified scientists to crunch numbers the correct way. There are different approaches to Level IV trading and analysis, and the discipline is a rapidly growing field.

Expert quants seek to determine if luck or intelligence is responsible for a trading system's performance. Often, the methods used to analyze systems in order to distinguish between luck and intelligence are more important than the methods used to generate those systems, and they are considered an integral part of the competitive advantage of expert quants. Specific examples are presented in Chapter Six, along with a set of rules for increasing the chances of success when using either analysis or synthesis of trading systems.

The four levels of technical analysis presented in this chapter will be used in Part II of this book as the foundation for exposing some of the myths, traps, and pitfalls of this method of trading the markets.

CHAPTER TWO
Trading Expectation

The first step in the path of a technical trader toward consistent profitability is to understand what trading means from a quantitative perspective. Essentially, the goal of trading is to consistently generate profits through the application of a clearly defined edge. Regardless of the traded market and timeframe, having an edge allows realizing a positive average trade, denoted in this book as AvgT, over some time t during which N trades are executed. The following equation provides the average trade:

$$AvgT = (\sum W - \sum L)/\, N \quad (2.1)$$

where $\sum W$ is the sum of winning trades, $\sum L$ is the sum of losing trades (in absolute value), and N is the number of trades.

The trading edge may come in the form of a well-defined algorithm that generates market entry and exit signals and maintains a sufficiently high average trade AvgT, as defined by Equation 2.1, over a sufficiently long period t, over which performance is evaluated. Although this definition of a trading edge satisfies the profitability requirement, it is nevertheless problematic. To demonstrate this, we will first show that the average trade defined in Equation 2.1 can also be expressed by the following equation:

$$AvgT = w \times avgW - (1\text{-}w) \times avgL \quad (2.2)$$

where w is the win ratio, avgW is the average winning trade, and avgL is the average losing trade (in absolute value). This definition of average trade assumes a finite number of independent trades N made in a period t.

Proof

Equation 2.1 is equivalent to:

$$AvgT = \sum W/N - \sum L/N \quad (2.3)$$

Note that avgW = ∑W/Nw and avgL = ∑L/NL, where Nw and NL are the number of winning and losing trades, respectively. Therefore, ∑W = avgW × Nw and ∑L = avgL × NL and after inserting these definitions into Equation 2.3, we obtain the following result:

$$AvgT = avgW \times Nw/N - avgL \times NL/N \quad (2.4)$$

Next, note that by definition, Nw + NL = N, i.e., the sum of the number of winning and losing trades yields the total trades. Then, with the use of this requirement, Equation 2.4 becomes

$$AvgT = avgW \times Nw/N - avgL \times (N - Nw)/N \quad (2.5)$$

Equation 2.5 is equivalent to:

$$AvgT = avgW \times Nw/N - avgL \times (1 - Nw/N) \quad (2.6)$$

Note that Nw/N = w, since the win fraction w is equal to the number of winning trades divided by the number of total trades. Then Equation 2.6 can be written as follows:

$$AvgT = avgW \times w - avgL \times (1 - w) \quad (2.7)$$

Thus, we have shown that Equations 2.1 and 2.2 are equivalent under the assumptions stated. Note that the right-hand side of Equation 2.7 is not the trade expectation E[T], as often stated in the trading literature, although it has a similar form. The trading expectation is the mean of the distribution of the trade profit/loss, which is defined as follows for n discrete trades:

$$E[T] = \sum T_i p_i \quad i = 1,2,\ldots,n \quad (2.8)$$

where T_i is the trade profit/loss of the ith trade and p_i is the probability of T_i.

The good news from the above result (Equation 2.7) is that the average trade can be calculated by summing all trades and then dividing the result by their number. The bad news is that the resulting quantity, AvgT, is not in general equal to the expectation E[T], which is the mean of the distribution, or the average of the population of the trades of the system, but only the arithmetic average of a sample of trades that was generated in a specific period t. These two quantities are different for the majority of systems developed via backtesting. The calculated expectation may be positive and large if the trade sample is not representative of the population and the distribution's mean is zero. Under actual trading conditions and as more trades are generated, the average trade AvgT may decrease significantly, and a trading system may lose any apparent edge based on a small sample of trades. In this book, we will delve deeper into this fundamental problem of trading system development and attempt to address it.

In practice, AvgT in Equation 2.1 will be different from E[T] in Equation 2.8, but we desire that it stay positive throughout the trading activity. We also desire that AvgT is sufficiently large, is not severely affected by trading friction, and results in a return above the "risk-free" interest rate or the rate realized by buying and holding a benchmark index. We also want the variance of trading system returns to be small so that the resulting equity curve is as smooth as possible and free of large swings. However, note that for any trading system, both the expectation and the variance of returns are path-dependent and have values that are, in general, not constant in time. Therefore, a trading system that has an average trade (AvgT) greater than 0 until time t = t1 may stop being profitable for times greater than t1 if market conditions change, which could lead to an average trade (AvgT) of less than or equal to 0. Certain tests can be performed to lower the chances of this occurring, which will be discussed in Chapter Six.

In Ref. 12, page 4, this author also discusses the issue of expectation convergence.

There is a fundamental problem with quantitative trading strategy evaluation that renders it ineffective in most cases. Consider the following two sequences of returns: {0.1, 0.1, -0.1, 0.1, 0.1, -0.1, 0.1, 0.1, -0.1, 0.1}, {-0.1, -0.1, -0.1, 0.1, 0.1, 0.1, 0.1, 0.1, 0.1, 0.1}. In both these cases, the win fraction is 0.7, the average return is 0.04 and the standard deviation is 0.0967. However, the maximum drop in equity for the first sequence is 10% but for the second sequence, it is about 33%. A drop over 20% to 25% could be a cause of abandoning a strategy or the closure of a fund. Therefore, when analyzing trading strategies we are not only interested in a positive average trade, which is a simple average, which will be achieved at some point in the future but whether time averages will not result in excessive losses. The latter is a much more difficult problem since trading strategy equity is path-dependent while realizing the true expectation of the population does not depend on the path but only on a sufficiently large sample of trades. The fundamental problem of strategy evaluation is that the average of a sample converges to the expected value, or mean of the distribution, only at the limit of sufficient samples (Papoulis, 1965).

Note that in the case of trading strategies, due to non-stationarity and path dependence, a sufficient sample might be absent. Therefore, another objective of a trading strategy developer is to identify strategies for which a sufficient sample already exists that allows for determining expectations.

The need for large trade samples

As shown in Equation 2.7, the average trade AvgT looks like the expectation E[T] of a random variable whose values are AvgW and -AvgL with probabilities w and w-1, respectively. But AvgT will only be the same as the expectation E[T], which is given by Equation 2.8, if the samples are big enough (Ref. 1, page 138). Only when the number of trades is sufficiently large does the average of their values converge to their distribution mean. If the trade sample is small and not representative of the population of trades, then AvgT may decrease towards zero or even turn negative after trading friction is accounted for, as more trades are generated forward in time and its value converges to the mean E[T]. In other words, the average may not be accurate if the number of trades is too low. In general, the number of trades required so that AvgT converges to the average of the population, also called the mean and denoted by E[T], depends on the form of the distribution. For a normal distribution, several thousand trades may be required for the calculated AvgT to be within 1% of the population average. But in reality, systems that are tested on historical data and found profitable usually generate a small sample of trades. In that case, hypothesis testing may be used to determine whether the calculated average trade AvgT is significant, and that may be achieved by calculating the t-statistic, which is equal to the Sharpe ratio times the square root of the number of years over which the trade sample was generated (Ref. 2).

$$\text{T-statistic} = \text{Sharpe ratio} \times \sqrt{\text{Number of years}} \quad (2.9)$$

The null hypothesis to test is that the system is not profitable. For example, if the t-statistic is about 3 and trade returns are normally distributed, then the probability that the system is a fluke is less than 1%. Therefore, tests on longer historical series are desirable because they help obtain a large t-statistic. It is important to realize that this statistical analysis assumes an independent test. In reality, data-mining bias occurs due to multiple tests that are not independent; specifically, the results of one test are used to enhance the results of subsequent tests. In that case, it has been suggested that the t-statistic is adjusted to account for the bias arising from multiple tests. This adjustment might be inadequate because a more fundamental issue exists: the test examines the profitability of backtesting results on specific historical data, rather than the null hypothesis of zero profitability. This argument is true even if it is assumed that the distribution of the population that has mean E[T] can be constructed using nonparametric methods such as bootstrapping of system returns, as was proposed in Ref. 10. Obtaining a normal distribution of the average trade AvgT via bootstrapping due to the application of the law of large numbers does not equate to knowing the trade distribution with the mean E[T]. This difference is crucial, and it makes the results of statistical hypothesis tests very unclear and even useless when it comes to trading systems. One can often curve-fit or "data mine" a system to attain a high Sharpe ratio, which is needed in Equation 2.9 to achieve a high t-statistic. This limitation makes it easy to cheat on these kinds of tests. Therefore, additional tests that detect curve-fitting and data-mining bias must be performed to ensure the significance of the results of trading system development, and such testing often requires large trade samples so that the average trade converges to the expectation E[T]. As we shall see in Chapter Six, one way of achieving these goals is by testing trading systems on a sufficiently large number of comparable securities.

In the case of trading systems, hypothesis testing is often the wrong application of statistics because the primary cause of system failures is changing market conditions that render optimized and data-mined systems unprofitable. All systems are optimized in some way or another with respect to some objective function, even if that function is not explicitly known. As a result of these facts, some trading system developers are more interested in the robustness of systems than in their statistical significance. In general, robustness and statistical significance are not directly related to each other. The more market conditions and trade samples encountered during development, the more robust a system will be. In simpler words, statistical hypothesis testing cannot compensate for, or even correct, the lack of exposure to a sufficient range of market conditions. In a similar way to how symmetrical but random patterns deceive Level I chartists, statistical hypothesis testing frequently fools Level III quants.

The trade sample size required in the case of an intraday trading system is much larger than that required in the case of daily trading systems, approximately by a factor equal to the square root of the number of intraday bars in a daily bar. For example, in the case of 5-minute stock trading during regular trading hours, this factor is approximately equal to 8.8, or the minimum sample size should be about 9 times the sample size required in the case of daily data (square root of 6.5 x 60/5). Note that if the win rate is close to 50%, as is the case with random trading, the difference between daily and intraday systems becomes less relevant as the required sample size for significance is huge anyway. However, a detailed analysis of the impact of small trade samples on trading system performance is outside the scope of this book. The key point for the reader to realize is that statistical hypothesis testing is valid only in the case of independent tests and sufficiently large representative samples of the population, but this is hardly the case in practical trading system development. Again, this is because an apparent statistical edge may be the result of data mining and cease to be profitable when market conditions change. When a quant realizes that, he is ready to move to the next level and towards profitability. Hypothesis testing has limited practical use in trading system development, which is why this book will not cover it in detail. In Chapter Six, we will employ other, more practical methods to test the significance of trading system results. This book aims to educate the reader about practical trading system development, rather than focusing on fancy hypothesis testing that is inapplicable and potentially misleading.

After introducing the notion of expectation and briefly discussing some fundamental issues associated with it, we can now proceed to discuss the paradox of inverting a trading system.

The trading system inversion paradox

After becoming frustrated with negative performance and the difficulty of maintaining a positive average trade profit/loss during actual trading conditions, a trader might hypothesize that it could be easier to find a system designed to lose and then reverse its signals for profit. However, as the trading system inversion paradox shows, identifying a consistently losing strategy to invert and profit from is as difficult as identifying a consistently profitable strategy. This is because the trade expectation from frictionless random trading must be exactly zero, i.e., $E[T] = 0$. Due to streaks of losing trades and the wealth-out effect brought on by trading friction, which includes commission fees, bid-ask spreads, and slippage, some traders frequently accumulate large losses. If enough time is allowed, the expectation ($E[T]$) may turn positive. But often, the trader is ruined before that due to capital constraints, and this is one reason why it is not an empirical fact that random traders under low friction conditions break even. Chapters Three and Four present specific examples of how trading friction affects profitability. There may also be instances of traders who perform worse than random, as they not only use a random strategy for entering and exiting the market but also implement poor risk and money management strategies. The choice of a risk and money management strategy may skew the distribution of returns for better or worse. For example, pyramiding positions when performance is persistently negative may cause ruin.

$$\text{AvgT} = w \times \text{avgW} - (1\text{-}w) \times \text{avgL} \quad (2.10)$$

where w is the win fraction, avgW denotes the average winning trade, and avgL indicates the average losing trade (in absolute value). Let us assume that we have a consistently losing system such that, over a sufficiently long time, the average trade is negative. Thus, from equation 2.10, we determine that:

$$w \times \text{avgW} - (1\text{-}w) \times \text{avgL} < 0 \quad (2.11)$$

Next, let us consider the following transformation:

$$T\text{: } \{z = (1\text{-}w),\ \text{avgW}' = \text{AvgL},\ \text{avgL}' = \text{avgW}\} \quad (2.12)$$

In the transformation *T* above, we define a win fraction *z* that is equal to 1-w and corresponding average win and average loss quantities. After applying the transformation 2.12 to Equation 2.11, we obtain the following:

$$(1\text{-}z) \times AvgL' - z \times AvgW' < 0 \quad (2.13)$$

After rearranging equation 2.13, we obtain:

$$z \times AvgW' - (1\text{-}z) \times AvgL' > 0 \quad (2.14)$$

Equation 2.14 gives the average trade AvgT' of a new system, where the win fraction of the losing system w in Equation 2.11 is now the loss fraction (1-z), and the average winner and average loser become the new average loser and new average winner, respectively. This is an inverted system with a positive average trade, even if the system in equation 2.1 has a negative average trade. If the original system in Equation 2.10 experienced losses over a sufficiently long period of time, then the inverted system described by Equation 2.14 will show gains over that same duration. Therefore, finding a consistent loser is as demanding as finding a consistent winner because of the transformation defined by Equation 2.12. This result does not take into account trading friction and undercapitalization since consistent losses may be due to undercapitalization combined with high commissions and slippage.

An important ramification of the above analysis is that fading a losing trader will only work if he is a consistent loser before trading friction is applied. However, this is difficult to establish from limited samples, as the trader may be a temporary loser due to a non-stationary average trade, AvgT, and his method may turn profitable in the future. Another important ramification of this analysis is that most traders that get ruined are not consistent losers but are instead victims of insufficient capitalization and bad risk and money management because being a consistent loser is as hard as being a consistent winner.

In the next chapter, we will discuss the risk of ruin in more detail. The risk of ruin is an important notion, although many traders are either unaware of it or underestimate its importance. However, as we will also show in Chapter Four, some markets and timeframes naturally drive to ruin traders that are not sufficiently capitalized, and this phenomenon occurs primarily due to the high cost of trading.

CHAPTER THREE

Risk of Ruin and Trading Capital Requirements

The risk of ruin, which is related to the probability of exhausting the trading capital, is a subject that lacks comprehensive treatment in the trading literature. One reason for this is the fact that determining the risk of ruin in trading systems is not as simple as determining the risk of ruin in a game of tossing a coin or in casino games with known payoffs. In general, the probability P(ruin) associated with the use of a specific trading system depends on the particular path that the system follows, the starting capital, and trading friction (commission and slippage). As a result, a complex stochastic function that describes P(ruin) may not even have a closed-form solution in most cases.

Below is a list of six causes of trading account ruin:

- Broker failures
- Company bankruptcies
- Exchange flash crashes
- Central Bank policy changes
- Undercapitalization
- Low win rate

Unpredictable events beyond the trader's control are the first four causes of trading account ruin. In the case of broker failures, such as those that have occurred in the last several years, the trader may never be able to recover account funds, and essentially, that amounts to total ruin. Company bankruptcies can result in significant losses related to stock investing and, in certain cases, a total account loss. Exchange flash crashes are rare events but can happen, as the recent past has shown. During a flash crash, there is the possibility of liquidation by the broker. That, combined with a decision by the exchanges not to cancel fills, can lead to total ruin. These are all low-probability events that are beyond the control of a trader.

The decision by the Swiss National Bank on January 15, 2015, to abandon the policy of a Swiss Franc peg to the euro created havoc in the forex market and caused the total ruin of forex trading accounts that exploited this market inefficiency. If a trading strategy depends on a specific policy and also uses leverage to take advantage of price differences from set targets, it can quickly result in complete loss when that policy ends, which often happens unexpectedly and without warning.

Another major cause of trading account ruin is undercapitalization, which leads to an excessive drawdown, especially in the presence of high trading friction. Undercapitalization is the main cause of trading system failures and the ruin of retail traders. As we shall see in the next chapter and with specific examples, undercapitalization along with trading friction makes it even harder to identify a profitable system that can avoid ruin in daily timeframes and seriously constrain the set of profitable systems in the case of intraday timeframes. Losses can accumulate when a trading system fails to perform as expected and its profit factor (the ratio of the total value of winning trades to the total value of losing trades) falls below 1, potentially leading to an excessive drawdown.

Equity drawdown depends on the number of losers as a percentage of total trades and streaks of consecutive losers. In turn, the number of losers during a certain period depends on the win ratio of the trading system, which is the ratio of the number of winning trades to the total number of trades. A low win ratio is a major cause of the ruin of traders. One way of minimizing the drawdown of a potentially profitable system is by maximizing its win rate, which is the win ratio times 100. Note that the closed trade drawdown of a trading system with a 100% win rate is equal to 0% when calculated based on closed trade profit. However, the maximum open trade drawdown can get so large that it could cause ruin depending on leverage and available equity, as in the case of a flash crash. Note that in this book, all references to drawdown levels refer to the maximum open trade drawdown calculated based on intraday highs and lows.

All traders must understand what is achievable within a timeframe and market of choice before putting the effort into developing a system and committing funds to trade it. Traders profit not only from the use of profitable and robust trading systems but also because some other traders lose money. If a market is such that it distributes profits and losses evenly among participants in the long term, regardless of the trading method used or skill level, then profiting from trading may be difficult or even impossible. Trading friction acts as a constant "wealth-out" effect, and thus profiting from some markets and timeframes in the longer term is impossible unless there is a substantial edge. The first objective of every trader should be to identify when opportunities for profit are present and when there are few or none. Examples of analyzing markets and timeframes for profitability are presented below, based on a method that allows establishing minimum requirements for account capitalization so that the probability of ruin is minimized.

Risk of ruin due to undercapitalization

Undercapitalization is the number one cause of trader failures, even in the presence of a theoretically sound trading methodology that possesses an edge. Every experienced trader knows that, but, as it turns out, many novice traders are often too optimistic about performance prospects in the short term, and they believe they can get away with an undercapitalized account. Things are worse when leverage is employed in addition.

In the summer of 2000, as an invited speaker, I delivered a presentation at a trading conference in New York City. Part of my presentation was on the subject of the risk of ruin and proper account capitalization. After explaining what consecutive losers are, how they contribute to drawdown, and that getting 4, 5, or even 7 consecutive losers is normal in trading, I wrote down the following simple formula that can be used during the initial phase of determining proper account capitalization in the special case when the percent risk is fixed, for example, 2% of starting capital:

$$\text{Minimum capital} = \text{Amount risked per trade} / \text{Percent risk}$$

Usually, the stop-loss determines the amount of risk per trade. The percent risk specifies what percentage of the account is risked on each trade. For example, if a swing trader of E-mini futures risks $500 on each trade, and each time only 2% of the initial equity should be at risk, then the required trading account equity is equal to $500/0.02 or $25,000 per contract traded. However, let us assume that the trader starts with $5,000 in the account instead of $25,000. The trader knows that the initial equity is low, and an attempt is made to set stops as tight as possible without severely impacting the profitability of the trading method. The modified trading system risks $350 on each trade instead of $500. The corresponding risk can be calculated after rearranging the above equation as follows:

Risk percent = Amount risked per trade/Minimum capital

In the case of the tighter stop of $350, the risk percent turns out to be $350/$5,000 = 0.07, or 7%. This means that 7% of the account is risked on each trade. With 7% of the initial capital risked on each trade, a $5,000 account will be reduced to $3,600 after 5 consecutive losers and to $2,550 after 7 consecutive losers. If the trader cannot cover margin requirements, then any open positions will be liquidated. A reduction of the probability of ruin requires lower risk, for example 2%, and in that case, the proper account equity is determined by the original formula and is equal to $350/0.02 or $17,500. The difference between the two accounts is a respectable 250%, or, in other words, a $5,000 account is undercapitalized by a factor of 2.5 for a 2% fixed percent risk.

I attempted to explain the above basic facts during the mentioned trading conference, along with some additional details that included the determination of minimum capital for futures trading systems that also take into account drawdown estimates. Shortly after I finished my presentation, someone from the organizing committee told me that a group of individuals rushed to her office and complained that I was discouraging them from trading because none of them had more than $5,000 to start with. That did not come as a surprise to me. I expected this type of reaction, especially from traders who were doomed to be fooled by technical analysis, given that the bulk of the presentations at the conference were about some ambiguous chart patterns, like triangles and wedges. As we shall see in more detail in Chapter Five, the use of chart patterns cannot lead to a profitable trading method unless the trader has a lot of experience with price action.

Around the time of my presentation, the Dow Jones Industrial Average index had reached a new all-time high. There was a dot-com bubble, but the bust had already started. Many technical traders, after failing in swing and position trading due to their low capitalization, decided to enter the day trading arena. They either discovered it on their own or received directions from those who realized that reducing the risk per trade to a few ticks was the only way to keep the capitalization requirements low. When the E-mini futures were launched, intraday traders were able to risk a few ticks on each trade, like the equivalent of \$50 to \$100. Some even tried and are still trying one tick stop, or \$12.5 per contract per trade. This technique certainly lowers the capitalization requirements. For example, a 4-tick stop with a \$50 loss and 4% risk per trade requires \$1,250 in account equity, which is less than the margin requirement. There is a catch here.

Volatility is the catch. All types of market participants, but particularly random traders and automated robots, generate a lot of noise in intraday timeframes, frequently in the form of a random walk. This effect neutralizes any small trading edges due to the commission wealth-out phenomenon. If, for example, the commission cost is about 10% of the average winner for scalpers (traders who chase a few ticks) and the winning bias is only 5%, or a win rate of 55%, then it is difficult to make money. One way to avoid ruin is by increasing the edge substantially or decreasing the risk-to-reward ratio, something that is challenging to achieve in those timeframes. These structural constraints doom the majority of scalpers with small edges. Only those with a substantial edge, a low commission cost, and a low risk-to-reward ratio manage to survive. Then, there is high-frequency trading (HFT). In markets where HFT operates, poorly capitalized traders are dealt with by rapid order placement that essentially creates an additional commission effect by front-running orders, thus increasing the demand for even larger winning edges to levels beyond what is realistically possible. Scalping the equity markets is considered dead at this point, and most active traders have increased their timeframes to beyond 5 minutes, some to 30-minute intervals, or even longer to avoid HFT algos.

An example of an undercapitalized system

An example of how an undercapitalized account can lead to ruin is the application of a simple strategy for trading overnight changes in daily SPY ETF data. The strategy fully invests all of the available equity at the close of the day and sells the full position at the following open. The pseudo-code for this system is shown in Pseudo Code 3-1. In the case of zero commission and $10,000 starting capital, this simple strategy has generated a net return of 385% in SPY ETF from 01/29/1993 to 02/03/2011, as shown by the equity curve plotted in Figure 3-1.

```
N=integer(equity/close) //calculate number of shares

Buy N shares at the close //buy signal

exit at the next open //exit signal, sell N shares;
```

Pseudocode 3-1. A system for trading overnight market changes

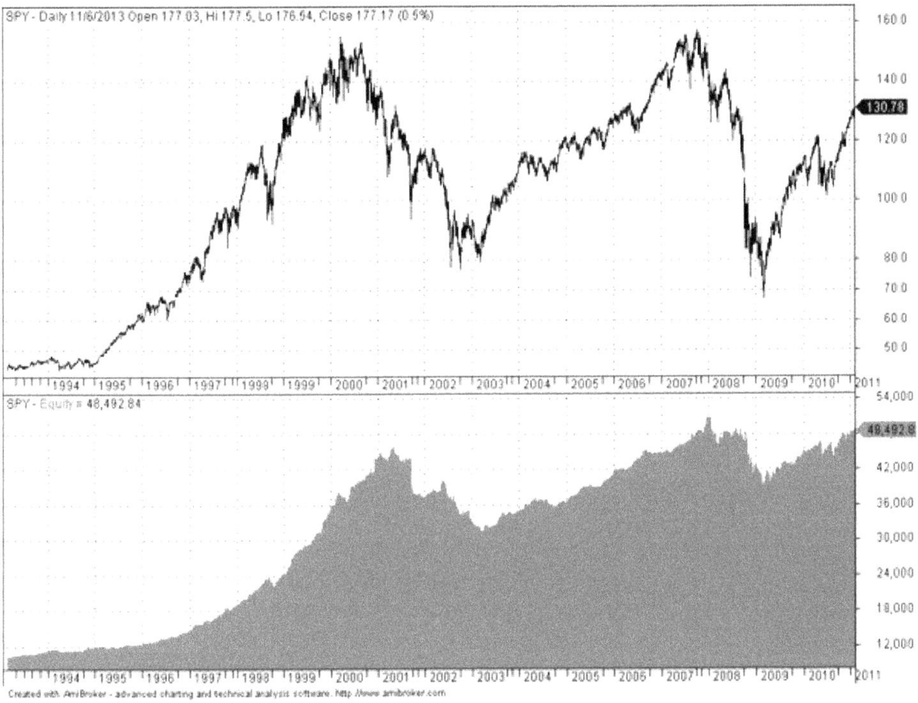

Figure 3-1. Equity Curve of a trivial SPY ETF trading system with $10,000 starting capital and $0 commission per trade. Net return: 385%. Period: 01/29/1993–02/03/2011

Next, if a commission rate of $7 per trade is introduced, which is a typical rate paid by users of some retail stock trading platforms, the equity of this system drops to zero fast, and ruin occurs, as shown in Figure 3-2. The equity curve is a straight line downward, and ruin takes place in about 3 years.

Figure 3-2. Equity Curve of a trivial SPY ETF trading system with $10,000 starting capital and $7 commission per trade. Ruin occurs. Period: 01/29/1993 –02/03/2011

Table 3-1 shows the values of a few key performance parameters of this system for various starting capital levels and a $7 commission rate. Even a starting capital of $20,000 can lead to ruin. For starting capital of $75,000 and $100,000, this trivial SPY ETF trading system has generated net returns of 214% and 257%, respectively. Figure 3-3 shows the equity performance in the latter case.

Starting Capital	Drawdown %	Ruin date	Return %
10,000	-100	04/09/1996	-
20,000	-100	05/13/2003	-
50,000	-38	-	128
75,000	-36	-	214
100,000	-38	-	257

Table 3-1. Performance of the SPY ETF trading system in Pseudocode 3-1 for various starting capital levels and $7 commission per trade

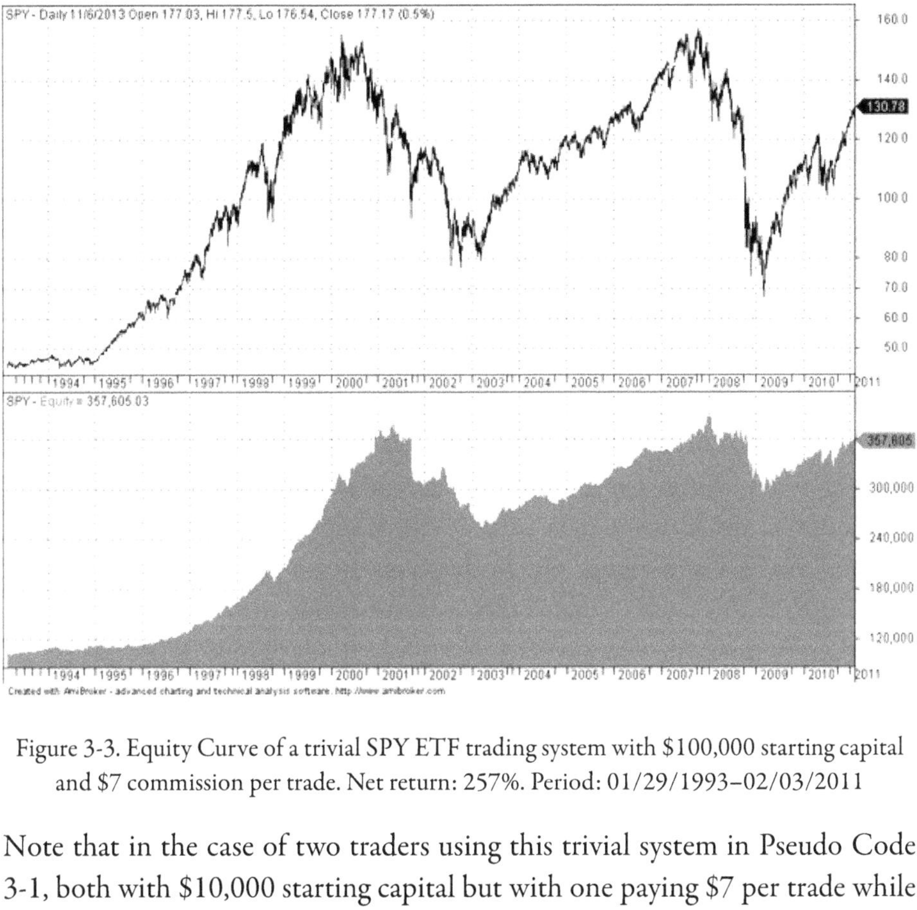

Figure 3-3. Equity Curve of a trivial SPY ETF trading system with $100,000 starting capital and $7 commission per trade. Net return: 257%. Period: 01/29/1993–02/03/2011

Note that in the case of two traders using this trivial system in Pseudo Code 3-1, both with $10,000 starting capital but with one paying $7 per trade while the other pays one cent per share, the former is ruined and ends up with no money in the account because he is undercapitalized for the specific market and trading friction levels, while the latter enjoys a compound annual return of close to 3.2% and a final equity of about $17,700.

Trading systems whose performance depends on starting capital and trading friction are often not scalable. They will only work well above a certain minimum starting capital level and when trading friction is low. An example of this is the simple system that trades overnight changes in Pseudo Code 3-1. In this example, it was undercapitalization combined with trading friction due to commissions that caused total ruin, as shown in Figure 3-2. Even in the case of a constant position size of 100 shares, this system would have generated a drawdown of -100% by March of 1996 for $10,000 in starting capital and a commission of $7 per trade. The commission charged per trade must drop below $2 for this system to break even and start making a profit.

The risk of ruin is path-dependent, which means it depends on how the price series changes over time. If there is insufficient capital and the trading friction is the same, a system that worked in some markets, like in Pseudo Code 3-1, may not work in others.

Risk of ruin and win rate

The risk of ruin for a trading system depends on several parameters, including its win rate. The lower the win rate, the higher the risk of ruin. In the ideal case where the commission was set to 0, the main cause of ruin for undercapitalized accounts was the low win rate of the SPY trading system, as illustrated in Pseudo Code 3-1 and Figure 3-1. In this case, the win rate was equal to 55%, meaning that 55% of the total trades were profitable. After the introduction of trading friction, the win rate dropped substantially because trades with tiny returns turned to losers when the position size was small. When the position size was large, as in the case of a $100,000 account, the relative impact of trading friction was small when a fixed cost was applied per trade and the win rate was preserved. The preservation of the win rate after the introduction of friction should be a primary objective of trading system developers in medium- to high-frequency trading. If the theoretical, friction-free win rate is adversely impacted after trading friction is introduced, then ruin is a possibility.

In the special case where ruin is caused by consecutive losers and fixed fractional position sizing is employed, the dependence on the win rate can be seen in the following equation:

$$P(\text{ruin}) = (1\text{-}w)^R \quad (3.1)$$

where P(ruin) is the probability of risk of ruin and it ranges from 0 to 1, w is the win ratio, and R is the inverse of risk percent, i.e., the inverse of the percentage of the initial capital at risk. Although this equation applies only in the special case when the risk percent is fixed, it nevertheless provides useful insight into how the win rate impacts the probability of ruin. For a fixed risk percent, the probability of ruin increases as the win ratio w decreases, in a power-law fashion. Ruin due to a streak of consecutive losers is a special case, but it is used here to illustrate the importance of a high win rate. A high percentage of traders get ruined because they believe that they can be profitable in the long term even if they are wrong more often than they are right in the short term, provided that they win multiples of what they lose on average. What they underestimate is how the win rate is related to the risk of ruin through generations of streaks of losing trades.

For example, let us consider an investor who follows a wrong analyst 70% of the time, but he claims to make four times as much as he loses when he wins. The investor puts at risk 20% of his capital each time he receives a call from the analyst. After applying Equation 3.1, we calculate the probability of five consecutive losers that will cause ruin, as follows:

$$P\{Ruin\} = (1 - 0.30)^5 = 0.17 \text{ or } 17\%$$

i.e., the investor's chances of losing his capital due to consecutive losers are 1 in 6, a high probability by all standards.

In the above example, the analyst is theoretically profitable in the long term, assuming infinite capital, because his average profit factor approaches 1.70 as the number of trades increases. But after five losing trades, ruin may come, and it doesn't help that the analyst can profit long-term. Five wrong calls in a row translate to ruin, even though the next 10 calls may be correct. The above scenario is a case where an appeal to average quantities, such as a high-profit factor or a high compound annual return (CAR), does not suffice for making an investment or trading decision because of the effect of short-term consecutive losers. When the win rate is low, ruin can strike before long-term averages are achieved.

It may be seen that P(ruin) in the above example is independent of capital but depends on risk percent and win rate. This is a simple case because, in general, the risk percent depends on the starting capital. In the majority of cases, P(ruin) is impossible to calculate, but it explicitly depends on the win rate. Therefore, contrary to common misconceptions that the win rate's value is insignificant as long as the profit factor remains positive, it is crucial and should be maximized to reduce the risk of ruin. Those who underestimate the importance of a high win rate do so because they underestimate trading risk. Some market wizards in the past hinted at the importance of win rate when they talked about *high-probability setups*. Chapter Five demonstrates the relationship between the win rate and several other crucial performance metrics.

Low win rate impact on trend-following system performance

A low win rate also adversely impacts the performance of hedge funds and CTAs (Commodity Trading Advisors) that operate in longer-term trading timeframes. Despite popular misconceptions, a low win rate does not only impact the probability of ruin of intraday and short-term trading systems but also that of longer-term trend-following systems. Choppy markets reduce the effectiveness of trend-following algorithms by accumulating short-term losses, and shorter trend durations reduce their profitability by reducing any gains from trends. The result is a lower payoff ratio (the ratio of the average winning trade to the average losing trade) and a low win rate. Note that these two quantities, the payoff ratio and win rate, uniquely determine the profit factor, as shown below. Trend-following system developers often believe they can get away with a low win rate, provided the profit factor is high enough. This fix worked well in equity and a few other markets during the strong uptrend of the 1990s. After the dot-com crash and the bear market that followed, volatility increased in the equity markets, and after another period of low volatility during the uptrend that led to the top of 2007, trend volatility increased, although this fact may not be reflected in popular volatility measures such as the VIX and annualized standard deviation of returns. In essence, trends in many markets have become choppier, although daily changes are smaller than in previous years.

There is a trade-off between the win ratio w and the payoff ratio R (the ratio of average win to average loss) that impacts trend-following systems. As one attempts to increase the win ratio, the payoff ratio usually decreases. As a consequence, the profit factor PF (the ratio of the sum of winners divided by the sum of losers) either remains constant or decreases. The profit factor PF is related to the win ratio w and payoff ratio R as follows (Ref. 3):

$$PF = w \times R / (1 - w) \quad (3.2)$$

The required value of R is obtained by rearranging Equation 3.2 to yield

$$R = (1-w) \times PF / w \quad (3.3)$$

If the win ratio is 0.35 and the profit factor PF is 2, then the required value of R is 3.175, obtained after plugging these values into Equation 3.3. If w is increased to 0.50, then, as a result, R must be at least equal to 2 to maintain the same profit factor of 2.

An example that shows how a change in market conditions has affected the win rate and robustness of trend-following systems is the well-known 50-200 moving average crossover system. This is a long/short symmetric system that establishes long positions when the 50-day simple moving average crosses above the 200-day simple moving average, and it exits and reverses to short positions when the opposite crossover occurs, as shown in Pseudo Code 3.2. This system has performed well in SPY ETF since its inception in 1993 and even during 2008, with a return of about 34% for that year. Figure 3-4 shows the equity performance of this system from 01/29/1993 to 04/23/2010. The starting capital is $100,000, the commission rate is 1 cent per share, and the equity is fully invested at all times.

N=integer(equity/close) //calculate number of shares

If MA(50) crosses above MA(200) then Buy N shares at the close //buy signal

If MA(50) crosses below MA(200) then Short N shares at the close //short signal

Pseudocode 3-2. The 50-200 moving average crossover system

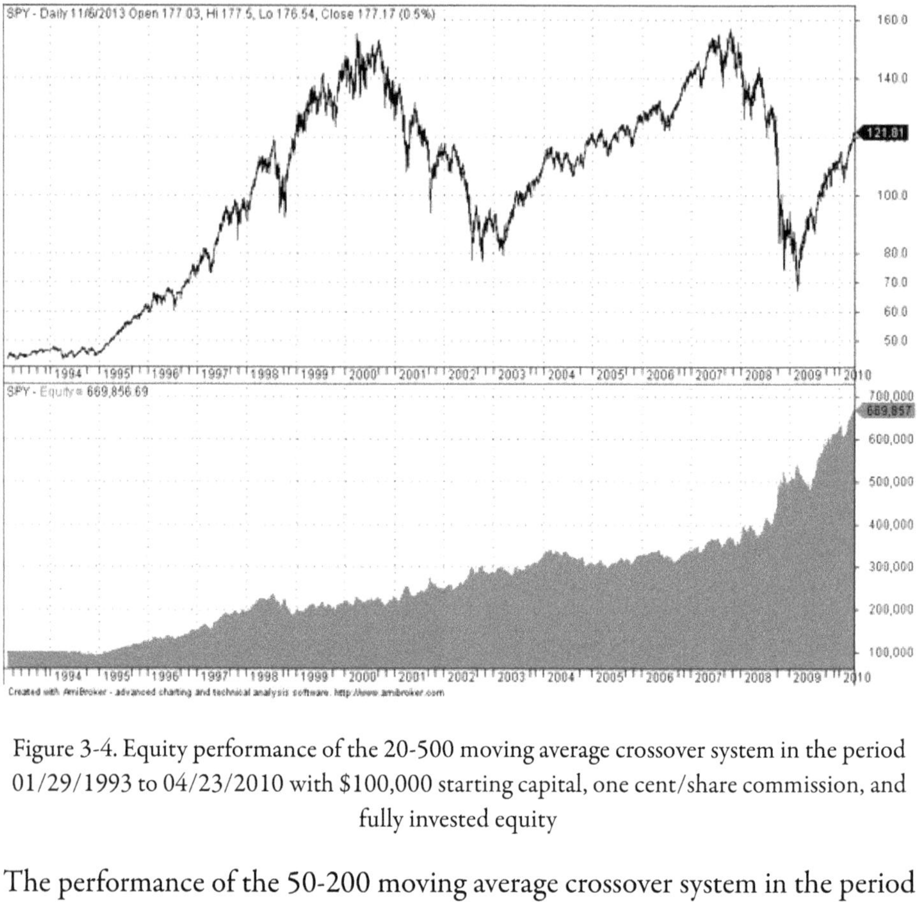

Figure 3-4. Equity performance of the 20-500 moving average crossover system in the period 01/29/1993 to 04/23/2010 with $100,000 starting capital, one cent/share commission, and fully invested equity

The performance of the 50-200 moving average crossover system in the period shown in Figure 3-4 is positive, although the maximum drawdown in 1999 was -29%. The win rate is 60% on a total of 15 trades, 8 long and 7 short; the profit factor is 8.39; the payoff ratio is 5.59; and the net return is 527%, which translates to a compound annual return of 11.44%. These results may appear excellent, but one must not rely solely on past performance because it is easy to be fooled by technical analysis and limited data samples.

In forward testing, from 04/23/2010 to 11/06/2013, the performance of this moving average crossover system deteriorated because market conditions and trend dynamics changed. Figure 3-5 shows the equity performance. The system equity dropped to produce a maximum drawdown of -38%. The net rerun is negative at -14%. The payoff ratio is only 0.94, and the win rate drops to 40%, resulting in a profit factor of 0.61.

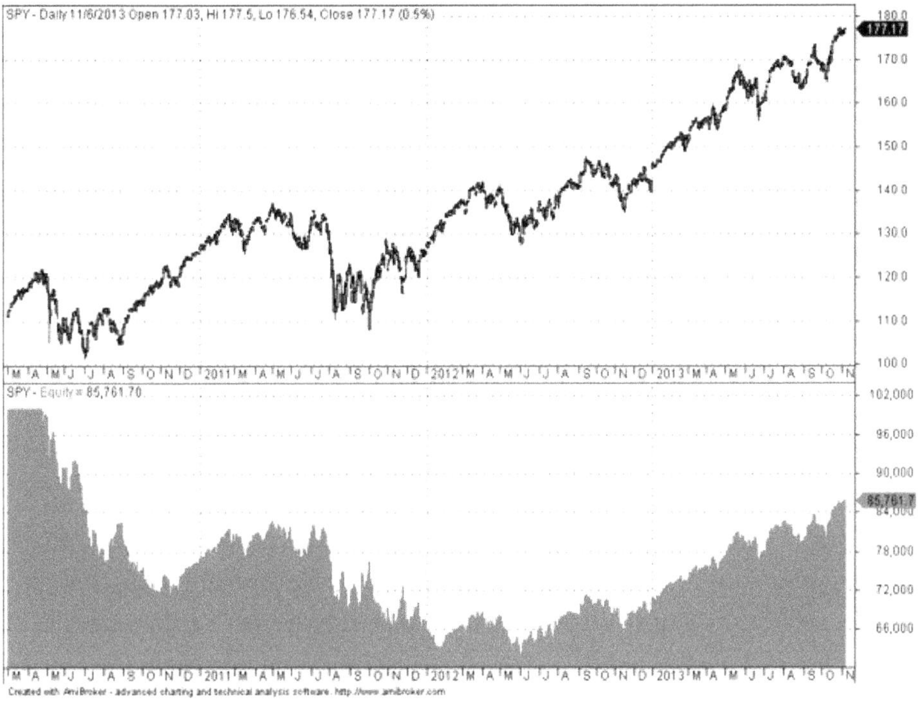

Figure 3-5. Equity performance of the 20-500 moving average crossover system in the period 04/23/2010 to 11/06/2013 with $100,000 starting capital, one cent/share commissions, and fully invested equity

One factor that contributed to the performance degradation of this popular moving average crossover system during the specific test period was its inability to maintain a high win rate during choppy market periods. Testing this system over the combined period from 01/29/1993 to 11/06/2013 reveals a win rate of approximately 58%. However, even for a trend-following system of this kind, 58% is a marginal win rate, and the system risks ruin in the future if markets stay choppy for an extended period. Even a starting win rate of about 60%, based on the performance in Figure 3-4, may not suffice to guarantee low drawdown levels in the future. After a -38% drawdown, as in the case of the results in Figure 3-4, some funds are liquidated or experience a high rate of redemption, and most retail traders are discouraged with the prospects of trading. These drawdown levels can result in devastating conditions, both financially and psychologically, that must be avoided in advance by careful analysis of the markets and their potential, as well as by ensuring that a system can maintain a high win rate during adverse market conditions. These tasks are not trivial, but achieving profitable trading requires hard work, knowledge, and skill.

Often, technical traders are fooled by randomness into believing that they have an edge that is robust enough to deliver consistent profits, but when market conditions change and the win rate decreases, there is significant performance degradation. Technical analysis is full of traps and pitfalls, as we shall see in the second part of the book, in Chapters Five and Six, where the former deals with traditional charting techniques and the latter with quantitative analysis.

Determining initial capital requirements

The correct determination of initial trading capital is of paramount importance to trading success. Many traders, especially novice ones, usually think that they can succeed by risking small amounts. However, as we saw in the example of the system in Pseudo Code 3-1, the choice of initial trading capital can make the difference between satisfactory performance and total ruin. In general, the objective is to determine the proper initial trading capital amount so that performance is maximized and the expected drawdown is minimized. This is a complex non-linear stochastic optimization problem of the general form:

$$max\text{CAR},\ min\text{DD}$$

with respect to C and subject to constraints

where CAR is the compound annual return, DD denotes the maximum drawdown, and C represents the initial capital. The constraints may include an upper limit on trading capital, a maximum drawdown (DD), and bounds for other variables and metrics. The solution to the above optimization problem, if it exists at all, depends on the path followed by the trading system.

In the past, several authors have recommended using the maximum drawdown for determining the minimum initial trading capital required. The maximum drawdown is determined by backtesting a trading method on historical data. However, the maximum drawdown is a random variable whose value depends on the path followed. Therefore, we need a measure of the expected maximum drawdown. We can only obtain this measure using historical data, and we have to ensure that we have explored as many adverse conditions as possible, but in ways that make sense and are guided by our problem. One method to determine the minimum initial trading capital required for a specific trading system is based on simulations that include:

1. Random entries, time-based exits
2. Random entries, actual exits
3. Random entries and random exits

Note that all three variations do not apply to all trading systems and timeframes. Deciding which method to apply is based on experience.

1. Random entries, time-based exits

This method can be used in the case of mean-reverting systems that do not use any stops. First, we determine the average bars in trade. Then, we perform a simulation with random entries and time-based exits using the average bars in a trade as the number of bars to exit after the entry. In the example below, we apply this method to the WR2 system. This strategy is a long-only mean-reverting system that takes long positions in a market when there are two consecutive losing days and exits the trade if there are two consecutive winning days, as shown in Pseudo Code 3-3.

N=integer(equity/close) //calculate number of shares

If two-day losing streak then Buy N shares at the next open //buy signal

If two-day winning streak then Exit at the next open//exit signal

Pseudocode 3-3. The WR2 mean-reverting system

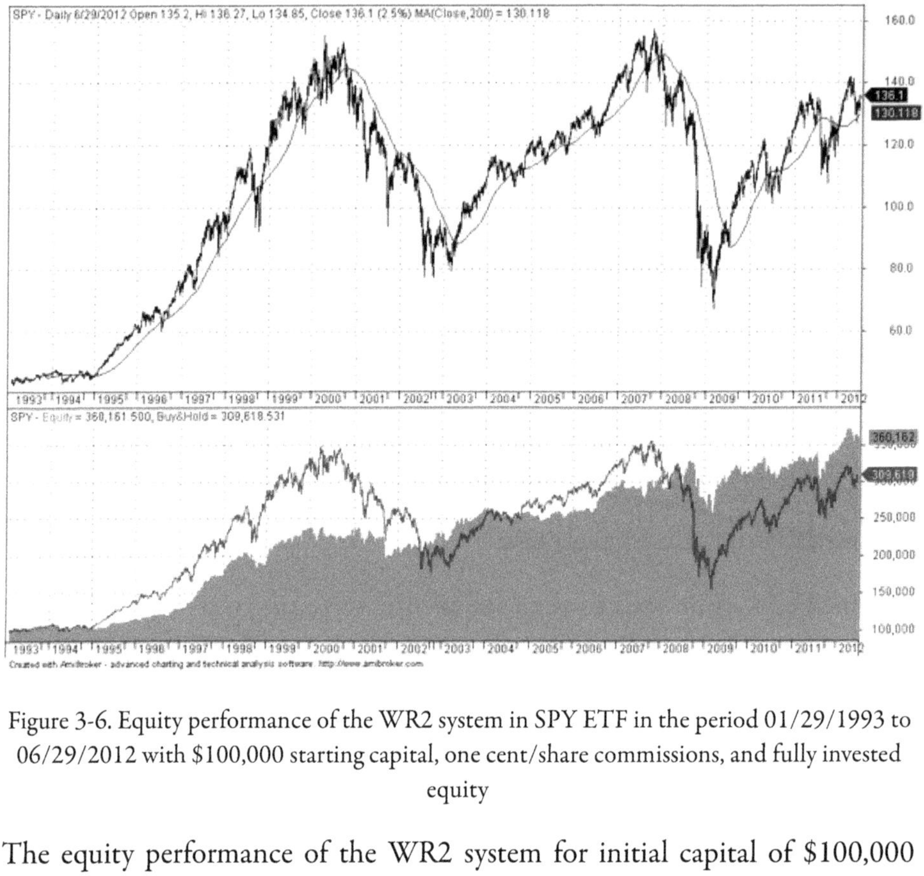

Figure 3-6. Equity performance of the WR2 system in SPY ETF in the period 01/29/1993 to 06/29/2012 with $100,000 starting capital, one cent/share commissions, and fully invested equity

The equity performance of the WR2 system for initial capital of $100,000 and $0.01/share commission in SPY ETF with data from 01/29/1993 to 06/29/2012 is shown in Figure 3.6. Note that this simple system has performed well, particularly during periods of low autocorrelation and mean-reversion conditions in SPY, such as the time after the financial crisis when its performance exceeded that of a buy-and-hold strategy.

The win rate is about 66%, and the maximum percent drawdown is about -27%, while CAR is 6.82%. However, the value for the drawdown is valid only for the particular entry and exit points. If the path the system follows is different, the drawdown may decrease or increase. The WR2 system stays in the market for an average of 6.42 bars, as the backtesting results indicated. We round this value to 7 days and use that number for the time-based exit in the simulation.

The simulation environment for determining the minimum initial trading capital is as follows:

- A biased coin with p{heads} = 0.66 (66%)
- Toss a coin after the close of each day
- Buy at the open of the next day if heads show up
- Exit long positions after 7 days at the open
- Repeat the coin-tossing until the end of the price history
- The trading commission is set at $0.01/share
- Equity is fully invested in each long position
- The simulation is repeated 20,000 times
- The average maximum percent drawdown is determined

The simulation generated the following statistics:

Mean: -55.67%

Median: -55.55%

Standard deviation: 7.6%

Kurtosis: -0.303

Skewness: -0.05

Therefore, according to this simulation, the mean percent drawdown is about -56%. The initial capital must be adjusted accordingly so that the maximum drawdown scales to acceptable levels. In this particular case, if one is willing to accept a -25% maximum drawdown, only about 44% of the available capital must be used as initial trading capital. As a result, in the original backtest, CAR will drop to about 3.1% from 6.82%, and the maximum percent drawdown is -12.4%.

The above results may not sound acceptable to a Level III quant who is fooled by satisfactory backtesting results, and the decision may be to go ahead and invest the full available capital. This type of decision is one of the main causes of trader failures. The future is not always the same as the past. Specifically, profitable systems become unprofitable due to changing market conditions. For instance, if a downtrend lasts a long time, like GLD's after 2013, the drawdown can be excessive. This phenomenon is shown in Figure 3-7, which shows the equity performance of the WR2 system in GLD in the period from February 1, 2003, to July 1, 2015.

Figure 3-7. Equity performance of the WR2 system in GLD ETF in the period 01/02/2003 to 07/01/2015 with $100,000 starting capital, one cent/share commissions, and fully invested equity

The maximum drawdown in the case of a fully invested WR2 system in GLD is -34%. This result is reduced to -16% when trading only 44% of the initial capital. In most cases, curve-fitted backtesting results lead Level III quants to believe that the system parameters will remain robust in the future. However, all curve-fitted systems—whether developed manually or generated via machine learning—almost always appear favorable on paper; yet when market conditions change, they often generate excessive drawdown levels that can either lead to financial ruin or cause traders to abandon trading altogether due to fear of further losses.

In the previous example, we considered a system that traded an ETF, a security that trades just like a stock. Most trading systems for stocks are less sensitive to commissions than the system in Pseudo Code 3-1, and the objective of determining the initial trading capital is to calculate the appropriate fraction of available initial capital needed to minimize drawdown and maximize return. However, margin requirements exist in futures and forex, necessitating the determination of initial trading capital on a per-contract basis. In the next example, we consider a futures contract and longer-term trading.

2. Random entries, actual exits

This method can be used when we would like to preserve an exit timing method or when we trust our exit logic. Longer-term trend-following systems are usually candidates for this test. In the example that follows, we consider a long/short 50–200 moving average crossover in E-mini futures shown in Pseudo Code 3-4.

N= 1 //number of contracts

If MA(50) crosses above MA(200) then Buy N contracts at the next open //buy signal

If MA(50) crosses below MA(200) then Short N contract at the next open //short signal

Pseudocode 3-4 represents a 50-200 moving average crossover system.

The equity performance of the moving average crossover system in Pseudo Code 3-4 is shown in Figure 3.7, for an initial capital of $30,000 per contract, a $5,000 margin, and a $5 commission one-way, in continuous E-mini data from 01/02/2001 to 10/25/2013. Equity performance is based on one traded contract and the specified initial capital. This example illustrates one method for calculating the initial trading capital, and we will focus solely on the maximum drawdown per contract traded. The drawdown in this particular case is -$20,265. However, this value of the drawdown is valid only for the particular entry and exit points. If the path the system follows is different, then the drawdown may decrease or increase.

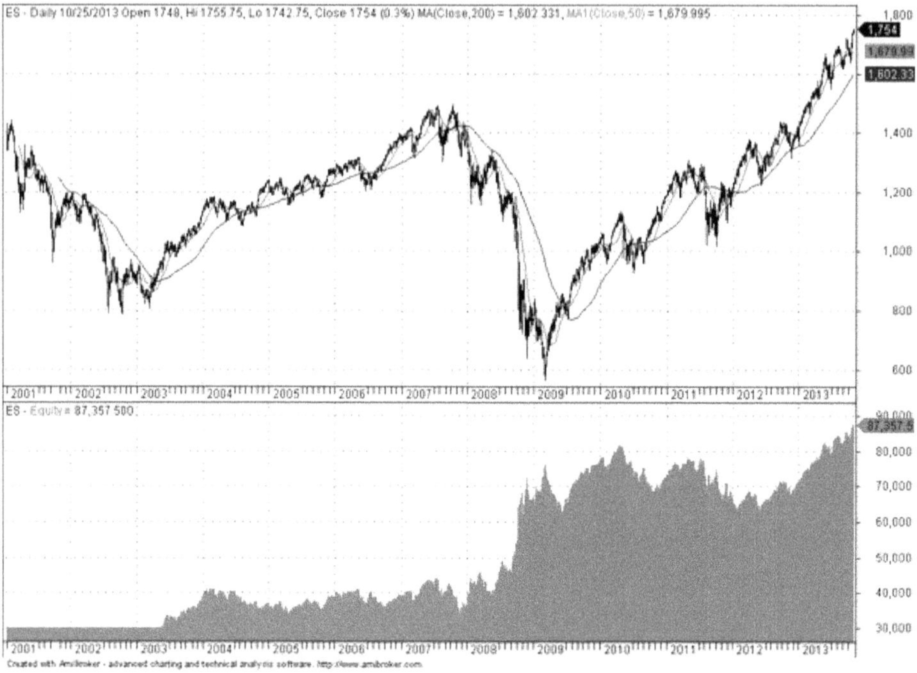

Figure 3-8 Equity performance of the system in Pseudo Code 3-4 in E-mini futures and the period 01/02/2001 to 10/25/2013 with $30,000 starting capital per contract and $5 commission

The simulation environment for determining the minimum initial trading capital is as follows:

- A coin with p{heads} = 0.50 (50%)
- Toss a coin after the close of each day
- Buy at the open of the next day if heads show up and 50-ma > 200-ma
- Exit long positions and reverse if tails show up and 50-ma < 200-ma
- Repeat the coin-tossing until the end of the price history
- Trading commission is set at $5/contract
- The simulation is repeated 20,000 times
- The average drawdown value is determined

The simulation generated the following statistics for the maximum drawdown per contract:

Mean: -21,364

Median: -20927

Standard deviation: 1,478

Kurtosis: -1.14

Skewness: -0.22

According to the simulation performed, the average drawdown per contract is -21,364, about $1,000 more than the value obtained from backtesting the system. In this case, the following formula determines the minimum initial capital per contract traded:

Minimum initial trading capital = expected drawdown level + margin

Therefore, if the expected drawdown is $21,364 (absolute value) and the margin is $5,000, the minimum trading capital per contract is $26,364. A value of $30,000 that was used for the initial trading capital in the backtest results of Figure 3-8 was sufficient based on these results.

A Level III quant may claim that the equity curve in the backtest in Figure 3-8 never falls below the initial capital of $30,000. This is true, but it's a random fact because of the backtest's start date. If one started the backtest just before the drawdown accumulation, then an account with $20,000 would be ruined. This is the point, and this is the reason for this exercise. Even this analysis can't save a system or account because it's based on past data. Future market conditions can change so drastically that they may cause significant outliers in the expected drawdown.

3. Random entries and exits

This method should be used when a trader is uncertain about the robustness of a short-term or intraday trading system. This includes situations where curve-fitting may occur or where the system was developed using data-mining techniques. As will be discussed in more detail in Chapter Six, trading systems developed via the use of data mining have a low chance of success due to high data-mining bias.

In the example that follows, we consider a forex trader with a short-term trading system for daily EURUSD. We aren't concerned about the specific algo because we suspect that the system is random, and we would like to determine the minimum trading capital that is compatible with market dynamics. As will be shown in the next chapter, in some markets, including forex, results are sensitive to initial trading capital and commission/spread cost due to the market structure.

The analysis below uses EURUSD daily data in the period from 01/02/2001 to 11/29/2013, as shown in Figure 3-9. The simulation environment for determining the minimum initial trading capital is as follows:

- A coin with p{heads} = 0.50 (50%)
- Toss a coin after the close of each day
- Buy one standard lot at the open of the next day if heads show up
- Exit long positions and reverse if tails show up
- Repeat the coin-tossing until the end of the price history
- The spread is set at 1 pip, and the leverage is 50:1
- The simulation is repeated 20,000 times
- The average maximum percent drawdown is determined

Figure 3-9. EURUSD spot from 01/02/2001 to 11/29/2013

The simulation generated the following statistics for the maximum drawdown per contract:

Mean: -27,856

Median: -25,750

Standard deviation: 7,301

Kurtosis: 2.5

Skewness: -1.47

According to the simulation just described, the average drawdown per standard lot is about -28,000 The minimum initial capital per standard lot traded in this case is given by the following formula:

Minimum initial trading capital = expected drawdown level + margin

Therefore, if the expected drawdown is $28,000 (absolute value) and the margin is $2,000 for 50:1 leverage, the minimum trading capital per contract is $30,000.

Note that the majority of retail forex traders start with small amounts, thinking that they have an edge. Approximately 95% of retail forex traders, lacking an edge, ultimately face financial ruin. Only the lucky ones or those few with an edge can escape ruin, but only if they are properly capitalized. More about these facts is discussed in the next chapter, where it is shown how the timeframe of choice and trading friction dictate whether there is potential for profit in a market. Such information is important to know in advance because many, especially quantitative traders, attempt to develop strategies in markets and timeframes that are too efficient to provide any profits. When friction is added to trading systems fitted with historical data or developed via data mining, the result is negative performance and losses.

CHAPTER FOUR

Trading Timeframes and the Impact of Friction

There is some confusion in the trading literature regarding trading timeframes, styles, and methods. For example, some refer to the trend-following trading style that attempts to catch extended price moves only in the context of longer time frames of weeks or even months. However, trend-following techniques are also applicable in intraday time frames. For example, trends may form in a 30-minute timeframe that lasts several days and can be followed using techniques similar to those used to follow trends in daily timeframes that last many months. Below, we attempt to clarify this often confusing relationship between timeframes and trading styles with a few definitions.

Trading Timeframes

Intraday trading timeframe: This is trading that initiates and exits positions using intraday data. The data can be for any period, including tick data. Low-frequency intraday trading became popular in the 1990s, and high-frequency intraday trading became popular in the mid-2000s when exchanges started to offer collocation services to reduce order execution latency.

Daily trading timeframe: This trading style uses end-of-day (EOD) data to initiate positions, usually at the open or close of the day. Positions are exited using end-of-day or intraday data.

Some traders also use higher timeframes, such as weekly or monthly.

Trading Styles

Day trading: This style involves trades that are opened and closed during a trading session. For example, high-frequency trading (HFT) is a day trading style, no matter how fast the trades are executed. Scalping is also a day trading style. Day trading can also occur in daily timeframes by opening a trade at the open and exiting it at the close. Therefore, for day trading, one may use data from any timeframe up to EOD.

Short-term trading: This style involves entails keeping trades open for several days or even weeks. It is primarily executed using EOD data but also intraday, especially in forex, where the use of 1-hour and 4-hour price bars is popular.

Longer-term trading: This style involves trades that last months or even years. Passive stock investors are essentially longer-term traders, although they may not be aware of that. This is because, in the absence of a method or system, buying stock for an extended period involves an entry and an exit point, and thus there is timing involved, regardless of whether it is arbitrary or based on technical or fundamental considerations. Note that some equate longer-term trading exclusively with trend-following, but in general, the two are not equivalent.

Trading methods

There are many trading methods, and some of them operate in both popular trading timeframes, intraday and daily. For example, there are intraday trend-followers and daily trend-followers. Both try to ride price moves in their base timeframe and often use similar methods, such as moving average crossovers or channel breakouts to enter the trade and a trailing stop to exit it. Some associate trend-following strictly with daily timeframes, but this is not the case.

Position and swing trading attempt to capture price moves using patterns, indicators, and other technical signals. For example, long positions are entered on strength to take advantage of momentum or on weakness to benefit from mean reversion. These methods are also applicable to all timeframes. Virtually all methods that apply to daily trading also apply to intraday trading, but not *vice versa*. Some of the methods that do not apply in daily timeframes are scalping, market making, and HFT.

Although most traders choose a timeframe, a specific trading style, and a method, for example, 5-minute E-mini S&P 500 index futures momentum trading or daily swing trading in forex, others use combinations of different timeframes, styles, and methods. The choices do not impact the definition of trading expectation, as what matters is the win rate and average win and average loss, while the timeframe, trading style, and method used are irrelevant for calculating its value. However, the required sample size for the significance of the results is impacted by the choice of timeframe, as already discussed in Chapter Two.

Convergent and divergent trading strategies

Quantitative traders often classify trading strategies as convergent or divergent. Trend-following strategies fall under the divergent classification, whereas mean-reversion strategies are usually referred to as convergent. If the price and an indicator move closer to each other, there is convergence, and if they diverge from each other, it is divergence, positive or negative. This classification assumes some independence of the two notions, i.e., convergence and divergence, but in reality price action is more complicated.

Trend-following aims to catch outlier trades that may remain open for months or even years. Since the payoff ratio is much higher than 1, the right strategies are usually profitable over time.

Mean reversion closes winning positions quickly to secure profits. The win rate is high, and although the payoff ratio tends to be lower than 1, the right strategies are profitable.

Trend-following encompasses a wide variety of strategies based on moving averages, momentum, and other indicators that follow price trends. Despite their purported simplicity, trend-following strategies have a vast optimization space due to a large number of parameters, and that makes them sensitive to overfitting.

Mean reversion also encompasses a broad spectrum of strategies based on their structure and includes reversion to an indicator, reversion to a price level, reversion from overbought to oversold and the other way, and statistical arbitrage and pairs trading. These strategies also have a vast optimization space due to a large number of parameters, and that makes them sensitive to overfitting.

The choice of a strategy depends on the comfort level and experience of a trader. Divergent strategies require a disciplined approach in following long trends, and convergent strategies demand being comfortable with realizing occasional large losses.

The Negative-Sum Game of Futures and Forex Trading

Retail intraday trading of futures, forex, and stocks flourished after the introduction of electronic orders via exchanges. This paradigm shift was quite profitable for brokerages and market makers but a massive loss for technical traders, who were oblivious to the microstructure of these markets. The cost associated with intraday trading in most cases transforms an inherently zero-sum intraday game into a negative-sum game with low chances of realizing consistent profits. Despite that, a giant industry emerged in the 1990s that provided data and tools to intraday traders, including charting software, real-time order book data, backtesting programs, and APIs that linked algorithms developed by the traders to brokerage execution platforms. Nowadays, it's believed that over 90% of intraday traders never made a profit, and the majority experienced financial ruin. Undercapitalization and the need for a significant edge to mitigate trading friction were the primary causes of the massive failures. In this chapter, specific examples from futures and forex markets are presented that illustrate how unskilled discretionary or system traders without an edge have low chances of succeeding in trading in intraday timeframes. It is also shown that stock trading via proxy ETFs provides better chances of success, but that is only due to the inherent positive bias of the stock market, something that is now known in hindsight.

Example 1: Daily E-mini trading

After the introduction of the E-mini futures contract, which allowed traders to speculate on the movements of the S&P 500 index at lower margin requirements, a new industry emerged for teaching retail traders how to trade futures intraday and for providing signals in real-time. However, simulations reveal that the majority of these traders faced no chance of success.

Figure 4-1 shows the distribution of net return, which is defined as 100×net profit/initial equity, and associated statistics of 20,000 random E-mini S&P 500 index futures trading systems based on daily data from 01/02/2001 to 10/25/2013. The starting capital of each trading system is $100,000 per contract traded, and no commission is included in the results. The simulation that generated the distribution was based on tossing a fair coin: if heads showed up, then any open short position was closed, and one contract was bought at the close. Any open long position was closed, and one contract was sold short when tails showed up. An initial margin of $3,000 was used in these simulations.

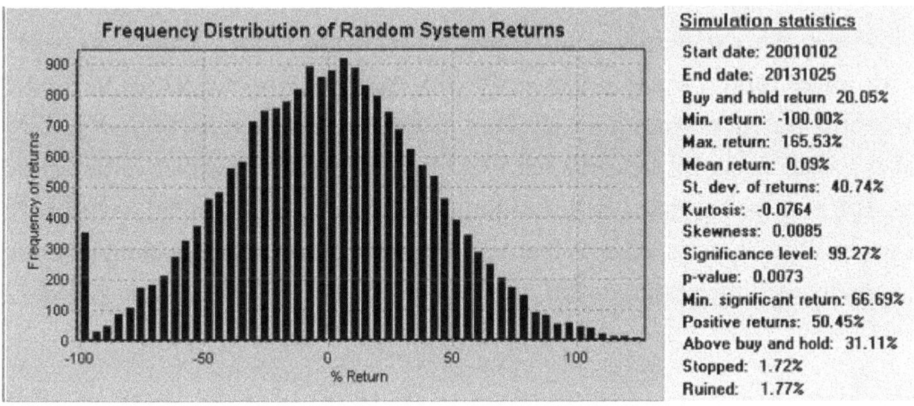

Figure 4-1. Frequency distribution of net returns of 20,000 random E-mini S&P 500 index futures daily trading systems, no commission, 100K starting capital, $3,000 margin. Generated by DLPAL software. www.priceactionlab.com

The distribution in Figure 4-1 is close to normal, with a mean return of 0.09% and a standard deviation of 40.74%. The kurtosis is -0.0764 and the skewness is 0.0085. The minimum return is -100%, which is equivalent to total ruin, and the maximum return achieved is 165.53%. Note that returns below -100% are not allowed because when the equity drops below a margin requirement of $3,000, trading stops. The significance level of 99.27% indicates the percentage of systems that made a return lower than a test return, which was set at 100% in this simulation. The p-value of 0.0073 is the probability of obtaining a return of 100%, assuming that the null hypothesis is true. In this case, the null hypothesis is that the true return of a system is zero. Furthermore, Figure 4-1's distribution shows that 1.72% of the 20,000 systems experienced a stop, while 50.45% generated a positive return. This type of futures trading, in the absence of trading friction and when participants trade randomly, should lead to these expected results.

After reducing the initial capital to $20,000 per traded contract, Figure 4-2 displays the results of the same simulation. In this case, 30.71% of the systems generate positive returns, and 65.39% are stopped because the equity drops below the required margin. This pattern occurs because of the drawdown and indicates that the $20,000 initial capital was not enough to cover equity swings for most of the random systems, even in the absence of trading friction. However, many traders have attempted to trade the E-mini S&P 500 futures with initial capital levels as low as $5,000. According to the results in Figure 4-2, only the lucky ones have survived. It may be seen that more than a third of the systems cluster near the left end of the distribution with a return close to -100%, meaning that a daily random trader with a small capital would have a probability of about 65% to lose the $20,000 initial capital, trading just one contract even when offered zero commission and charged no bid-ask spread

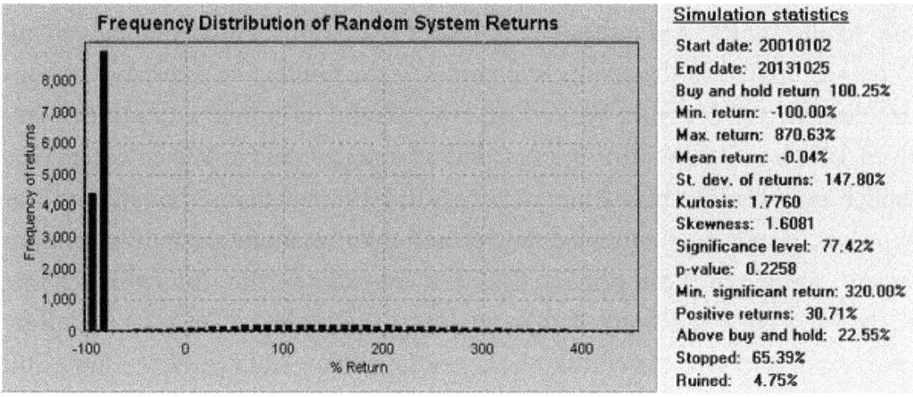

Figure 4-2. Frequency distribution of net returns of 20,000 random E-mini S&P 500 Index futures daily trading systems, no commission, 20K starting capital, $3,000 initial margin. Outliers are not shown on the graph. Generated by DLPAL software. www.priceactionlab.com

It should be clear that as the trading capital decreases, the minimum return for significance increases. In the simulation shown in Figure 4-2, a reduction of initial capital by a factor of five, from $100,000 to $20,000, caused an increase in the minimum return for significance from 67.22% to 320% as compared with the simulation in Figure 4-1, also by about a factor of five. Therefore, the high returns realized by small accounts, usually in the order of 50% to 100%, are often not statistically significant and are a result of luck. Such an outcome is a frequent phenomenon in trading contests. Despite that, the lucky winners are often presented as trading geniuses when in fact they were only lucky to survive a negative-sum trading game and end up on the right side of the return distribution. To prove skill, in most cases, the returns should be higher by a large factor. However, the brokerage industry often uses those lucky winners out of a large pool of random traders to correlate returns to skill. Such evidence is not possible from contest results because when there is a large pool of random traders, there is a high probability that someone will be lucky. It would take several years of significant returns to demonstrate the difference between skill and luck.

Figure 4-3 shows the effect of adding a $3 commission per contract traded per side to the trades of the random systems with $100K initial trading capital. When compared to the results in Figure 4-1, the number of profitable systems decreases to 40.95% from 50.45%, and the number of ruined systems increases from 1.72% to 2.90%. This implies that a large percentage of well-capitalized daily E-mini traders could generate profits in 10 years if the trading friction was kept low, even if they possessed no skill and their methods resulted in random signals, similar to those generated by the coin toss in the simulations. Some traders and their followers, if they provide a signal service, may be misled by these random results into thinking there was an edge when there was none and any positive performance was just luck.

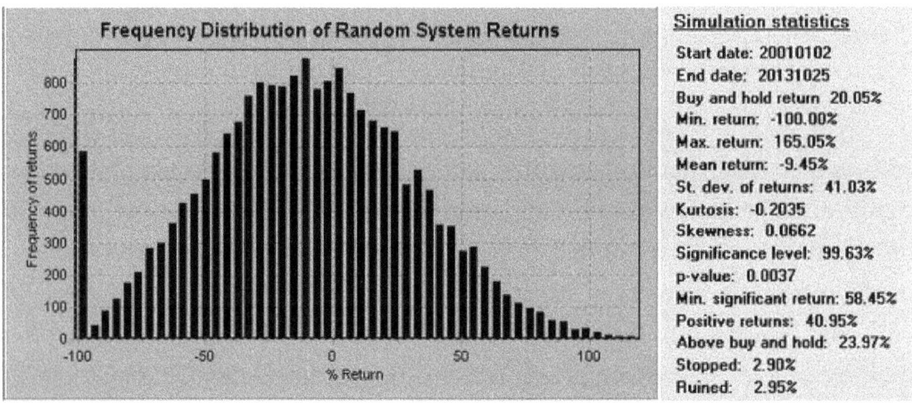

Figure 4-3. Frequency distribution of net returns of 20,000 random E-mini S&P 500 index futures daily trading systems, $3 commission, 100K starting capital, $3,000 margin. Generated by DLPAL software. www.priceactionlab.com

Would it be possible to distinguish between a skilled trader with an edge and a lucky trader? The answer is that, in principle, this is difficult to do. The random systems simulation based on E-mini S&P 500 futures daily data concludes that initial capital, along with the level of commissions paid, plays an important role in daily trading. The point is that a substantial percentage of random and unskilled daily traders possessing no edge may realize profits just by luck alone if they are well-capitalized and have low trading costs. Traders with low capital and high trading costs have little chance of profit.

Example 2: Intraday E-mini trading

The next example involves intraday E-mini S&P 500 futures trading. Figure 4-4 shows the distribution of net return, which is defined as 100×net profit/initial equity, and associated statistics of 20,000 random E-mini trading systems on 15-minute data spanning 8 years, from 01/2001 to 12/2008, with the intraday bars numbered from 10000001 to 10198750. The starting capital is $100,000 per contract traded, and no commission was included in the simulation. The margin was set at $3,000 per contract.

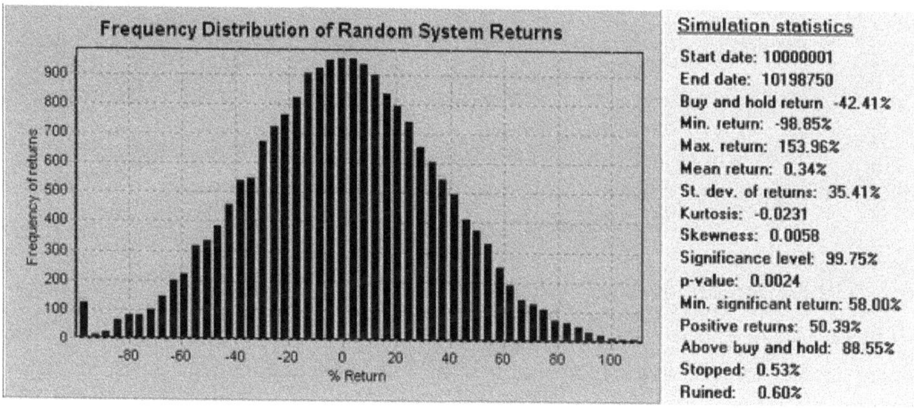

Figure 4-4. Frequency distribution of net returns of 20,000 random E-mini S&P 500 index futures intraday trading systems, no commission, 100K starting capital, $3,000 margin. Generated by DLPAL software. www.priceactionlab.com

The distribution in Figure 4-4 is close to normal, with a mean return of 0.34% and a standard deviation equal to 35.41%. The kurtosis is equal to -0.0231 and the skewness is 0.0058. The minimum return is -98.85%, and the maximum is +153.96%. Note that returns below -100% are not allowed because when the equity drops below a margin requirement of $3,000, trading stops. According to the results in Figure 4-4, 0.53% of the 20,000 systems were stopped, and 50.39% produced a positive return. This outcome was expected due to the zero-sum nature of futures trading in the absence of trading friction, and the results of the analysis may look promising for intraday traders. But this is not the case when $1 of commission and slippage is added to each transaction, as shown in Figure 4-5.

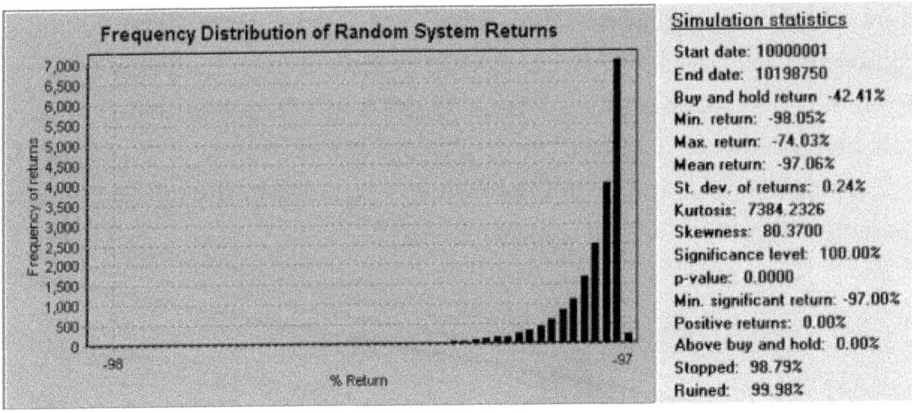

Figure 4-5. Frequency distribution of net returns of 20,000 random E-mini S&P 500 index futures intraday trading systems, $1 commission, 100K capital, $3,000 margin. Generated by DLPAL software. www.priceactionlab.com

All 20,000 random systems became unprofitable after a small commission charge, as shown in Figure 4-5. The average return was -97.06%, and 99.98% of the systems were ruined. Given that just the exchange fee for trading the E-mini S&P 500 futures contract is about $1.14 per side for retail, one can understand claims that 99% of intraday futures traders are losers. The winners are either extraordinarily lucky or exceptionally skilled, but if they stay long enough in the game, they may lose everything because, due to its nature and by design, the process is a negative-sum game.

One could attempt to object to any inferences made from the results in Figures 4-1 to 4-5 by arguing that the systems based on a fair coin toss generate too many trades. To counter such claims, the simulation was repeated with position trades along with a strong uptrend. Figure 4-7 displays the results obtained by manipulating the coin to be unfair, resulting in a probability of heads of 0.745; this means that the coin toss experiment favored heads, indicating long positions. In addition, the simulation was performed on a segment of the data that corresponds to the uptrend in this market from approximately the start of 2004 to the end of 2007, and only long positions were taken that were closed when a sell signal was generated. The result was long-only intraday positions that lasted several bars on average until closed along with a strong uptrend, as shown in Figure 4–6, but in a daily timeframe.

Figure 4-6. E-mini S&P 500 index futures uptrend in the period 2004–2007 (Daily adjusted data)

Under the condition of intraday long-only positions along with a strong uptrend, one would expect that a large percentage of random systems would stay profitable. But when just $1 of commission per side is introduced, only 0.62% of the random systems manage to stay profitable, as shown in Figure 4-7. Although no random systems were ruined when the coin was biased, the distribution shifted to the left with a maximum return of +8.27% and a minimum return of -39.92%. The mean return was -15.53% and the standard deviation decreased to 6.06%.

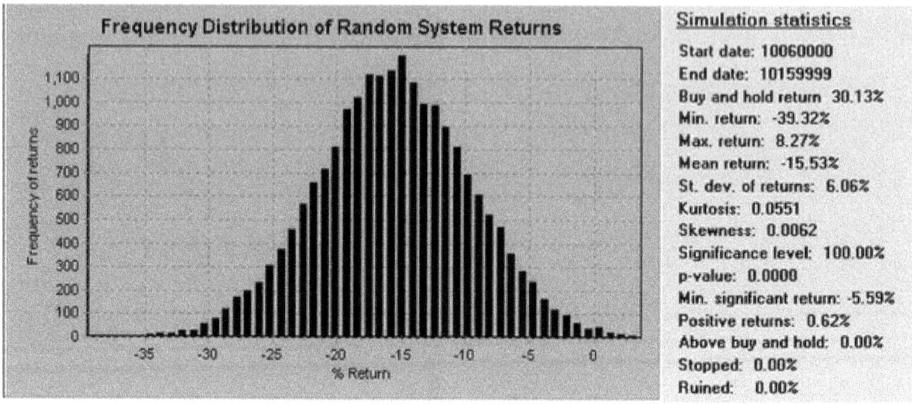

Figure 4-7. Frequency distribution of net returns of 20,000 random E-mini S&P 500 index futures intraday long-only, position trading systems with a long bias, $1 commission, 100K capital, $3,000 margin. Generated by DLPAL software. www.priceactionlab.com

The conclusion from the intraday E-mini S&P 500 futures simulations is that, after adding low trading costs, profitable intraday trading is unattainable for the majority of traders who cannot perform better than random systems, i.e., they have no edge or skill. We will see below that in forex, the same conclusions hold, and in some respects, things are even worse in that market for intraday traders.

Example 3: Daily Forex trading

A simulation of 20,000 random long/short systems was performed using daily EURUSD data (bid prices) from 01/02/2001 to 11/29/2013. The simulation was based on tossing a fair coin; if heads showed up, then any open short position was closed, and one standard lot was bought at the close. Any long position was closed and reversed by selling short one standard lot when tails showed up. Starting capital was $100K per standard lot, resulting in 1:1 leverage. No spread cost was added in this simulation, and the bid price was the traded price for both long and short positions, something that is not the case in reality, as retail traders can buy at the ask and sell at the bid. Using the bid price makes the simulation more optimistic for the long term, and any conclusions from these results are conservative in that respect.

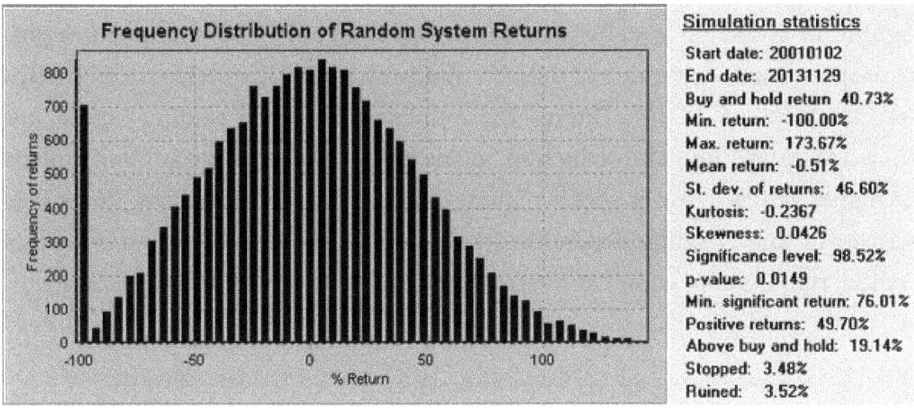

Figure 4-8. Frequency distribution of net returns of 20,000 random daily EURUSD trading systems, no spread charged, 100K capital, one standard lot per position, \$2,000 margin. Generated by DLPAL software. www.priceactionlab.com

Figure 4-8 shows the frequency distribution of the net return of the random systems in the simulation, which is calculated as 100×net profit/starting capital. The spike at the far left of the graph near the -100% return corresponds to a situation when the equity drops below the required margin (\$2,000 in this case for 50:1 leverage). At that point, any open positions are closed, and the system no longer trades. The statistics confirm the zero-sum game nature of the forex market. The mean return is -0.51% with a standard deviation of 46.40%, the kurtosis is -0.2367, and there is a positive skewness of 0.0426. Nearly half of the systems generated positive returns; 3.48% of systems were stopped, while 3.52% of systems were liquidated. The significance level of 98.52% represents the number of systems with returns lower than 100%, and the corresponding p-value for this threshold was 0.0149. The minimum return for significance at the 5% level was 76.01% for this simulation period, with a buy-and-hold return of 40.73% and 19.14% of systems generated more than that.

When the initial capital is reduced to \$20,000 per standard lot and the simulation is repeated, the impact of this change is catastrophic, with 69.02% of systems stopped because of equity dropping below the required margin of \$2,000 and 16.13% of systems ruined with their equity dropping below 95% of starting capital, as shown in Figure 4-9. Note that the mean return is -0.37%, but the standard deviation is 164.55%. In this case, a 100% net return is not significant at the 5% level because it is higher than only 77.83% of the systems, corresponding to a p-value of 0.2217. The percentage of systems with positive returns drops to 28.63% due to the reduction in initial trading capital per traded standard lot. The reduction in the initial trading capital also resulted in higher returns, but at much higher variability, as was expected. Note that returns in forex trading depend on the initial capital and the number of lots traded; therefore, to compare systems, leverage must be taken into account.

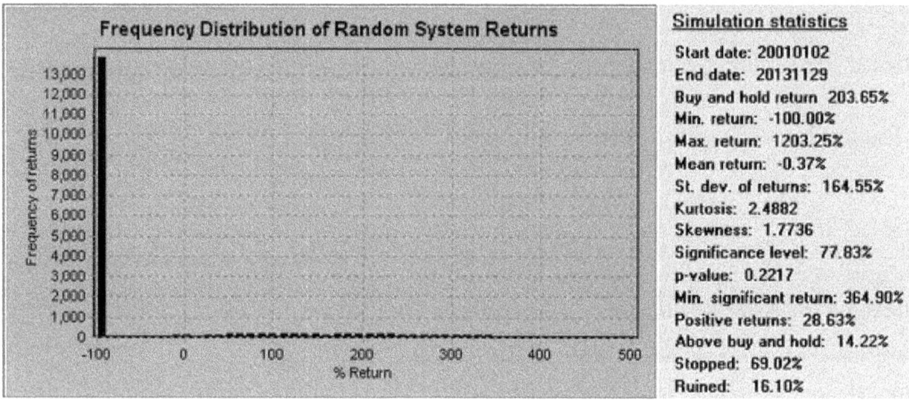

Figure 4-9. Frequency distribution of net returns of 20,000 random daily EURUSD trading systems, no spread charged, 20K capital, one standard lot per position, $2,000 margin. Outliers are not shown on the graph. Generated by DLPAL software. www.priceactionlab.com

Under actual retail trading conditions, buy orders are usually filled at the asking price, and sell orders are usually filled at the bid because this is how the market maker profits. The difference between the bid and the asking price is called the *spread*. The average spread of some popular retail brokers in the case of EURUSD is between 0.5 and 4 pips, although some claim tighter spreads, but only during normal market conditions. Figure 4-10 illustrates the impact of incorporating a spread of 2 pips per trade on the simulation results from Figure 4-8. Initial capital is 100K. The distribution of returns changes remarkably from that in Figure 4-8 after the introduction of an average spread cost.

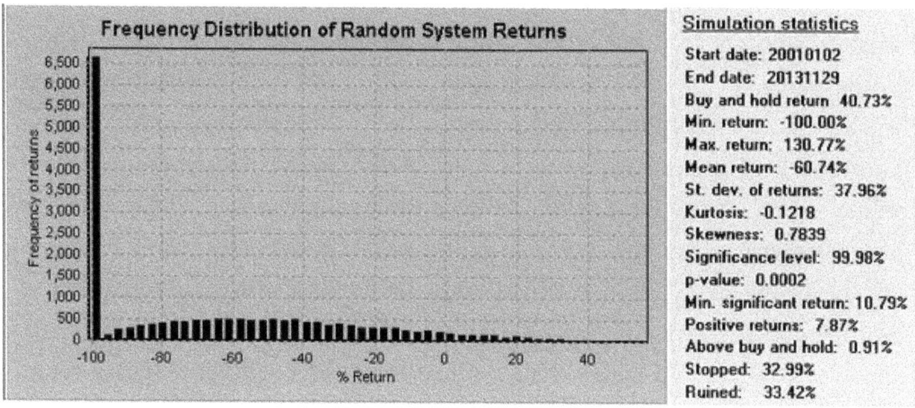

Figure 4-10. Frequency distribution of net returns of 20,000 random daily EURUSD trading systems, 2 pips spread charged, 100K capital, one standard lot per position, $2,000 margin. Outliers are not shown on the graph. Generated by DLPAL software. www.priceactionlab.com

After the introduction of a spread of two pips, the drop in mean return is dramatic, from -0.51% in Figure 4-8 to -60.74% in Figure 4-10. Only 7.87% of the systems generate a positive return, rather than nearly 50% when the spread is set to 0. The number of ruined systems surges to 32.99% due to the introduction of a 2-pip spread, which occurs with 1:1 leverage. There is no point in considering lower initial capital levels and higher leverage because the results will be worse, but we will only mention that in the case of 10K initial capital and a spread of one pip, 95% of the random systems were ruined. Note that the typical starting capital levels of retail forex traders are even lower, and some offshore brokers offer 400:1 leverage. These results are in agreement with the empirical fact that 95% of all small-account retail forex traders lose money. As the simulations showed, a loss is an inescapable reality of this negative-sum game unless a trader is skilled or lucky.

Since intraday futures and forex trading have a high rate of unsuccessful traders, particularly among those lacking skill or an edge—such as naïve chartists (referred to as Level I traders) and quants (referred to as Level III traders)—there will always be a few who achieve high returns purely by luck due to the sheer number of these traders. These lucky outcomes usually occur in trading contests, where some traders manage extraordinary returns. These statistical outliers are used by the contest organizers to promote this kind of trading when, in reality, those who profit do so by luck in most cases, and the chances of anyone unskilled achieving similar profits are often less than winning a lotto ticket. All references to traders who profited from intraday trading in any market overlook the fact that many similar traders incurred losses. One way of establishing the significance of positive results is by proving that the trader possesses a verifiable skill or edge. Usually, there is no skill, and the edge cannot be identified because it cannot be formulated into rules. It is also impossible to verify the significance of the edge because that would involve an extended period of trading to generate a sufficient sample of trades. Therefore, unless the significance of an assumed edge or skill is established, outstanding returns from trading contests should only be viewed with skepticism and in the context of randomness. This statement pertains to actual trading results, while simulated results are deemed worthless since they resemble unvalidated backtest results based on historical data.

The results from the forex simulations confirmed those obtained for the E-mini S&P 500 futures simulation. Only well-capitalized and skilled traders can survive, given that the trading cost is low. These results may appear obvious to market professionals, but retail traders who use or plan to use technical analysis are often not aware of them. Most books on technical trading overstate profit potential because they focus on methods that assume an edge. An edge is unattainable unless one is either experienced with the markets, a Level II trader, or uses advanced quantitative techniques to discover one that effectively deals with data-mining bias, a Level IV technical trader, as discussed in Chapter One. An edge is unattainable unless one is either experienced with the markets, a Level II trader, or uses advanced quantitative techniques to discover one that effectively deals with data-mining bias, a Level IV technical trader, as discussed in Chapter One.

The impact of a long-term market bias

Certain markets display a structural bias, which can provide an advantage if one trades exclusively in its direction and within the appropriate timeframe.

In these situations, people often mistake bias-driven returns for those resulting from skill and an edge. This phenomenon is especially true in the equity markets and when trading major stock indexes, such as the S&P 500, its derivatives, such as the E-mini contract, or exchange-traded funds, such as the SPY.

Figure 4-11 displays the net return distribution and related statistics of 20,000 random trading systems using SPY ETF daily data from January 29, 1993, to December 31, 2014. The net return is equal to 100 times the net profit over the initial equity. The starting capital of each random system is $100,000, and the available equity is fully invested in each position. No commission was included in this simulation example, which was based on tossing a fair coin. If heads showed up, then any short position was closed, and SPY ETF shares equal to the available equity divided by price were bought at the close. Any open long position was closed and reversed to short when tails showed up, and SPY ETF shares equal to the available equity divided by price were sold short at the close. The results in Figure 4-11 show that 34.16% of the systems had positive returns, while only 0.13% of them were ruined. Note that the maximum return is +2,039.44%, but the minimum return is negative at -97.08% because below that, the system cannot buy any more shares. The minimum return for a significant performance at the top 5% level was 208.57%, and a test return of 100% was significant at about the 12% level, with 87.82% of returns below it. Only 1.63% of the random systems made more than the buy-and-hold return of 367.77%.

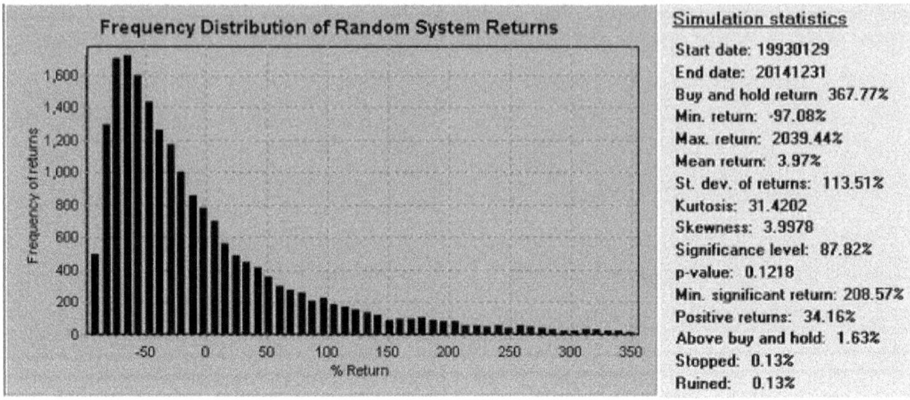

Figure 4-11. Frequency distribution of net returns of 20,000 random, fully invested SPY ETF trading systems, no commission, 100K initial trading capital. Outliers are not displayed on the graph. Generated by DLPAL software. www.priceactionlab.com

The results depict a different distribution of returns than in the futures and forex cases considered previously, where the distributions were close to normal when no trading friction was applied and there was enough capital to cover the drawdown, such as in Figure 4-3 This case exhibits a long right tail, leading to a distribution characterized by a power law. Going into the details of this phenomenon is beyond the scope of this book, but in general, it is known that equity market returns obey a power distribution. This means, among other things, that equity markets allow much higher returns to be realized due to luck, and such results may be partly attributed to the presence of autocorrelation in daily changes. Note that autocorrelation was positive in the 1990s, and since then it has turned negative due to arbitrage, a fact mentioned in Chapter Five and illustrated in Figure 5-2.

Next, we repeat the simulation in Figure 4-11 after adding a commission of one per share traded. Figure 4-12 displays the results.

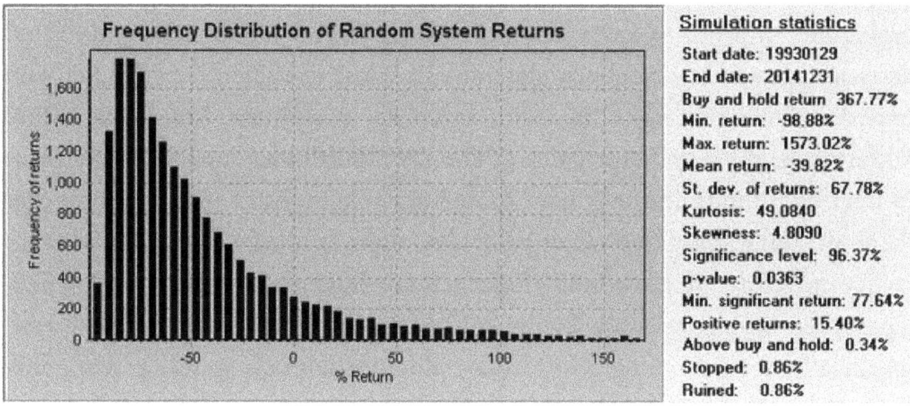

Figure 4-12. Frequency distribution of net returns of 20,000 random, fully invested SPY ETF trading systems, $0.01 commission, 100K initial capital. Outliers are not shown on the graph. Generated by DLPAL software. www.priceactionlab.com

The results in Figure 4-12 imply that a large percentage of unskilled and random traders in stock index-related products, such as SPY, could have profited just by luck. About 16% of the random traders profited. They could have been fooled into believing that it was the tools, systems, or skills that contributed to the positive results after many years of trading.

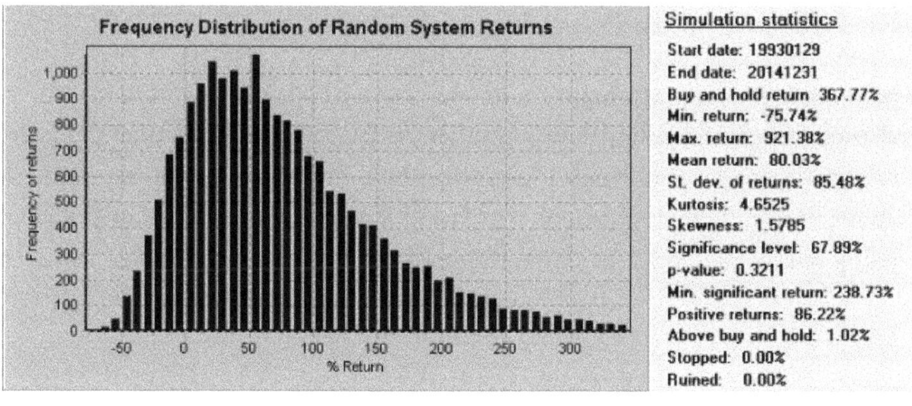

Figure 4-13. Frequency distribution of net returns of 20,000 random, fully invested SPY ETF long-only trading systems, $0.01 comm., 100K initial capital. Outliers are not shown on the graph. Generated by DLPAL software. www.priceactionlab.com

The simulations show that a structurally positive bias in prices increases the probability of profiting from random trading. The S&P 500 index and related derivative products have been generous to those unskilled participants who traded them with end-of-day data, especially during the late 1990s. More importantly, these characteristics of the S&P 500 index have been generous to long-only funds and may have fooled a whole industry into believing that there was some skill involved, or profitable algos, that offered an edge when in reality the results were random. These facts are illustrated in Figure 4-13, which repeats the simulation from Figure 4-12 but focuses solely on long positions; specifically, any open long positions are closed when tails appear and are only reopened when heads appear.

In Figure 4-13, the percentage of profitable long-only random systems increased to 86.22%. In this simulation, the minimum return for significance at the top 5% level is 238.73%, and a 100% return over the simulation period is only significant at about the 32% level, with 67.99% of returns above it. These results tell us that unskilled, long-only random traders in SPY ETF possessing no edge had high chances of realizing positive returns by luck alone. But only 1% of them beat the 367.77% buy-and-hold return on SPY (excluding dividends) in that time. The results in Figure 4-13 are an example of how markets with a structural bias can fool traders, especially those who use technical analysis, into believing that they have an edge.

The simulation shown in Figure 4-13 was repeated with an unfair coin, where the probability of landing heads was set to 0.745, indicating that the coin toss experiment favored heads (long positions). The result is that the random systems took only long positions that lasted longer, the equivalent of position trading systems. Figure 4-14 shows the results of this new simulation.

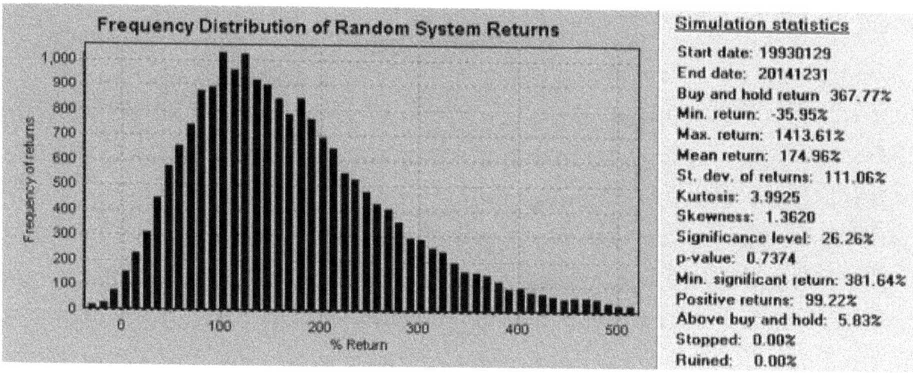

Figure 4-14. Frequency distribution of net returns of 20,000 random, fully invested SPY ETF long-only trading systems with a bias, $0.01 commission, 100K initial capital. Outliers are not shown on the graph. Generated by DLPAL software. www.priceactionlab.com

After a long bias was introduced, 99.22% of all long-only random systems were profitable, but the minimum return for significance at the top 5% level increased to 381.64%, slightly above the buy-and-hold return of 367.77%. These results suggest two conclusions: (A) Long-only SPY position traders could profit in the period considered even without an edge, and (B) Exceeding buy and hold is required to prove skill or edge, but that may not be enough. Many professionals over the years have managed to make more than buy-and-hold by timing the market. However, they may not possess an edge because, by luck alone, one could have realized high net returns, as shown in Figure 4-14, with the maximum return of the random systems being 1,413.61%.

One could argue against the significance of the simulation results presented in the chapter by claiming that random systems are not intelligent enough to capture returns. But how is "intelligence" exactly defined? We know that at the quantum level, the world is random, as particles appear suddenly and vanish quickly, in some cases without any apparent reason. The result of this random microcosm is our observed, deterministic macrocosm. One could counter the argument against random systems by claiming that all systems are actually random but disguise themselves as intelligent within the vast array of random data. This is not a fallacy of reversing the burden of proof but arises from the fact that "randomness" lacks a precise definition. We could argue for a long time and never conclude because the ultimate nature of reality is unknown to us.

One important conclusion from the results in this chapter is that when one adds commission cost to trading, underestimates capitalization requirements, or both, close to efficient trading markets become difficult to trade for daily traders and mostly unprofitable for intraday traders unless there is substantial skill or edge involved in generating trade entry and exit sequences or there is some structural bias that benefits random traders (or monkeys throwing darts on stock quotes). Some traders may possess skill or an edge, but the majority of traders perform similarly to random systems. General conclusions about trading should be about the majority and not about the few skilled or lucky ones that are exceptions or statistical outliers. One of the aims of this book is to present the facts about the perils of trading the markets with technical analysis to those retail traders who will never succeed in mastering a skill or discovering an edge. Those who are already skilled enough or possess a market edge may consider the material interesting in some other respects, especially in improving their results. The second part of the book unveils the fundamental technical analysis methods employed by Level I and III traders. These methods lead to random or even worse-than-random trading, which is the same as flipping a coin in the simulations in this chapter. Guidelines are offered on how the naïve methodologies can be modified and improved to allow one to become a Level II or Level IV trader, i.e., an expert chartist or an expert quant.

PART II

Fooled by Technical Analysis

CHAPTER FIVE
Naïve and Expert Chartists

Chartists use price and volume charts in an attempt to profit from price action. Implicit in this discipline is the idea that prices reflect all the information about a particular security but also that there are causal relationships in the market that can be exploited. In the past, the term "chartist" referred to traders that used classical patterns to visually analyze price action, but in recently, it has been extended to also include the use of indicators such as moving averages and oscillators of price, Fibonacci levels, Elliot waves, and candlesticks, just to name a few. Most traders who use technical analysis are visual chartists. The primary reason for that is that this practice has been well-established and supported by the *availability cascade* cognitive bias: new analysts and traders adopt it because other analysts and traders adopted it in the past. The availability cascade is one of the cognitive biases that has contributed most to the high rate of failure of traders who use technical analysis, as will be discussed in more detail later in this chapter.

Fooled by random chart patterns

Chart patterns became popular in the mid-1900s [Ref. 4] as a method for trading stocks, during a time when futures exchanges did not exist and currencies were still pegged to gold. This trading method was based on the assumption that there was some hidden order in the markets that could manifest itself through the formation of regular patterns. In turn, the patterns and their analysis would signal moves in price, often of predictable magnitude. The first books that were published exercised selection bias by providing many examples where specific chart formations, such as head and shoulders, double tops, bottoms, triangles, wedges, and flags, to name a few, worked well and mostly omitted cases where they did not perform as expected. More importantly, there was no analysis offered that quantified the long-term expectation arising from using chart patterns to trade the markets.

If we assume that an individual analyzes thousands of similar formations of a specific chart pattern C, then the expectation E[C], which represents the average amount won per trade from that chart pattern formation, will be approximately equal to the average trade (see Chapter Two):

$$E[C] \approx w \times avgW - (1\text{-}w) \times avgL \quad (5.1)$$

In this equation, w represents the win ratio (the number of winning trades divided by the total number of trades), avgW denotes the average amount won per winning trade, and avgL indicates the average amount lost per losing trade (measured in absolute value). If the expectation E[C] is sufficiently large to cover trading costs, then it is possible to profit from such formations; however, the expectation can only be realized in the long term. In the short term, there may be a streak of losing trades that results in a significant drawdown or even ruin, as discussed in Chapter Two.

To determine the expectation of chart pattern formations, you need to obtain a large sample that is representative of the population and measure the average win, average loss, and win ratio, as shown in Equation 5.1. During the mid-1900s, a manual search made it impossible to accomplish such a task. As a result, the expectation of using chart pattern formations was unclear, making it unjustifiable to promote them for trading in the markets based solely on this information. Despite that, many traders were attracted to chart patterns primarily because they were easy to learn and apply; all that was needed was a chart and the rules of pattern formation, as described in the published books.

Usually, chartists identify a small number of formations of a particular chart pattern that has been profitable in the past and hope that the expectation will be positive in the future. However, if the actual trade sample is unrepresentative of the population, then the pattern may fail to realize a positive expectation. To understand this problem, consider a study that involves calculating statistics for the population height of residents of a specific city. A sample taken from an elementary school is not representative of the population and will produce false results, usually a biased mean and standard deviation. In some markets, certain chart patterns that were effective in the past may generate many losing trades for years or even decades. For instance, when there is a strong upward trend in stock prices due to strong fundamentals, bear pattern formations like double tops and head and shoulders are more likely to be caused by random price action than to be signs of an impending reversal. They contribute to the continuation of the trend, not its reversal.

Figure 5-1. A failed double top in IWM during October 2009

An example in the case of IWM (Russell 2000 ETF) is shown in Figure 5-1 and involves a double top that was completed by October 30, 2009. Prices reversed direction and made successive new highs after a short break below the pattern base, culminating in a failed double-top formation.

What is fascinating is not that traders without any computer power at their disposal in the 1950s, 1960s, and 1970s applied ad hoc trading techniques, such as chart patterns, to profit, but that this continued when personal computers became available and software that could in principle be used to measure the expectation of those formations could be developed. Many still use such ad hoc formations nowadays, and even diplomas are issued after examinations to those that learn the rules of charting. It's not surprising that this practice continues, given that astrology is still widely used and some schools even issue diplomas in it. Nevertheless, none of the schools can offer a measure of the success rate of their discipline.

Several academic papers with limited application scope are the only studies that measure the expectation of chart pattern formations comprehensively. At least one book author [Ref. 5] has put an honest effort into trying to compile the success rate of such patterns, but this parameter is not enough for determining the expectation, as may be seen from equation 5.1. Our objective in this book is not to provide such a study, as it would be an exercise in futility; instead, we aim to warn chartists about how easily they can be misled by technical analysis, particularly by random price formations known as chart patterns, and the lack of rigor associated with their application in trading. This author believes that trading with chart patterns without significant experience with price action leads to failure with high probability, and it is indistinguishable from gambling.

The use of chart patterns defies logic

Some technical analysts often employ *argumentum ad verecundiam,* or what is also known as an *argument from authority*, in an attempt to assign credibility to chart patterns. The reader should be aware that in most cases, an argument from authority is a fallacy, also known as an *appeal to authority*. This type of informal logical fallacy is widespread in technical analysis. Any appeal to authority, i.e., to an author of a book on technical analysis or to an academic paper, that claims the success of chart patterns without being accompanied by reproducible results has no real value. Two factors jointly determine the strength of arguments from authority:

- The authority is a legitimate expert on the subject
- A consensus exists among many legitimate experts on the matter under discussion

In certain instances, such as [Ref. 5], the author meets the first condition and is considered a legitimate expert. However, a consensus does not exist in areas that are not sciences, such as technical analysis, and any arguments supporting technical analysis that rely on an appeal to authority are logical fallacies. In science, things are different because of the existence of consensus. For example, there is a strong consensus in science that quantum mechanics is a successful theory that allows reproducible, verifiable experiments. Most of the papers and books on charting can't be reproduced, and some hidden assumptions are unknown even to their authors. Therefore, although the author of this book could write 10 more pages in this chapter talking about specific publications that support or deny the effectiveness of chart patterns, that would be a waste of the time of the reader because such trading methods can be in principle refuted based on logic alone, and it is quite interesting why the academic community has spent any time at all with them.

In principle, chart analysis tells us that if pattern C is formed and confirmed, the market will move in a certain direction x% of time, which is a logical implication of the form:

If pattern C is confirmed, then the market will move in a certain direction x% of the time (5.2)

Note that X% is not known in general. This is an implication of the form: if P, then Q. The antecedent P is a sufficient condition for the consequent Q, meaning that knowing P to be true is sufficient to conclude that Q is true. However, we also know from the paradox of material implication that anything implies a true proposition, i.e., the implication below is true:

If there are unicorns, then the Empire State Building is in New York (5.3)

The above implication is true regardless of whether or not there are unicorns. Accordingly, the market could move in a certain direction x% of the time because of some other cause(s) not related to the formation of pattern C. To establish the causality required in an inductive sense and prove that implication 5.2 is true in the context of probability theory, the pattern's statistical significance must be analyzed, and this is the point made here. This involves looking at a representative sample of pattern formations and analyzing their statistics, rather than just claiming without proof, or by just showing selected examples, that certain patterns imply certain price moves, which is exactly what the pioneers of technical analysis have done and many technical analysts still do nowadays. Since there is no proof, anything could make the price change after the pattern formation in implication 5.2, which is what the paradox of material implication in 5.3 says must happen. One of the problems of inferring statistics from small samples is that the population is very large, as already discussed in Chapter Two.

It is only fair to present at this point the counterargument, which is often made by proponents of the charting method. To defend their practice, they argue that even when x% (Equation 5-2) equals 50%, i.e., the chances of the market moving in the direction dictated by the chart pattern C are determined by a fair coin toss, if they can make more than they lose on average in the long term, then they will profit. Furthermore, they claim that they can essentially achieve profitability because the patterns allow for a higher average win than an average loss, and according to equation 5.1, the expectation is positive. One of the problems with this argument, which is analyzed in more detail later in this chapter, is that even if it is true that the average win-to-average loss ratio will be sufficiently large, a streak of losers can wipe out the trader before the longer-term expectation is realized, and this is actually what happens in many cases.

In reality, even if the above counterargument in support of chart patterns is sound, trading a representative sample requires monitoring many different markets and identifying many uncorrelated chart patterns. Furthermore, the burden of proof is on those who present the counterargument to prove that the average win-to-average loss ratio (payoff ratio) can be much higher than 1 with such patterns. A high payoff ratio may or may not be possible, but the point of this book is that such proof does not exist in an easily reproducible way, and those who claim they have profited from chart patterns must prove that their results were not due to luck, as in the examples of the simulations in Chapter Four, but due to the predictive ability of chart patterns. Given the fact that often even the formation of a certain chart pattern may be subjective or in conflict with other patterns that signal price moves in the opposite direction, any evidence of the predictive power of chart patterns may be impossible to provide, and one may have to resort to showing specific examples that demonstrate failure. In other words, the burden of proof is on those who make the claims that charting can work in the longer term, and they must prove that any positive results are significant and could not be obtained by luck. Nothing of this sort has been demonstrated to the best knowledge of this author.

Chart patterns and self-fulfilling prophecies

When the boom in the use of technical analysis occurred in the 1980s, the number of technical traders also increased, while at the same time, passive investing was not as popular as it is nowadays, and active management through market timing was gaining ground. As a result, some of the patterns of technical analysis worked well because a large number of traders would sell, for example, when a double top formed, or they would buy when an inverse head and shoulders was confirmed. This effect generated momentum, and, especially in the case of chart patterns that indicated a reversal in stock to the downside, price action accelerated because there were not enough buyers of dips to cause a rebound. This momentum effect initially offered some justification for chart patterns, but soon professionals started to realize that the moves were mainly due to the retail action of small account traders and not related to the actions of value investors. Thus, by the early 1990s professionals started "fading" patterns after they realized that retail traders were "weak hands" and could not withstand large losses. This author recalls meeting a professional trader in New York City in the late 1980s who was developing software that would identify chart patterns and indicator formations to bet against them. The self-fulfilling chart pattern prophecy soon stopped working, as is the case with most positive feedback systems that suddenly break down either due to a chaotic mode or due to saturation.

The self-fulfilling prophecy of chart patterns contributed to a positive autocorrelation in stock prices during an extended period. Autocorrelation dropped because of arbitrage in the late 1990s, making it harder to use traditional chart pattern rules and technical analysis indicators. By 2007, it was mostly gone, making trading methods that relied on it mostly useless. Figure 5-2 shows a daily chart of the S&P 500 index from January 1, 1960, to September 5, 2014, with the rolling 120-day autocorrelation of lag 1 (shifted by one day) of the daily arithmetic returns. The return for period i is given as [Close(i)/Close(i-1) - 1]. It may be seen that for about 24 years, the autocorrelation was high (blue area), with few and short periods of negative autocorrelation. That was a good time for technical methods because price action was persistent. During that time, technical traders in the stock market may have gotten the (false) impression that their methods were significant, although their success could be mostly attributed to the high autocorrelation. Note that high autocorrelation is not required to have trends, as was the case in the 2000s and especially in the uptrend that started after the Great Recession in March of 2009. Prices can rise even if autocorrelation is negative (red area).

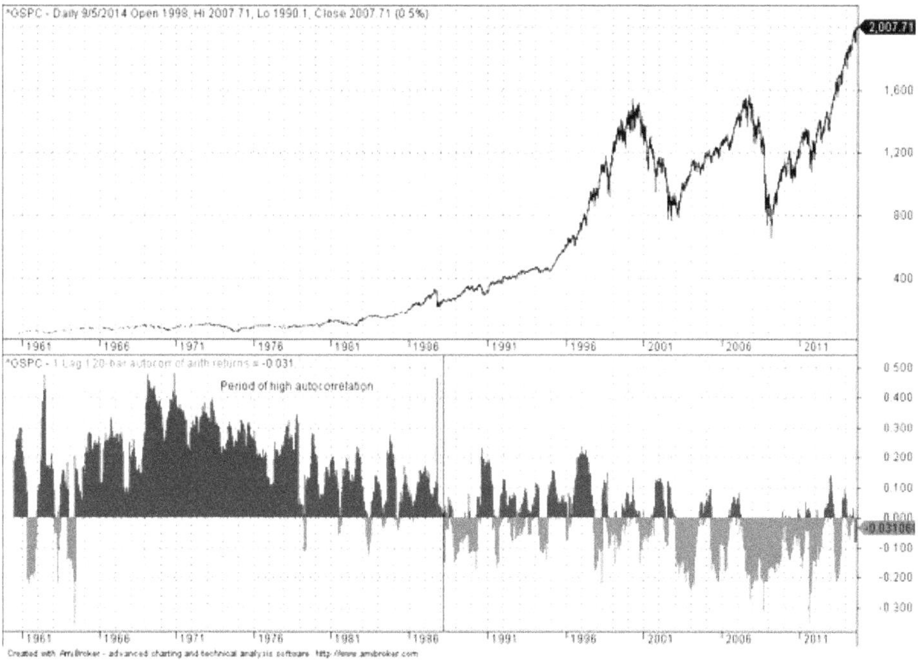

Figure 5-2. 1-Lag, 120-day autocorrelation of S&P 500 index daily arithmetic returns

It's quite possible that high autocorrelation deceived chart pattern traders in the 1960s, 1970s, and early 1980s into attributing nonexistent causal relationships to some random chart formations. Later, other technical traders and book authors raised these methods developed for the equity markets to general trading rules for all markets using an unsound induction process. The rules developed had the general form of implication 5.2. However, the conditions that made these rules profitable in the equity markets for some time were not present in those other markets with the same frequency and persistence, and as a result, a high percentage of commodity and currency traders that used them in the 1980s and 1990s lost a lot of money to locals and market makers.

The profitability of chart patterns in the equity markets fell steadily in the late 1980s, and by the mid-2000s, it was gone, as the autocorrelation of the daily returns was arbitraged out by fast traders and algos. It is quite unlikely that autocorrelation will increase again to the levels required for these technical methods to be profitable. High-frequency trading (HFT) is the basic mechanism that is currently in place to arbitrage out autocorrelation, and its profits come mainly from technical traders that trade using methods developed when there were pits and traders compiled charts manually to be made available in publications on a weekly or monthly basis. Nowadays, these technical trading methods do not have any inherent predictive power, and they have been abandoned by the majority of technical traders in favor of other technical methods, such as scalping, price pattern trading, arbitrage, and pairs trading. Some of these methods rely on mean reversion rather than on persisting autocorrelation.

Chart Patterns are mostly flukes

Chart patterns are mostly random price formations. Figure 5-3 shows a tilted head and shoulders pattern that was formed in random price data. The lesson from this chart is that regular chart patterns can form in random data, the type one finds in books that were published 60 years ago. Since price action is random in the example of Figure 5-3, there is no causality, and prices can move in any direction after the break below the neckline. Note that a chartist could claim that market price action is not entirely random. This claim may be true, but the point is to distinguish random price action from non-random price action because patterns that form during random price action are insignificant, as the price can continue on its previous trend or reverse with equal probability. Although in the longer term the expectation of such random chart formations should theoretically be exactly 0 before trading friction is accounted for, in the short term, a large drawdown can ruin a chart trader. In other words, the losses from these random patterns can cluster, and a streak of losers can cause a large loss. Therefore, each time a trader identifies a chart pattern, such as the head and shoulders in Figure 5-3, or any other chart pattern everyone else can also identify, the first question that must come to mind is the following: *Am I looking at a random formation?* Unless one can show with high statistical significance that the formation is not random, any trading based on it is indistinguishable from gambling.

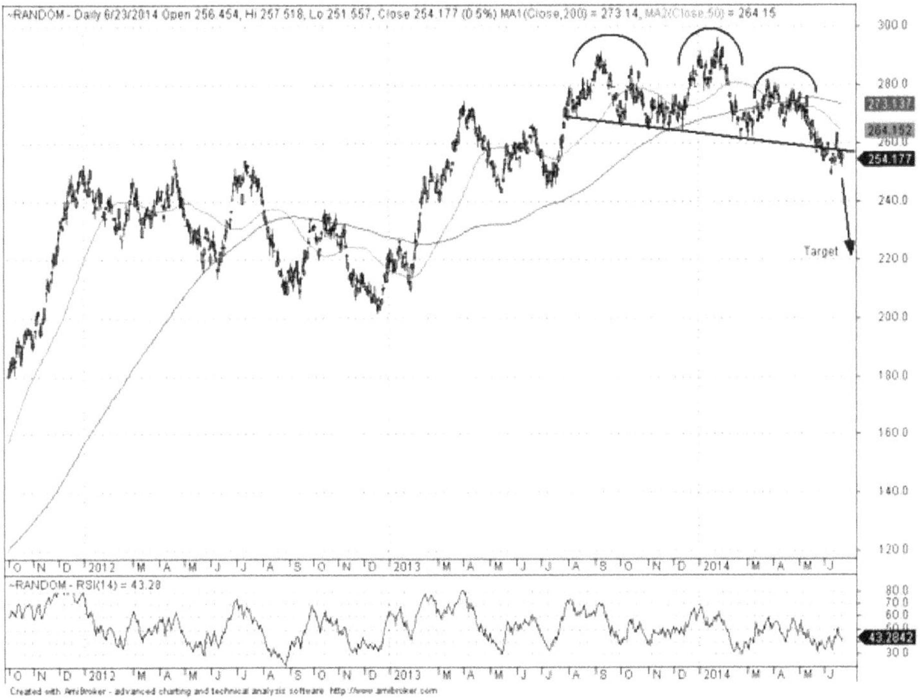

Figure 5-3. A head and shoulders pattern formed in randomly generated price data

Figure 5-4 shows an example of successive failed patterns in the iShares 20+ Year Treasury Bond ETF (TLT). The first pattern was a failed double bottom, followed by a failed head and shoulders. When this particular chart was posted on the author's blog in March of 2014, the fate of the third pattern shown, a double top formation, was unknown. Prices rallied during the following six months to a high of 120, invalidating that pattern too. This example shows how a streak of losers from chart patterns can develop, which can cause a high drawdown and possibly ruin.

Figure 5-4. Successive failed chart patterns in TLT ETF

The bond market has dealt chartists several blows recently, primarily because fundamentals rather than technical trading drive it. The most notable incident of a classic chart pattern failure was that of a complex head and shoulders top formed between November 2011 and March 2012, as shown in Figure 5-5. During that time, chartists had high expectations, and the pattern formed in TLT was extensively discussed in the blogosphere. Its failure caused disappointment but also a *backfire effect* in a large group of chartists, i.e., a tendency to defend chart patterns more strongly. This and other cognitive biases contribute to another adverse effect of using such trading methods, as will be discussed below.

Figure 5-5. Massive complex head and shoulders top in TLT ETF

Another chart pattern that has recently caused massive losses to chartists was a head and shoulders in the stock of Google formed between May and October of 2013, as shown in Figure 5-6.

The head and shoulders top in Figure 5-6 compelled many chartists to short the stock in anticipation of a large down move. Instead, a large up move occurred with a $44 opening gap on the split-adjusted chart shown ($88 before the stock split), and that was a real shock to many chartists who relied on the particular head and shoulders pattern to short the stock. Note that the head-and-shoulders pattern is considered the flagship of classical chart pattern analysis. However, its many recent failures have had a large impact because nowadays, due to social media and blogging, technical analysis has a large audience, yet many do not realize that they are getting fooled by randomness.

Figure 5-6. A failed head and shoulders pattern in the stock of Google was followed by a price gap.

Figure 5-7 shows a major failure of a head and shoulders pattern that was formed in the first half of 2012 in the Russell 2000 index. Actually, after the failure of this pattern, the index rose about 50% and reached the 1200 level in the first half of 2014. Only those who took profits from a short position based on the head and shoulders top earlier than classical chart analysis suggested avoided the losses. This is one reason that this trading method can foster a lack of discipline; traders who exit earlier than the suggested target to avoid losses may begin to do so out of fear of losing money. Slowly, this leads to erratic actions and a loss of trading discipline, as well as reinforcing several cognitive biases in the trader.

Similar conclusions as those related to chart patterns hold in the case of other geometric formations chartists use, such as trendlines, support and resistance levels, and channels, to name a few. There is simply no logical basis for using any such geometric constructs in price action analysis because, in most cases, they are artifacts of randomness. In the case of trendlines, there is also subjectivity in drawing them, and in many cases, they conflict with other chart patterns. In the case of support and resistance, classical analysis rules assert that when broken and a trend is in place, support turns to resistance and resistance to support. However, in many cases, what chartists think is a support or resistance level is derived from wishful thinking. Anyone who is not convinced could generate random data and see how many trendlines and support and resistance levels appear in the chart. Figure 5-8 shows several up-and-down trendlines and support and resistance lines formed in random price data.

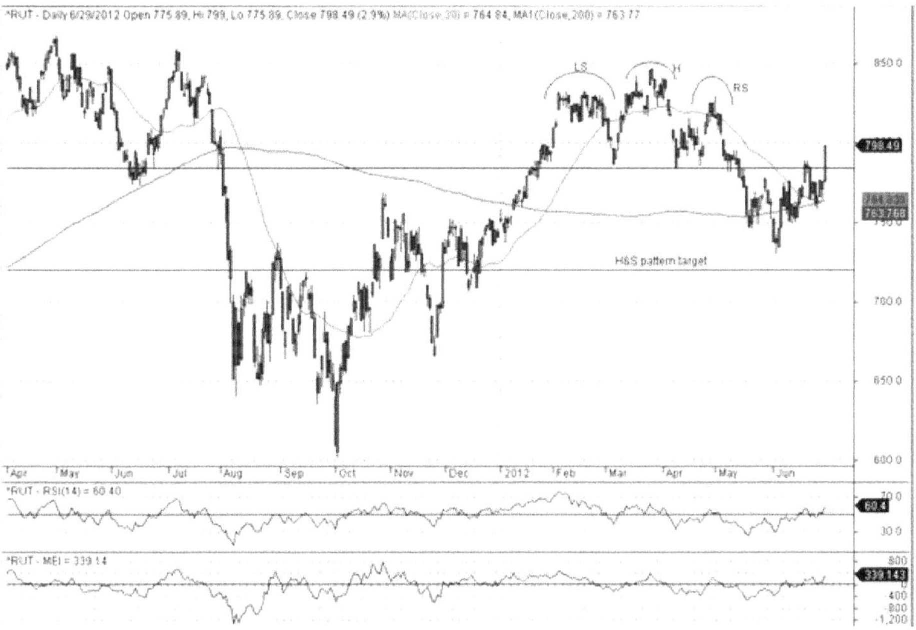

Figure 5-7. A major failure of a head and shoulders pattern in the Russell 2000 index during 2012

Technical analysis rules cannot assign any significance to lines drawn on charts as related to the future direction of prices because that depends on information that was not available at the time of their formation. Uncovering a causal relationship between some pattern, a classical chart pattern, or some other geometric formation, such as a trendline or a support level, and price action goes beyond visual chart inspection and into the realms of quantitative analysis based on probability and statistical inference. Chartists get fooled by randomness because markets are random most of the time.

Figure 5-8. Trendlines and support and resistance levels in random price data

Claims of Chartists Debunked With Simple Math

It can be shown that traders in classical chart formations that take several months to form have to trade more frequently than even short-term traders to realize the same profit. Given the relevant timeframes, more frequent trading requires trading in many different uncorrelated markets, and that may be impractical. To see that, let us consider a chartist and a short-term trader with the following parameters:

Chartist: win rate = 20%, reward = 5, risk = 1

The chartist has a low win rate, but the claim is that he makes five times more than he loses on average.

Short-term trader: win rate = 70%, reward =1, risk = 1

The short-term trader has a payoff ratio of 1 but at a higher win rate.

The average trade for the chartist, avgTc, is given by:

$$AvgTc = 0.2 \times 5 - 0.8 \times 1 = 0.2 \quad (5\text{-}4)$$

The average trade for the short-term trader, avgTs, is given by:

$$AvgTs = 0.70 \times 1 - 0.3 \times 1 = 0.4 \quad (5\text{-}5)$$

Note that the average trade is equal to the mean of the population only for sufficient samples (Ref. 1, page 138), and only in that case does it become the expectation. From Equations 5-3 and 5-4, it may be seen that the average trade of the chartist is half that of the short-term trader, 0.2 versus 0.4. Therefore, the chartist needs to trade twice as much to achieve the same profit. Furthermore, since the average number of bars when trading classical chart patterns is several weeks or even months, the average trade will converge to the expected value after a long time. For example, if we assume that a typical chart pattern takes 3 months to form, then for a sufficient sample of 30 trades, it will take 7.5 years of data in all markets combined. In contrast, a short-term trader needs a few months to accumulate a sufficient sample to profit from a winning strategy or test a strategy moving forward.

The conclusion from the above simple analysis is that any claims of high payoff ratios (average win to average loss) to justify charting and trading based on formations that take several months to form come in conflict with simple math and common sense. Ruin, when trading with a low win rate, is highly probable and most likely to occur before the average trade converges to the expectation.

Fooled by random indicator patterns

The use of technical analysis indicators became widespread among traders with the advent of the personal computer. Before that, only those with access to expensive mainframe computers could calculate a simple indicator in real time. Even with end-of-day data, it was time-consuming to calculate a moving average for more than a few securities. The advent of the personal computer made possible the development of retail software that could scan data in any timeframe and calculate a set of indicators and patterns based on them, such as moving average crossovers, the Moving Average Convergence Divergence (MACD) indicator, the Relative Strength Indicator (RSI), and a host of others, including the identification of Fibonacci levels, Elliot Waves, candlestick patterns, etc. This is when data-mining bias started emerging, and its impact on analysis became important, as it will be discussed in more detail in Chapter Six.

As in the case of classical chart patterns, the use of indicators and patterns formed by them, such as an oversold condition or a moving average crossover, does not provide sufficient conditions for price action. Unless one knows the expectation of indicator patterns, their use is not justified. However, every day, a lot of technical analysis reports are released that focus on these kinds of patterns. For example, a pattern where the price falls below the 200-day simple moving average or a pattern where the RSI rises above 70. These reports are often based on wishful thinking and not on facts. The following implication is true regardless of the truth value of the antecedent

If indicator pattern XYZ occurs, then prices will move up (or down)

Indicators are neither necessary nor sufficient conditions for price action, as movements in security prices usually take place due to fundamental factors. However, there are times when certain indicator patterns can realize positive expectation in the long term, given sufficient samples. Proper statistical analysis must be used to identify such patterns, but this is not what Level I chartists do when they use indicators. In the longer term, Level I trading based on indicator patterns is random, and in the absence of trading friction, it will break even regardless of the risk/reward ratio. The rationale for this rule is as follows: if the risk/reward ratio is 1, i.e., the average gain is equal to the average loss, then the win rate will approach 50% in the longer term and the profit factor will be 1, which is a break-even condition. In reality, however, the performance is negative due to trading friction.

If the risk/reward ratio is much lower than 1, as some chartists suggest, and if X is risked to earn n times X, then the win ratio decreases accordingly because the stop-loss is smaller than the profit target, resulting in more losing trades than winning ones. Furthermore, the paradox of reversing trading systems in

Chapter Two dictates this break-even condition as follows: If a chartist is doomed to lose money consistently, then one could reverse his method and profit. Then, charting would be profitable because the same patterns would signal the reverse positions with high expectation. Not understanding these facts fools many chartists who break even with low trading costs and sufficiently large samples of trades into thinking that they possessed some skill in some tough trading environment and managed not to lose money. But in reality, the break-even occurred because statistics demanded it, and there was no skill involved; it was all random trading.

There have been several academic studies on the subject of the effectiveness of technical indicators, some involving the use of thousands of indicator patterns. Most have concluded that indicator patterns possess no predictive power that suffices to overcome trading friction. The objective of this book is not to present the results of such studies, although that would add a few dozen pages because there is no way in virtually all the cases to reproduce the results and know all of the assumptions made. A key message of this book is that charting lacks a fundamental logical basis, as any pattern or indicator can signal a price change in a security; additionally, determining which chart or indicator patterns to use in advance for signaling changes requires either Level II expert chart analysis or Level IV expert quantitative analysis. In the former case, it is the experience with price action that allows a chartist to pick the appropriate patterns to use from a large selection, and in the latter, it is the proper statistical analysis that increases the probability of a positive expectation.

In the case of an indicator pattern IP, the expectation E[IP], which is the amount won per trade on average for large samples, will be approximately equal to the average trade (see Chapter Two).

$$E[IP] \approx w \times avgW - (1-w) \times avgL \quad (5.6)$$

where w is the win ratio, avgW is the average winning trade, and avgL is the average losing trade (in absolute value). If the expectation is sufficiently large to cover trading costs, then one could profit from indicator patterns, but only in the long term, as in the short term, there can be a streak of losers resulting in a significant drawdown.

Calculating the expectation of indicator patterns given by Equation 5.6 requires identifying a sufficiently large representative sample and measuring the average win, average loss, and win rate, as already discussed in Chapter Two. Such a task was difficult for retail traders to accomplish before personal computers became available, and it was only possible for investment firms with access to expensive mainframe computers. Nevertheless, although nowadays there is even free software available that allows programming and backtesting indicator patterns on historical data, the majority of retail traders pick random occurrences, such as a moving average crossover or an oversold RSI, and use them to forecast future price moves without measuring the expectation E[IP]. One of the reasons for that is that testing indicator patterns requires programming skills and it takes time to code them. Then, the interpretation of the results of the backtesting analysis is not trivial because it is plagued by small samples and by hidden assumptions, such as that what worked in the past has a higher chance of working in the future or that what did not work in the past should not be used. There are ways of dealing with these problems, but that is done properly by Level IV quant traders, as discussed in Chapter Six.

As with the case of random chart pattern formations, even if the expectation of an indicator pattern is positive, the trader's account may be ruined in the short term because of excessive drawdown, which is the result of a long period of adverse market conditions during which losses accumulate. Therefore, an understanding of the risk of ruin (Chapter Three) and how capitalization requirements and trading friction affect profitability (Chapter Four) should be part of the analysis. Nevertheless, most chartists using classical chart patterns or indicator patterns neither know the expectation nor exercise proper risk and money management. The reasons for that include undercapitalization, a lack of understanding of the issues involved, wishful thinking, and a lack of discipline. The high failure rate of Level I traders, which is often claimed to be close to 95% or even higher, is a result of getting fooled by naïve technical analysis practices. Probably, the rate would be close to 100% if the lucky ones stayed in the markets long enough to realize a negative expectation. Unless a Level I trader is lucky, as demonstrated with the simulations of random systems in Chapter Four, ruin is certain if enough time is allowed. Level I trading is a game that transfers nearly 100% of wealth from naïve participants to market makers, brokers, and other well-informed and skilled professionals.

Indicator patterns and self-fulfilling prophecies

When traders who use simplistic technical analysis dominate the market, technical indicator patterns become self-fulfilling prophecies. An example is the 200-day moving average, which acts as a resistance or support level. This average became popular in the mid-1980s when the financial media and a few analysts who were presented as indisputable authorities constantly referred to it as an important technical level, possibly to convince the public that they were following some rules. But quants could not determine any special significance that could be attributed to this average, and on top of that, its use would often result in trading strategies with large drawdown levels. Despite that, the use of the 200-day moving average in the last 30 years has increased its significance to the point that it has become a self-fulfilling prophecy.

There is no clear explanation or justification for the use of most indicators. Choosing the 200-day simple moving average as an important trend indicator is arbitrary. A 201-day simple moving average indicates almost the same condition as a 200-day simple moving average, so the latter was probably chosen because it involved a nice round number. More importantly, technical traders pay attention when prices find support at the 200-day moving average but rarely do that when they touch a 207-day moving average and bounce back. Why is the 207-day average not called a support level but only round numbers, such as the 20-day, 30-day, 50-day, 100-day, or 200-day? There is nothing special about those round numbers, as they have the same probability of being selected from any finite set of numbers. This illustrates how unsound the foundation and practice of classical technical analysis are.

Figure 5-9. 200-day moving average (solid line) versus 240-day moving average (dashed line)

Figure 5-9 shows a daily chart of the S&P 500 index from September 2009 to December 2011. In June 2011, prices found support at the 200-day moving average (solid line) and bounced back for a few days. There were many reports on social media by technical analysts of the following form: "The S&P 500 found support at its 200-day moving average and bounced back strongly." Some chartists would even add that the second bounce off the 200-day moving average contributed to a double-bottom formation. However, in May 2010, the same index found support at its 240-day moving average (dashed line), and nobody paid attention to that. This situation is a classic case of selection bias at work. Chartists look at the 200-day moving average more than the 240-day moving average because, at some point, someone fell victim to the *clustering illusion* fallacy and attributed the former a special status. Then, some others continued to promote that average and managed to convince traders that it possessed a special place among all possible averages. The truth is that the 200-day moving average possesses no such special place except for the fact that if many people believe it does, then it will, but only occasionally and when the market permits that. This is what a self-fulfilling prophecy in technical analysis means. The efforts by a whole industry developed around the technical analysis to convert it into a self-fulfilling prophecy have failed because ultimately prices are not determined by chartists but by value investors, who rarely pay attention to technical levels but only to valuations.

Indicators and wishful thinking

Traders' wishful thinking led to the idea that certain indicator levels or patterns of indicators can predict price direction. This was done to make the subject of technical analysis more interesting to traders. For example, the "golden cross" pattern, which describes a situation when a fast-moving average crosses above a slow-moving average, and the related pattern of a "death cross," which describes a situation when a fast-moving average crosses below a slow-moving average, are known not to have any forecasting power unless the moving average periods are fitted to the data. Another example is the Relative Strength Index (RSI), which is used to indicate overbought and oversold levels. The idea is that when the n-period RSI rises above a certain level, that is a signal of an overbought market, and when it falls below a certain level, that is a signal of an oversold market. Thus, the RSI indicator, which is usually calculated over 14 days, along with a group of other similar indicators, was labeled an overbought/oversold indicator. This, however, is a clear indication that wishful thinking and selection bias plague the foundation of technical analysis. In the case of the RSI, it was probably called an oversold or overbought indicator after applying the gambler's fallacy. The RSI is an indicator of market strength, as its name implies. But a gambler may think that if the market has been strong for several days, then at some point it must correct, as is the case with the tossing of a fair coin when one may assume that tails should interrupt a long streak of heads. The problem with this thinking is that the probability of heads and tails does not depend on how many have already occurred in a row. Each time a fair coin is tossed, the probability of heads (tails) is 0.5. Thus, tails after 14 consecutive heads have a probability of 0.5 and not a higher probability, as some gamblers may falsely think.

Below is the definition of the Relative Strength Indication [Ref. 6]:

"A technical momentum indicator that compares the magnitude of recent gains to recent losses in an attempt to determine the overbought and oversold conditions of an asset. It is calculated using the following formula:

$$RSI = 100 - 100/(1 + RS^*)$$

*Where RS = Average of x days' up closes / Average of x days' down closes."

It may be seen that the above definition involves two parts: The first part explains the fundamental characteristics of the RSI, a momentum indicator. The next part describes the forecasting capability technical analysis practitioners ascribe to this indicator: "...compares the magnitude of recent gains to recent losses in an attempt to determine the overbought and oversold conditions of an asset." The definition attempts to raise technical analysis to the level of a forecasting method that traders can use. Possibly someone did that in the past after exercising selection bias, and then the claims were repeated in publications and articles. Many novice traders obey these rules because they are convinced that they are part of a concrete method for trading the markets. If they make profits, technical analysis is praised, but if they lose, they are blamed for not applying it correctly. In the case of the RSI, a few tests should suffice to convince even a skeptic that the reference to overbought and oversold levels is motivated by wishful thinking, possibly combined with past performance results.

Figure 5-10 shows the results of backtesting a trading system that enters a short position at the open of the next day after the RSI(n) crosses above 70 and exits when either a 3% profit target or a 3% stop-loss is reached. Unadjusted (not adjusted for dividends) daily data for SPY ETF from inception to 09/30/2014 was used in the backtest. The value of n, which is the RSI period, varied from 5 to 40 in increments of 1, and the system was fully invested. No commission was applied for simplicity. The pseudo-code of the system is shown in Pseudo Code 5-1.

M = integer (equity/entry price);

If RSI(n) > 70 then short M shares at the open of the next day //short signal

Pseudocode 5-1. A trading system for going short when the RSI(n) is greater than 70

No.	RSI	CAR	Sharpe Ratio	# Trades	% of Winners	Net Profit	Avg Bars Held	# of winners	# of losers
24	28	0.26	0.80	8	62.50	5,817.72	21.88	5	3
26	30	0.26	0.77	8	62.50	5,795.20	22.00	5	3
25	29	0.26	0.77	8	62.50	5,795.20	22.13	5	3
28	32	-0.01	-0.10	4	50.00	-191.89	22.00	2	2
29	33	-0.01	-0.10	4	50.00	-197.02	20.25	2	2
30	34	-0.01	-0.10	4	50.00	-197.02	20.25	2	2
36	40	-0.10	-0.73	3	33.33	-2,197.07	27.67	1	2
35	39	-0.10	-0.73	3	33.33	-2,197.07	27.67	1	2
34	38	-0.10	-0.73	3	33.33	-2,197.07	27.67	1	2
33	37	-0.10	-0.73	3	33.33	-2,197.07	27.67	1	2
32	36	-0.10	-0.76	3	33.33	-2,203.41	25.00	1	2
31	35	-0.15	-1.24	3	33.33	-3,116.66	25.33	1	2
17	21	-0.15	-0.20	23	47.83	-3,167.87	20.78	11	12
27	31	-0.15	-0.77	5	40.00	-3,191.08	24.80	2	3
18	22	-0.40	-0.53	19	42.11	-8,255.49	22.26	8	11
23	27	-0.44	-1.15	11	36.36	-9,083.46	18.45	4	7
22	26	-0.50	-0.93	14	35.71	-10,316.28	20.64	5	9
16	20	-0.53	-0.50	28	42.86	-10,951.99	22.29	12	16
21	25	-0.65	-1.16	15	33.33	-13,208.84	19.33	5	10
14	18	-0.75	-0.50	38	42.11	-15,121.99	23.53	16	22
19	23	-0.80	-1.24	16	31.25	-15,948.11	23.19	5	11
20	24	-0.80	-1.24	16	31.25	-15,948.59	23.06	5	11
15	19	-0.81	-0.63	32	40.63	-16,089.34	24.28	13	19
9	13	-0.85	-0.35	68	45.59	-16,806.63	18.84	31	37
13	17	-0.87	-0.60	37	40.54	-17,304.10	22.35	15	22
12	16	-1.14	-0.73	41	39.02	-21,970.75	20.88	16	25
1	5	-1.41	-0.24	189	47.62	-26,560.34	15.51	90	99
11	15	-1.44	-0.83	47	38.30	-26,946.54	19.47	18	29
10	14	-1.65	-0.75	58	39.66	-30,254.72	20.00	23	35
5	9	-2.15	-0.58	104	43.27	-37,527.28	19.38	45	59
8	12	-2.34	-0.91	72	38.89	-40,210.02	19.49	28	44
2	6	-2.39	-0.44	163	44.79	-40,857.85	16.67	73	90
7	11	-2.48	-0.83	83	39.76	-41,923.35	19.65	33	50
4	8	-2.52	-0.59	120	43.33	-42,535.67	19.73	52	68
3	7	-2.83	-0.58	140	42.86	-46,327.52	18.76	60	80
6	10	-2.85	-0.84	93	39.78	-46,545.53	20.48	37	56

Figure 5-10. Backtest results for the system in Pseudo Code 5-1 on daily SPY ETF data and n = 5 to 40. Created with Amibroker – advanced charting and technical analysis software: www.amibroker.com

In Figure 5–10, the backtesting results are sorted by the highest net profit. This short-only system was profitable only for values of n between 28 and 30 and unprofitable for values less than 28 and greater than 30. For n = 14, a popular choice among chartists, the win rate is 39.66%, and the compound annual return (CAR) is -1.65% on a sample of 58 trades, i.e., this choice for the RSI period results in a losing system. Thus, in the case of SPY ETF, the RSI(14) has acted as a strength indicator, as was expected, due to the longer-term structural positive bias of this ETF. One could reverse the system in Pseudo Code 5-1 and profit with a 3% profit target and stop-loss.

An important observation from the results in Figure 5–15 is that the system based on the RSI(n) was profitable for just three values of n in the interval [5, 40]. Therefore, a selection of n = 30 to claim that the RS(30) > 70 provides profitable short signals in SPY ETF amounts to curve-fitting the indicator signals to the price series. This is what might have happened in the past, with RSI(14) > 70. Probably someone determined that, from n equal to 13, this indicator performed well in some markets for some time. Then, a self-fulfilling prophecy worked for a while until market conditions changed. The RSI alone is not always a useful indicator for detecting overbought or oversold conditions because it is, by design, an indicator of strength.

	RSI	CAR	Sharpe Ratio	# Trades	% of Winners	Net Profit	Avg Bars Held	# of winners	# of losers
1	5	-1.70	-0.44	111	45.05	-31,078.62	18.44	50	61
2	6	-2.53	-0.99	70	37.14	-42,613.92	19.59	26	44
3	7	-1.23	-0.61	55	41.82	-23,468.13	19.65	23	32
4	8	-1.81	-1.18	43	34.88	-32,680.15	19.09	15	28
5	9	-1.30	-1.18	31	35.48	-24,749.80	19.65	11	20
6	10	-0.77	-0.71	27	40.74	-15,368.21	26.56	11	16
7	11	-0.46	-0.65	19	42.11	-9,536.09	22.89	8	11
8	12	-0.30	-0.71	12	41.67	-6,331.49	19.08	5	7
9	13	-0.43	-1.33	9	33.33	-8,991.04	21.33	3	6
10	14	-0.25	-0.98	6	33.33	-5,191.09	24.17	2	4
11	15	-0.25	-1.00	6	33.33	-5,195.25	23.83	2	4
12	16	0.04	0.33	2	50.00	838.01	27.00	1	1
13	17	0.04	0.33	2	50.00	838.01	27.00	1	1
14	18	0.18	N/A	1	100.00	3,969.30	8.00	1	0
15	19	0.00	0.00	0	N/A	0.00	N/A	0	0
16	20	0.00	0.00	0	N/A	0.00	N/A	0	0
17	21	0.00	0.00	0	N/A	0.00	N/A	0	0
18	22	0.00	0.00	0	N/A	0.00	N/A	0	0
19	23	0.00	0.00	0	N/A	0.00	N/A	0	0
20	24	0.00	0.00	0	N/A	0.00	N/A	0	0
21	25	0.00	0.00	0	N/A	0.00	N/A	0	0
22	26	0.00	0.00	0	N/A	0.00	N/A	0	0
23	27	0.00	0.00	0	N/A	0.00	N/A	0	0
24	28	0.00	0.00	0	N/A	0.00	N/A	0	0
25	29	0.00	0.00	0	N/A	0.00	N/A	0	0
26	30	0.00	0.00	0	N/A	0.00	N/A	0	0
27	31	0.00	0.00	0	N/A	0.00	N/A	0	0
28	32	0.00	0.00	0	N/A	0.00	N/A	0	0
29	33	0.00	0.00	0	N/A	0.00	N/A	0	0
30	34	0.00	0.00	0	N/A	0.00	N/A	0	0
31	35	0.00	0.00	0	N/A	0.00	N/A	0	0
32	36	0.00	0.00	0	N/A	0.00	N/A	0	0
33	37	0.00	0.00	0	N/A	0.00	N/A	0	0
34	38	0.00	0.00	0	N/A	0.00	N/A	0	0
35	39	0.00	0.00	0	N/A	0.00	N/A	0	0
36	40	0.00	0.00	0	N/A	0.00	N/A	0	0

Number of rows: 36

Figure 5-11: Backtest results for the system in Pseudo Code 5-2 on daily SPY ETF data and n = 6 to 40. Created with Amibroker – advanced charting and technical analysis software: www.amibroker.com

Figure 5-11 shows the results of the same backtest as in Figure 5-10, but after the overbought level is raised to 80, as shown in Pseudo Code 5-2.

M = integer (equity/entry price);

If RSI(n) > 80 then short M shares at the open of the next day //short signal

Pseudocode 5-2. A trading system for going short when the RSI(n) is greater than 80

The system is profitable for values of n equal to 16, 17, and 18, with small trade samples. For n = 14, only 6 trades were generated, and the system was unprofitable. Therefore, the condition RSI(14) > 80 signaled continuation rather than reversal. The profitable cases arise from a few values of n, and must be curve-fitted to the data to support an overbought indicator.

	RSI	CAR	Sharpe Ratio	# Trades	% of Winners	Net Profit	Avg Bars Held	# of winners	# of losers
1	5	-5.04	-0.55	111	41.44	-67,426.12	35.37	46	65
2	6	-6.41	-0.83	93	35.48	-76,214.30	39.85	33	60
3	7	-4.89	-0.64	92	39.13	-66,280.07	37.67	36	56
4	8	-5.02	-0.75	83	37.35	-67,242.82	36.23	31	52
5	9	-5.84	-0.97	75	33.33	-72,892.72	38.08	25	50
6	10	-4.38	-0.77	66	36.36	-62,105.96	42.83	24	42
7	11	-3.77	-0.74	60	38.33	-56,496.74	40.72	23	37
8	12	-3.32	-0.78	50	36.00	-51,910.96	41.58	18	32
9	13	-3.12	-0.72	51	37.25	-49,724.99	40.12	19	32
10	14	-2.86	-0.74	44	36.36	-46,673.23	43.93	16	28
11	15	-3.25	-0.97	38	31.58	-51,136.93	47.24	12	26
12	16	-3.21	-1.03	34	29.41	-50,745.33	54.26	10	24
13	17	-3.63	-1.33	30	23.33	-55,146.01	62.60	7	23
14	18	-3.61	-1.30	30	23.33	-54,983.08	66.03	7	23
15	19	-3.10	-1.29	25	24.00	-49,437.12	68.68	6	19
16	20	-3.08	-1.51	23	21.74	-49,294.80	61.30	5	18
17	21	-2.62	-1.93	17	17.65	-43,775.14	56.00	3	14
18	22	-2.14	-1.71	15	20.00	-37,465.85	56.80	3	12
19	23	-1.90	-2.07	12	16.67	-34,017.34	53.75	2	10
20	24	-1.90	-2.06	12	16.67	-34,022.40	54.33	2	10
21	25	-1.68	-1.51	13	23.08	-30,696.78	52.31	3	10
22	26	-1.90	-2.04	12	16.67	-33,998.32	55.67	2	10
23	27	-1.43	-1.69	10	20.00	-26,877.08	57.60	2	8
24	28	-0.93	-1.37	8	25.00	-18,361.28	44.88	2	6
25	29	-0.51	-0.73	8	37.50	-10,427.39	40.75	3	5
26	30	-0.51	-0.73	8	37.50	-10,427.39	40.63	3	5
27	31	-0.72	-1.88	5	20.00	-14,488.08	45.00	1	4
28	32	-0.48	-1.59	4	25.00	-9,994.42	37.50	1	3
29	33	-0.49	-1.60	4	25.00	-10,043.71	37.50	1	3
30	34	-0.49	-1.60	4	25.00	-10,043.71	37.50	1	3
31	35	-0.71	-498.89	3	0.00	-14,336.57	44.00	0	3
32	36	-0.25	-1.04	3	33.33	-5,253.14	34.67	1	2
33	37	-0.25	-1.02	3	33.33	-5,249.10	36.67	1	2
34	38	-0.25	-1.02	3	33.33	-5,249.10	36.67	1	2
35	39	-0.25	-1.02	3	33.33	-5,249.10	36.67	1	2
36	40	-0.25	-1.02	3	33.33	-5,249.10	36.67	1	2

Number of rows: 36

Figure 5-12: Backtest results for the system in Pseudo Code 5-1 on daily SPY ETF data and n = 6 to 40. Created with Amibroker – advanced charting and technical analysis software: www.amibroker.com

Figure 5-12 shows what happens if the same backtest is repeated for the system in Pseudocode 5-1, but with the profit target and stop-loss set to 5%. In this case, the system is unprofitable for all values of n. Therefore, the condition RSI(n) > 70, for n = 5 to 40, does not signal any overbought conditions but market strength in the short term for the specified exit levels in the market considered. Nevertheless, many traders in the past three decades were told by book authors and technical analysis gurus that the RSI indicator provides overbought and oversold levels. As the backtests show, nothing can be further from the truth in the case of SPY ETF using reasonable exit levels.

Figure 5-13 shows the backtest results of the system in Pseudo Code 5-1 with a 5% profit target and stop-loss applied to GLD daily data from inception to 09/30/2014. Only values of n greater than 30 generated profitable results, and the samples of trades were small, less than 10 in all cases. As a result, one could not even be sure whether the positive results were significant. The RSI(14) > 70 condition in GLD resulted in a win rate of 33.33% and a CAR of -5.15%, which translates to a losing system.

	RSI	CAR	Sharpe Ratio	# Trades	% of Winners	Net Profit	Avg Bars Held	# of winners	# of losers
1	5	-7.30	-0.69	73	41.10	-52,650.24	19.52	30	43
2	6	-10.08	-1.13	63	34.92	-64,968.01	21.06	22	41
3	7	-9.86	-1.26	56	33.93	-64,103.60	21.43	19	37
4	8	-11.96	-1.91	49	26.53	-71,550.66	21.71	13	36
5	9	-9.81	-1.59	48	31.25	-63,889.91	19.77	15	33
6	10	-5.78	-0.90	44	38.64	-44,443.79	20.59	17	27
7	11	-6.35	-1.08	41	36.59	-47,634.87	20.83	15	26
8	12	-7.34	-1.29	39	33.33	-52,891.26	23.59	13	26
9	13	-4.32	-0.74	39	41.03	-35,323.35	20.77	16	23
10	14	-6.15	-1.28	33	33.33	-46,524.61	21.97	11	22
11	15	-7.65	-1.98	28	25.00	-54,387.34	23.39	7	21
12	16	-8.20	-2.81	25	20.00	-57,015.29	20.72	5	20
13	17	-6.75	-2.62	22	22.73	-49,800.19	18.86	5	17
14	18	-6.32	-2.93	18	16.67	-47,476.90	22.11	3	15
15	19	-5.39	-2.77	16	18.75	-42,119.79	20.19	3	13
16	20	-4.85	-2.42	15	20.00	-38,798.69	23.67	3	12
17	21	-4.85	-2.42	15	20.00	-38,784.15	23.20	3	12
18	22	-5.18	-3.42	13	15.38	-40,835.40	23.23	2	11
19	23	-5.78	-5.11	12	8.33	-44,444.71	24.33	1	11
20	24	-5.29	-4.87	11	9.09	-41,519.27	24.18	1	10
21	25	-5.29	-4.87	11	9.09	-41,500.04	24.18	1	10
22	26	-4.05	-3.06	11	18.18	-33,523.54	21.09	2	9
23	27	-2.89	-1.88	11	27.27	-25,151.09	22.18	3	8
24	28	-0.89	-0.57	11	45.45	-8,416.04	15.91	5	6
25	29	-0.84	-0.54	11	45.45	-8,012.95	15.00	5	6
26	30	0.14	0.20	9	55.56	1,390.44	13.89	5	4
27	31	0.66	0.88	8	62.50	6,743.17	10.13	5	3
28	32	1.19	1.75	7	71.43	12,356.06	10.29	5	2
29	33	1.18	1.84	7	71.43	12,300.45	9.43	5	2
30	34	1.24	1.76	7	71.43	12,921.01	11.14	5	2
31	35	0.74	1.15	6	66.67	7,543.53	12.33	4	2
32	36	0.74	1.15	6	66.67	7,543.53	12.33	4	2
33	37	0.91	1.05	6	66.67	9,344.78	23.67	4	2
34	38	0.91	1.08	6	66.67	9,350.48	22.83	4	2
35	39	1.44	5.01	5	80.00	15,099.80	5.80	4	1
36	40	0.40	1.44	5	60.00	4,063.74	4.60	3	2

Number of rows: 36

Figure 5-13: Backtest results for the system in Pseudo Code 5-1 on daily GLD ETF data and n = 6 to 40. Created with Amibroker – advanced charting and technical analysis software: www.amibroker.com

Figure 5-14 shows the backtest results of the system in Pseudo Code 5-1 with a 5% profit target and stop-loss applied to XLE ETF daily data from inception to 09/30/2014. In this case, the effect of curve-fitting is even more pronounced, with values of n equal to 8, 11, 37, 38, 39, and 40 generating positive results. Note that the RSI(8) > 70 system generated 91 short trades with a CAR of 0.25%, while the RSI(9) > 70 generated 81 trades with a CAR of -0.81%. These variations show the high sensitivity of the results depending on the choice of the value for the parameter n.

	RSI	CAR	Sharpe Ratio	# Trades	% of Winners	Net Profit	Avg Bars Held	# of winners	# of losers
1	5	-6.43	-0.58	136	43.38	-64,941.87	14.72	59	77
2	6	-3.00	-0.27	121	47.11	-38,184.57	14.91	57	64
3	7	-2.04	-0.19	102	48.04	-27,794.00	16.29	49	53
4	8	0.25	0.08	91	51.65	4,072.13	17.31	47	44
5	9	-0.81	-0.07	81	49.38	-12,051.87	18.09	40	41
6	10	-0.39	-0.03	68	50.00	-6,011.46	20.34	34	34
7	11	0.23	0.09	60	51.67	3,719.22	18.78	31	29
8	12	-0.68	-0.11	53	49.06	-10,191.44	19.36	26	27
9	13	-1.28	-0.25	49	46.94	-18,373.88	21.04	23	26
10	14	-1.33	-0.33	43	46.51	-19,099.82	18.16	20	23
11	15	-0.96	-0.26	38	47.37	-14,149.54	18.50	18	20
12	16	-1.54	-0.52	32	43.75	-21,761.19	19.75	14	18
13	17	-2.76	-1.17	26	34.62	-35,675.15	22.54	9	17
14	18	-3.04	-1.76	21	28.57	-38,523.14	20.38	6	15
15	19	-1.78	-1.08	19	36.84	-24,708.36	19.11	7	12
16	20	-1.44	-0.92	18	38.89	-20,400.39	18.39	7	11
17	21	-1.74	-1.22	17	35.29	-24,195.35	18.94	6	11
18	22	-1.42	-0.97	16	37.50	-20,217.84	21.50	6	10
19	23	-1.42	-1.06	16	37.50	-20,236.91	17.69	6	10
20	24	-1.71	-1.60	13	30.77	-23,866.00	19.31	4	9
21	25	-1.05	-0.94	13	38.46	-15,354.98	18.92	5	8
22	26	-1.05	-0.94	13	38.46	-15,369.35	18.77	5	8
23	27	-0.73	-0.69	12	41.67	-10,897.22	18.83	5	7
24	28	-0.73	-0.67	12	41.67	-10,893.10	19.75	5	7
25	29	-0.73	-0.67	12	41.67	-10,890.70	19.83	5	7
26	30	-0.73	-0.67	12	41.67	-10,886.64	19.67	5	7
27	31	-0.71	-0.80	10	40.00	-10,666.41	19.90	4	6
28	32	-0.45	-0.54	9	44.44	-6,859.92	18.11	4	5
29	33	-0.45	-0.54	9	44.44	-6,851.07	18.11	4	5
30	34	-0.05	-0.06	6	50.00	-756.04	25.00	3	3
31	35	-0.36	-0.68	5	40.00	-5,501.75	28.00	2	3
32	36	-0.36	-0.68	5	40.00	-5,501.75	28.00	2	3
33	37	0.28	0.76	5	60.00	4,484.41	16.60	3	2
34	38	0.28	0.76	5	60.00	4,484.41	16.60	3	2
35	39	0.28	0.71	5	60.00	4,467.41	18.80	3	2
36	40	0.28	0.67	5	60.00	4,494.51	20.00	3	2

Number of rows: 36

Figure 5-14: Backtest results for the system in Pseudo Code 5-1 on daily XLE ETF data and n = 6 to 40. Created with Amibroker – advanced charting and technical analysis software: www.amibroker.com

The examples involving the RSI indicator were used to illustrate how a rule of technical analysis used by chartists turns out not to indicate what they expect after quantitative analysis is performed. The examples also indicate that the foundations of technical analysis were probably set by exercising selection bias and wishful thinking while maybe hoping that if many traders would apply the rules, then they would become a self-fulfilling prophecy.

Many other indicators that chartists use in a specific context can yield similar results. Most indicators signal continuation or reversal depending on price action dynamics, and it is difficult to determine the outcome from charts because all derivatives of price lag price by definition. It takes detailed quantitative Level IV analysis to decide whether some indicators and patterns based on them have an edge. Unless one is a Level II expert chartist with significant experience trading price action, the use of indicators plotted on charts and signals derived from them offers no edge. The results are erratic trading with no potential for profit but with losses accumulating due to friction effects.

Chart analysis and cognitive biases

The most hazardous side effect of chart analysis is the enforcement of cognitive biases that diminish the probability of success as time passes. The type of chart analysis that the majority of retail traders and even some professionals perform not only lacks a logical foundation but, in addition, causes damage to trading psychology through the random treatment of markets and price action. Below are five cognitive biases that plague chart analysis:

- Availability cascade
- Clustering illusion
- Selective perception
- Confirmation bias
- Backfire effect

An *availability cascade* occurs when simple solutions to complex problems are adopted by groups of people because others adopt them. Most traders who use technical analysis do so because others adopt it too. The herd behavior acts as a feedback-reinforcing mechanism that can explain collective beliefs, such as the belief that chart analysis can provide profitable trading signals. More importantly, such adoption is done without proof that chart analysis can indeed be profitable. The need to adopt a widely used technique overpowers logic and demands proof. One of the central notions of this cognitive bias is that traders believe that if they can observe something, it must be important. However, what is being observed in most cases is a random pattern.

Clustering illusion is the tendency to see patterns in samples of random data. Figures 5-3 and 5-8 illustrate how patterns can form in random data. Any pattern identified on a chart in any timeframe has a high probability of being random. Nevertheless, there is a proliferation of software tools and online services that identify patterns traders can use in making trading decisions without offering any statistical analysis. Head and shoulders, double tops and bottoms, flags and triangles, wedges, moving average crossovers, and overbought/oversold indicators, to name a few, are mostly random formations. That also applies to trendlines, resistance, support levels, channels, and many other geometric formations. Only a tiny percentage of the occurrences of such patterns signal the future direction of price action, and the rest are due to random price moves. Chartists who try to forecast the future direction of prices using patterns drawn on charts have no chance of succeeding because they frequently deal with some form of noise.

Selective perception is the bias toward what one wants or likes to see while ignoring other possibilities. For example, a chartist sees a head and shoulders while ignoring a wedge. Focusing on what is perceived as important is probably the cardinal mistake of technical analysts and visual chartists. Normally, what is overlooked may be even more important. Usually, what is more important is hard to see with the naked eye or found by software that searches for such patterns. This is true in medium- to high-frequency data but also true in daily and even weekly data, where multiple patterns can form, signaling opposite directions according to established rules of technical analysis.

Confirmation bias is involved when there is an underlying belief in market direction. This is related to *wishful thinking*. There is no way to demonstrate that any decisions made using chart analysis were not subject to confirmation bias. The reader should be able to make the following observation from social media posts and technical analysis blogs: after highly negative news about a company becomes public information, there is a spike in technical analysis of its stock price with references to bearish formations, such as double bottoms or flags, for example. The fact is that a double bottom can be either a continuation or a reversal formation, depending on the underlined market bias. This fact is also true for all chart patterns. Chartists who rush to confirm the news with their analysis are often victims of confirmation bias. It is also a sad fact that this behavior is so widespread. The motivation behind this naïve type of analysis is that the news supports the practice of technical analysis, but in reality, it is an attempt to accomplish exactly the opposite, i.e., to provide support to technical analysis after the fact, which is the release of the news.

The *backfire effect* is the tendency to hold a position even more strongly when presented with evidence that contradicts it. Challenging the established gurus and book authors of technical analysis seems not appropriate to most practitioners of technical analysis, and this backfires when it occurs, causing them to hold an even stronger position that their method is correct and what traders need to do is try harder to apply it correctly. The backfire effect is mainly responsible for the windfall profits of locals and pit traders in the past and of market makers and trading robots in recent years, at the expense of retail traders who believe that they only need to spot a pattern or two or draw a few lines and then pocket the profits.

The practice of chart analysis reinforces the five cognitive biases mentioned above. The chances of success in trading diminish as their influence grows stronger. Level I chartists usually do not realize that their failure has its root in their methodology but, after a while, put the blame on themselves, their bad luck, or even on the market. They hesitate to challenge a huge industry that has been developed around naïve trading methods to mostly benefit educators, brokerages, and analysts.

Expert chart analysis

Naïve chartists, defined in this book as Level I traders (see Chapter One), are doomed to fail because they try to uncover causal relationships that are almost nonexistent. The proper use of chart analysis by a Level II expert chartist is fundamentally different from that of the naïve type because it is based on experience with price action. The primary use of chart analysis at this level is as a risk and money management tool rather than a market timing method. A Level II technical trader has a professional approach to markets and uses technical rules and methods as a filter to establish exit levels or reduce exposure. Those who are successful with Level II analysis have usually worked in financial firms before starting trading; they did not just read a few books on technical analysis and decide to become traders. However, they also find it difficult to convey their knowledge to other traders because dealing with the market in this way also involves eliminating cognitive biases and managing emotions, a process that has to do more with psychology than with technical trading. It is not the objective of this book to offer a methodology for expert chart analysis of Level II type because there is simply none that can be formalized. Each expert chart trader uses her own rules and relies on her experience. This is another reason this type of analysis is hard to teach, and students cannot easily benefit from learning its principles because they often lack key elements that depend on experience.

Level II technical traders do not perceive classical chart patterns along the same lines as Level I chartists but their analysis can provide prior subjective probabilities that are subsequently updated as new information becomes available. Chart patterns and analysis are also used as a guide to filter out the noise and assist in gauging risk. Chart analysis, the way it is often presented in introductory trading books and courses, does not constitute a trading method because it is a highly subjective process and lacks a logical foundation, as already discussed in this chapter and demonstrated with examples.

Figure 5-15. A much-discussed but failed diamond pattern in QQQ during 2011

Figure 5-15 shows a pattern that was extensively talked about in the blogosphere but then failed spectacularly: a diamond pattern in QQQ (Nasdaq-100 ETF) during 2011. The expectation of a market reversal among many Level I traders was high during that time since this pattern is taught as being rare but providing a high win rate for a trend reversal. However, the reversal did not come, mainly because fundamentals were stronger than any technical signals at that point, and specifically, the Fed was committed to continuing its quantitative easing program. Level II chartists, after identifying the pattern, could use it to reduce any long position exposure just in case the reversal materialized, as shown in Figure 5-15. Then, after the pattern failed, they could increase exposure again to normal levels. Varying exposure based on chart patterns is one way that Level II technical traders use such formations. However, going short because of a pattern such as a diamond formation is usually not justified. The Nasdaq-100 index and the QQQ ETF rallied to new highs after the failed diamond pattern in Figure 5-15 and continued making new multi-year highs.

Figure 5-16. A failed diamond top in SPY ETF during 2014

In the second quarter of 2014, another rare diamond pattern was formed, but this time in SPY ETF, as shown in Figure 5-16. The expectations for a reversal based on that pattern were again high among Level I chartists, despite continuing reassurances by the Fed of low interest rates. This pattern also failed, with SPY ETF reaching new all-time highs after a few months. Also, in this case, Level II expert chart traders could have reduced exposure as the pattern completed its formation and then could have increased it back to initial levels after it failed.

Chart analysis can be used in the context of a Bayesian probability framework to update prior probabilities about price action direction. The mechanics of such a process are intriguing but fall beyond the scope of this book. Chart analysis, the way it is often taught, does not constitute a winning trading method, and on the contrary, its application can result in large losses.

Figure 5-17. A 50-200 death cross forming in GLD ETF

Figure 5-17 shows how, by the end of May 2014, the 50-day moving average in GLD (gold ETF) was about to cross below the 200-day moving average, forming a "death cross" pattern that is believed to signal a downtrend. Readers of the blog of this author were warned during that time that experienced traders would rush to sell before the death cross occurred and then cover when there was enough selling by chartists who blindly followed technical analysis signals. Figure 5-18 shows that this is what happened, and the day following the warning in the author's blog, GLD ETF gapped down, and in a few days it lost about $4, reaching the $120 price level. Prices started moving up immediately after the death cross occurred because those who went short early began to cover their positions. Those who shorted GLD ETF right after the death cross occurred were squeezed out of the market.

Figure 5-18. A 50-200 death cross and subsequent bottoming price action in GLD ETF

Figure 5-19 shows how prices suddenly gapped up above the 200-day moving average, with price action forming an island reversal pattern that essentially crashed the death cross shorts. The price kept going higher for about two more weeks to reach the $128 price level, and that was enough to squeeze out most late shorts due to the death cross. Then, after about two months of sideways action, prices started trending down, as naïve chartists were expecting in the first place due to the death cross.

Figure 5-19. An island reversal pattern squeezed out death cross traders in GLD ETF.

The GLD death cross example was used to illustrate how one can become a victim of naïve technical analysis and remain trapped in a game of negative mathematical expectation. On the other hand, deciding to always do the opposite of what these traditional technical analysis signals suggest is not an optimal solution because of the reversal paradox in trading systems discussed in Chapter Two. On some occasions, chartists are wrong, and on others, they are right, but on average and in the longer term, with no trading friction accounted for, the expectation of the group must be exactly 0; otherwise, one could fade its signals and profit. The important lesson here is that one can never know which direction a certain pattern will take after it is formed, but only its probability. Some formations will behave the way technical analysis expects, and some will not. Lucky Level I traders are those who accidentally come across a streak of patterns that behave the way they are expected to, and the unlucky ones are those who trade a streak of patterns that behave the opposite of what technical analysis claims. However, on average, the expectation of all traders combined will be 0 before the trading cost is included.

On average, Level II traders achieve a positive expectation from technical analysis patterns because of their experience with price action. They are rewarded with profits not because they learned technical analysis but because they have the experience to use it properly to reduce risk. The worst thing to do is to confuse a level II trader for Level I, and then try to fade her signals. This may happen during times when a Level II trader is experiencing a streak of losers before a streak of winners. One may try to identify a Level II trader by noticing that she often takes contrarian positions in classical technical analysis. On the other hand, most Level I traders cannot follow the actions of a Level II trader because they are under the influence of the backfire effect, and they tend to hold their views about traditional technical analysis even stronger.

Becoming a Level II expert trader requires a fresh look at technical analysis and experience with price action from an objective perspective free from cognitive biases. Only a small percentage of technical traders will ever manage to become Level II expert chartists because this is not something that can be easily taught, as already mentioned. Most courses and seminars deal with classical technical analysis because they need to present the audience with rules that can be memorized. In Level II charting, there are no such rules, as this is trading based on experience.

Another principle that those who desire to become Level II traders must learn and understand is that it is difficult or even impossible to make money from patterns everyone can find in books and identify visually with software. Using scanners to find classical chart patterns and trading based on them according to established rules leads to a doomed path. Drawing lines in the sand and hoping they will act as support or resistance does not work because there is nothing special about most lines that can be drawn on charts, and they are just artifacts of random price action. Occasionally, some lines will act as expected, but the success rate is not enough to provide the profits one needs to be a successful trader. Only Level II chartists can identify significant lines, but there are no fixed rules for that, as it is based on experience and a complex, bias-free cognitive process.

Countless traders in the last several decades have been fooled by technical analysis into believing that they can profit by trading chart patterns and indicators everyone else can identify on a chart. They perceived the patterns they read about in books or were taught in seminars as drivers of prices, especially things such as the head and shoulders and the moving average crossover that are considered flagships of technical analysis. Due to disappointment caused by the failures, many withdrew from trading after losing small fortunes, convinced that the game was rigged or that there was no way of profiting from the markets, when the reality is that they had unrealistic expectations: it is difficult to profit from patterns everyone else can see. Although such obvious patterns sometimes work because other conditions drive prices, in the long term, the expectation of trading them is equal to zero before commissions are applied. Unfortunately, traders often concentrate on occasions when patterns worked well in the past and ignore failures. This practice of selection bias played a key role in the development of chart analysis in the early years. One assumption was that the trader would be able to select the winning trades ex ante in the same way they are selected *post hoc*. However, this is not possible in the real world.

An alternative to charting is quant trading, whether discretionary or automated. However, as we shall see in the next chapter, naïve quants, called in this book Level III technical traders, have as low or even lower chances to succeed than Level I technical traders because of the wrong application of backtesting and their involvement with a process that is plagued by data-mining bias. Although the effort in becoming a Level III technical trader is often substantial and requires additional skills, such as programming knowledge and the capability of working with backtesting software, there are usually no benefits from that other than those realized by a giant industry that was developed to provide the tools and data. Those who decide to trade either as a hobby or for a living before getting involved with quant trading should know that the path to a Level IV expert quant is long and full of pitfalls.

In this book, I try to expose some of the most important pitfalls that prevent traders from becoming expert quants, but I will not provide a step-by-step procedure for achieving this objective because it does not exist. Anyone who claims that this process exists is selling unrealistic hopes and dreams, similar to those offered by certain gurus who assert they can transform inexperienced traders into experts in just a few weeks. The primary objective of this book is to identify the holes in logic and expose the pitfalls. Ironically, most traders believe that working harder and longer with technical analysis will lead to success; however, the opposite often occurs. Specifically, the longer they engage with it, the stronger their cognitive biases become in charting, and the larger the data-mining bias grows for quants, making all efforts to gain an edge futile. Going into Chapter Six, I suggest that the reader keep these facts in mind because they are important but also counterintuitive. For example, it is assumed that the longer one drives a car, the more driving skills are improved. However, this is not necessarily true with technical trading, as the longer one backtests systems, the larger the data-mining bias grows. The next chapter provides a few guidelines for minimizing the adverse effects of data-mining bias.

CHAPTER SIX

Naïve and Expert Quants

Quantitative trading is a broad term that refers to the use of mathematical models to identify an edge and profit from the market. Statistical arbitrage algorithms, liquidity-seeking algorithms, portfolio allocation, risk analysis, and high-frequency trading are all parts of quantitative trading at the institutional level. At the individual trader or fund management level, quantitative trading usually refers to the use of an edge that has been identified through the analysis of historical price data. The edge may be in the form of a single indicator, a pattern that repeats in the data, or a more complex set of rules that combine several indicators and patterns of price, volume, and even fundamental information about a security or a group of securities. In this book, we deal with the latter definition of quantitative trading. There is a large group of traders, called Level III technical traders, that have suffered significant losses due to a wrong application of quantitative analysis. We will discuss some of the major causes of the failure of these traders and then provide guidelines for a transition to Level IV, which is the group of expert quants.

Quant traders emerged in the early 1980s after personal computers became available and affordable. They coded their systems in some high-level programming language, such as Basic, and then tested their performance on historical data. The author of this book used FORTRAN 77 and Pascal during that time to program and backtest price patterns after identifying them visually on charts. Many tests during those earlier times provided solid evidence about the existence of statistically significant edges for trading the markets. During that period, a quant's work was arduous and time-consuming as they had to code each idea from the ground up. By the late 1980s, the first backtesting software packages had become available for sale to retail traders. One of the first such programs was System Writer Plus by Omega Research, Inc., a company that in the late 1990s changed its name to Tradestation Technologies. System Writer Plus offered a high-level trading language, called EasyLanguage, that one could use to code trading ideas and test them on a large database of historical data that came with the program. The invention was a significant development that allowed traders with basic programming skills to become quants. Additionally, it marked the beginning of a new era and the emergence of a new class of traders who had been deceived by technical analysis due to their ignorance of its drawbacks and limitations. Backtesting was not the main problem, but rather the lack of knowledge of its proper use that contributed to the losses of many of its users.

During the years that followed the advent of backtesting programs, the market for such software exploded, and more chartists started transitioning to quant trading to determine whether their methods possessed a quantifiable edge. Unfortunately, in the case of chart patterns, it was soon realized that it was difficult to describe them objectively in computer language as well as implement associated trading methods. As a result, many chartists abandoned quant trading and returned to their visual chart analysis. Those who preferred indicators and mathematical models continued using backtesting programs in an attempt to confirm or discover an edge. Gradually, two large groups emerged, with a small one in between. The first large group involved traders who strictly adhered to charting, i.e., to the visual identification of trading opportunities, either manually or with the help of a data scanner, and the second large group involved quant traders who would only employ trading systems that were tested on historical data and also allowed automation of signal generation. In between, a small group used both methods, switching back and forth without any success. But the new quant method had more issues than the chartist method, and becoming an expert quant was as challenging as becoming an expert chartist. Therefore, anyone familiar with market operations and statistical analysis could have anticipated that backtesting software was not a panacea. Technical analysis misled the second generation of traders, primarily due to backtesting. To understand why and how these events happened, the details of the two main methods used for discovering a trading edge via backtesting will be discussed next, after a brief introduction to the subject.

What exactly is backtesting?

Backtesting has also been called historical *testing* or *historical simulation* in the past. The term "simulation" refers to the process of driving some mathematical model with input and observing its output. Backtesting only provides a historical simulation of the performance that is *likely* to have been achieved had a system been used in actual trading in the past. Thus, the use of the term "historical simulation" may not be appropriate in the case of trading systems. Simulation means running a lot more tests with different kinds of inputs, like random prices, instead of just historical data. The term "historical testing" can also mislead, as it may imply that the system was used to trade in the past. The term "hypothetical historical performance testing" is a more accurate description of what backtesting is all about.

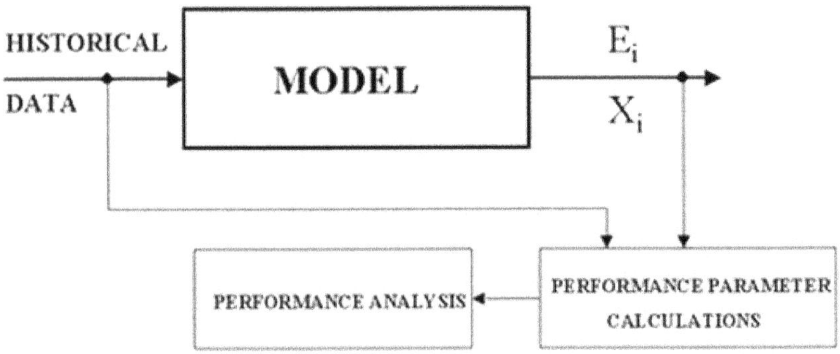

Figure 6-1. The process of trading system backtesting

Figure 6-1 shows how the process of backtesting works in principle at a high level. The mathematical model of the trading system is driven by historical data input, and the output is the sequence of market entry (E_i) and corresponding exit (X_i) levels. Then, the output is used in conjunction with the input to calculate a set of performance parameters that are in turn analyzed to decide whether the model qualifies as a viable trading system (see Ref. 3 for more details).

Some naïve quants may think that backtesting is a process of finding a system that will be profitable in the future, but that is a gross misconception. All one can achieve with backtesting is to determine historical profitability. If one assumes that systems that did not perform well in the past have a high probability of failing in the future in actual trading, then backtesting can facilitate some form of *hypothesis testing*. The hypothesis to test is whether a specific trading system will perform poorly in the future. If the results are not acceptable, then the hypothesis is supported and the system is rejected. However, backtesting results say little about future performance, meaning that regardless of whether the trading system's historical performance is acceptable or not, little can be said about its future performance. The problem is that we only have one assumption for supporting the hypothesis but not for rejecting it. Furthermore, rejecting the hypothesis is not equivalent to accepting some alternative hypothesis that the system will perform well in the future. When the hypothesis lacks support, the system's future profitability is uncertain. In practice, failure occurs when future market conditions prevent the system from performing well. These conditions are either absent or more severe than those in the backtest, which the system passed.

If the performance from backtesting is acceptable, then the system has a probability p of remaining profitable and a probability (1-p) of failing. Expert quants have devised methods of selecting systems with a high probability of staying profitable for an extended period, some of which will be discussed later in this chapter.

Table 6-11 provides a partial list of some of the most important parameters calculated during backtesting.

Parameter	Symbol	Types and Values
Win ratio	w	Real: 0 to 1
Compound Annual Return	CAR	Real
Total Profit	P	Real
Total Trades	N	Integer: 0 - N
Number of winning trades	N_W	Integer: 0 - N
Number of losing trades	N_L	Integer: 0 - N
Sum of winning trades	ΣW	Real
Sum of losing trades	ΣL	Real
Profit factor	P_f	Real
Average winning trade	avgW	Real
Average losing trade	avgL	Real
Average trade	AvgT	Real
Payoff ratio	R_{WL}	Real
Sharpe ratio	S	Real
Maximum consecutive losers	C_L	Integer: 0 - N
Maximum consecutive winners	C_W	Integer: 0 - N
Average bars in winners	B_W	Real
Average bars in losers	B_L	Real
Average bars in trades	B_T	Real
Maximum equity drawdown	D_R	Real

Table 6-1. A partial list of parameters calculated during backtesting

Pitfalls of backtesting

Besides data-mining bias, there are three major pitfalls of backtesting that could lead to misleading results even when a trading system has been coded correctly and the simulation of its performance on historical data is realistic and does not involve basic errors such as "look-ahead bias," for example, buying or selling at the high or low of a bar, or other common programming mistakes. These are:

- Backtester limitations

- Historical data integrity
- Lack of an effect on price action

Reference 3 provides a more detailed discussion of the first two pitfalls. Backtester limitations, or errors in the software, can affect the reliability of the results in many different ways, some of which are challenging to detect. For example, when backtesting programs were first released for sale to the public, some of them would not open a new position on a bar where an exit occurred. This limitation, sometimes referred to as a bug, frequently leads to unrealistic results when backtesting mid-frequency positions or swing trading systems. Most users of the two most popular backtesting programs from the 1990s were unaware of these limitations because they assumed the results were accurate, believing that the programs had been thoroughly tested before their public release. Only when intraday trading gained popularity did these errors become evident and warranted fixing.

Historical data integrity is an important issue. Data errors can affect backtesting results, including adjustments or differences in price series provided by different vendors. Data vendors often clean up errors due to misprints, but the issue of adjusted versus unadjusted data remains unresolved. For instance, data vendors adjust stock data for splits and dividends, and they adjust futures data for rollovers. In all cases, backtesting results using the adjusted and unadjusted series may vary depending on entry and exit logic. In the case of futures, the best way of performing backtests is via the use of front contracts and handling the rollovers in the software. However, this way of backtesting is cumbersome because it involves handling multiple price series, and, as a result, continuous, backward-adjusted data in the form of a single price series is used instead. The result is that certain types of exits produce unrealistic backtesting results, for example, percent profit targets and stop-loss levels. When setting exit levels as points in equities, using adjusted data for dividends often yields unrealistic backtest results. In the case of forex, there are no issues with data adjustments, but results may vary significantly when using historical data from different vendors because of the lack of a centralized exchange. It is suggested that forex trading systems be backtested using data from different vendors to establish their robustness because the variations in performance can be significant.

The lack of an effect on price action is the most serious pitfall of backtesting, and it especially affects intraday and high-frequency trading systems. This pitfall arises because a backtested trading system, using historical data, does not participate in the market and therefore cannot affect order book liquidity. A simulated system cannot cause reactions from other market participants as it happens in reality. The adverse effects of this pitfall are often taken into account by including additional trading friction in the form of slippage for each trade executed during the backtest, but that may not be sufficient in fast timeframes because the impact on performance ultimately depends on the nature of the trading system. In slower timeframes, such as when backtesting with hourly or daily bars in long holding periods, the effect due to the lack of actual trading participation is minimal in liquid markets. Backtesting scalping systems using order book historical data or high-frequency systems using tick data leads to unrealistic and, at times, misleading results because of the lack of an effect on price action. Although backtesting high-frequency trading systems is common these days, the majority of those who do it are susceptible to randomness unless they have a precise mathematical model of how their system affects price action. Thus, another model is required on top of a trading system model in some cases, and the number of assumptions and parameters increases along with the danger of curve-fitting performance to historical data. Trading systems tested on daily timeframes and with data from liquid markets usually function well despite not accounting for an effect on price action if the profit per trade greatly exceeds the security tick value and stop-loss levels are sufficiently far from the entry price.

Backtesting is an integral part of system development at every level of quant trading and of the two methods of discovering models that are discussed in more detail below.

Methods for discovering a trading edge

In Chapter Two, we learned that a trading edge is a set of rules, sometimes called a trading system, that keeps a positive expectation for a long enough time and makes profits at a risk level that is acceptable and usually higher than what could be obtained by following a benchmark index. There are two ways of discovering an edge: (a) conceiving a strategy and then backtesting it, and (b) discovering a strategy by data-mining historical data. These are also referred to as *trading system analysis* and *trading system synthesis*, respectively [Ref. 7].

Single strategy backtesting (Analysis)

A single strategy, or hypothesis, is a set of rules that can be tested on historical data and then applied to actual trading. For example, a simple strategy may involve entering a long position if the 5-day moving average crosses above the 25-day moving average and then exiting the long position and reversing to short when the opposite occurs. This strategy can be expressed in mathematical form, as shown in Pseudo Code 6-1. A trading strategy is also referred to as a *trading model.*

If MA(5) crosses above MA(25) then Buy at the close //buy signal

If MA(5) crosses below MA(25) then Short at the close //short signal

Pseudocode 6-1. 5-25 moving average crossover system

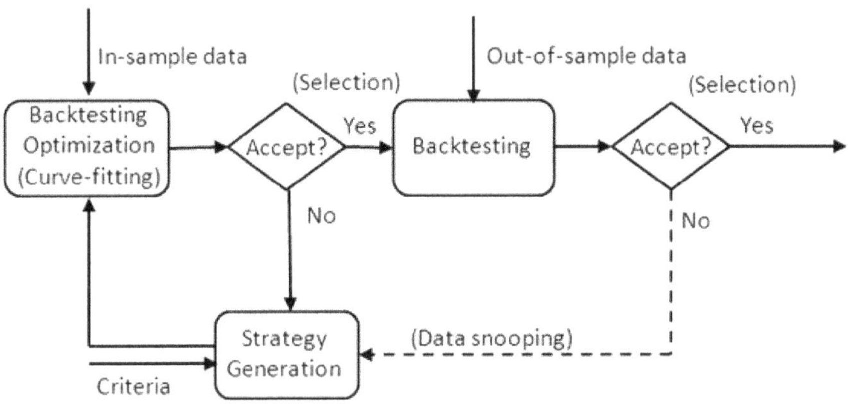

Figure 6-2. Backtesting (analysis) for developing a trading strategy

A complete system for actual trading based on some model usually involves additional rules for determining position size and incorporates rules for risk control, but the objective is to first determine whether the concept is sound and can deliver an edge. This book uses the terms "trading strategy," "trading model," and "trading system" interchangeably.

Figure 6-2 outlines the primary steps for conducting a single strategy analysis. The strategy is first backtested on a portion of the available data, called the in-sample, which usually covers 75% of the available history of the price series. This step may also involve optimization of the model's parameters, but it's optional since some trading models lack optimizable parameters (for example, the close of today is greater than the high of 10 days).

A selection is made if the model generates acceptable performance results in the in-sample; otherwise, the model is discarded. If chosen, the model is tested on an out-of-sample with the parameter values from the first step. If the performance in the out-of-sample is satisfactory, then it is accepted; otherwise, it is discarded. There is no consensus about what constitutes acceptable out-of-sample performance. Some say a model is acceptable if its out-of-sample performance is at least half of its in-sample performance. Others look for out-of-sample performance that is at least as satisfactory as that from the in-sample. There are other more complex criteria one could use, such as a metric that combines the return, drawdown, and other parameters calculated during the backtest, including the Sharpe ratio and the win rate, to name a few. But the choice of criteria to judge out-of-sample performance may not matter because this process is flawed.

If the model's out-of-sample performance is poor, it is either changed or discarded, or a new strategy is used. This is where the method of discovering trading systems becomes problematic due to the introduction of data-snooping bias; specifically, the developer knows how a particular model performed in the out-of-sample and uses that information to try to create a better model. In addition to that, the process involves model selection after the in-sample backtest, as shown in Figure 6-2. When curve-fitting, if any selection and data-snooping are used together, they cause what is called "data-mining bias":

any results that are accepted (the final selection in Figure 6-2) do not take into account the fact that other results were rejected.

Data mining is a dangerous practice because as the number of trials to identify an edge increases, the probability of accepting a model that possesses no market timing ability but performs well in the out-of-sample just by chance tends to 1, and after a while, it becomes a certain event. The risk of data mining bias and false correlations goes up when you do the steps in Figure 6-2 over and over again—that is, when you test models and throw them out based on how well they do outside of the sample. Expert quants attempt to minimize these negative effects, as discussed later in this chapter, but naïve quants, or Level III technical traders, according to this book, do not employ them because they either underestimate the negative impact of data-mining bias or are simply unaware of it. Level III quants who do a lot of backtesting are more likely to fall for randomness and false correlations because data-mining bias slowly builds up to high levels and grows worse with each new test. Even in the case of a single independent backtest, there is the possibility that the strategy that was analyzed was at some point discovered via data mining. Most strategies included in trading publications fall into this category. Using such strategies as an input to the process in Figure 6-2 will amplify the problems and most likely lead nowhere.

Naïve backtesting has resulted in a massive wealth transfer from Level III technical traders to market professionals and other well-informed or highly skilled market participants, such as Level II chartists and Level IV quants. Yet, technical analysis books rarely challenge this practice; instead, they highly promote it because no alternatives are present. There is a massive industry developed around backtesting that hesitates to educate its customers of its dangers for fear of losing them, apart from posting a few disclaimers in the fine print. Finding an edge through backtesting or a method like the one in Figure 6-2, on the other hand, will lead to a dead end if data-mining bias is not kept to a minimum. A person with little trading experience but a fresh strategy idea has better chances of success than an experienced trader who has spent years seeking an edge through backtesting, as the data-mining bias is smaller in the former case and much larger in the latter. This phenomenon is another angle of looking at *beginner's luck*. Technical traders should use backtesting only when they have a promising strategy to test. Using backtesting in ways similar to a computer game transforms it into a generator of spurious correlations and decreases the chances of success in the future.

Automated data-mining (Synthesis)

Figure 6-3 shows a schematic of how the process of discovering a market edge can be automated.

The automated process of discovering a trading edge is exploratory and based on some criteria for generating strategies combined with automation settings. Some examples of criteria are the rules of arithmetic and Boolean operators, the basic rules of technical analysis indicators, ways to manage risk and money, performance goals in the form of metrics, and ways to set up an objective function to optimize. The automation settings may involve things such as the maximum number of rules in a strategy, the maximum number of free parameters in a model, and the number of iterations to perform to combine rules. The creation of strategies may involve the random permutation of rules or a more complex algorithm based on neural networks or evolutionary biology principles, such as genetic programming algorithms.

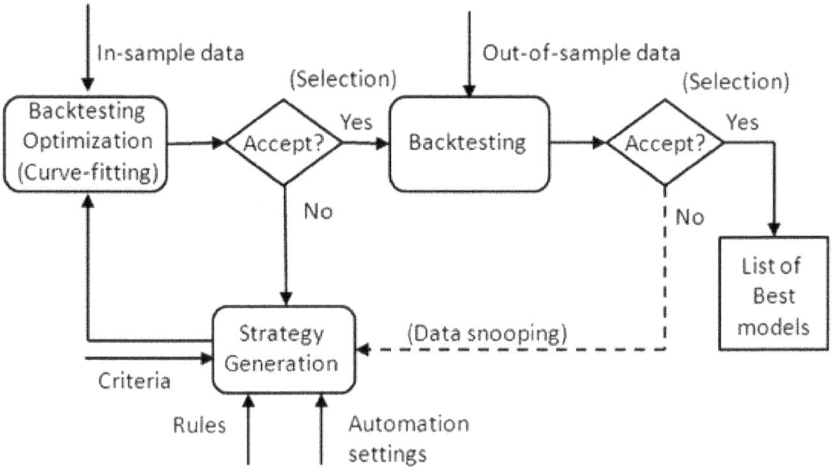

Figure 6-3. Data-mining (synthesis) for discovering a trading edge

After a strategy is generated by the procedure described in Figure 6-3, it is backtested on an in-sample of data, and if it has any parameters, those are optimized based on defined objectives. This process often introduces curve-fitting. If the results of the backtest are not satisfactory according to the performance objectives defined, then a new strategy is generated after modifying the previous one, which is a process that introduces selection bias. When convergence occurs in the sense of the particular objective function used, the best strategy is tested out-of-sample, and if it passes the performance tests, it is added to a list of best-performing models, a step that introduces additional selection bias. If the information that a particular strategy is not performing satisfactorily in the out-of-sample is used to modify the strategy generation process, or worse, to restart it, then data-snooping bias is introduced in addition to selection bias. The combination of any curve-fitting, selection, and data-snooping is what leads to what is commonly referred to as *data-mining bias*: any accepted results (the final selection as shown in Figure 6-3) ignore the fact that many other results were rejected, and the probability of discovering spurious models that perform well on the out-of-sample is high.

Note that the process in Figure 6-3 has an advantage over the process in Figure 6-2, where the developer tests new strategies sequentially until one is found that performs well in the out-of-sample. In analysis, data-snooping bias is necessarily introduced because the human developer is aware of the out-of-sample performance results along the way to a final system, while in synthesis, data-snooping will not be introduced unless the developer elects to modify or restart strategy generation based on out-of-sample results. Although this seems to be an advantage of automated data-mining methods for developing trading systems, it is not a significant one because these methods can generate millions or even billions—and in some cases, depending on the number of rules used, trillions—of strategies to backtest. The selection-related data-mining bias is so substantial that the lack of data-snooping bias only has a minor positive effect. A human developer is only able to test a limited number of distinct strategies in a lifetime, but an automated data-mining process can test a vast number of strategies in a matter of a few hours. There are ways of reducing the data-mining bias and increasing the probability of a final system not being a fluke, but that is what expert quants try to achieve by following certain procedures and guidelines that are discussed later in this chapter. The majority of Level III quants that use data-mining software to discover a trading edge are getting fooled by randomness because the probability of finding spurious correlation is for all practical purposes, equal to 1.

Fooled by hypothesis testing

Attempts to present statistical hypothesis testing as a solution to the problem of finding a significant edge have deceived many quants. When multiple comparisons uncover the edge, data-mining bias renders simple hypothesis testing ineffective (Ref. 2). Hypothesis testing is also problematic for a single independent. There are different ways to test a hypothesis in the literature. One way is to use procedures like bootstrapping or Monte Carlo simulation to make a sampling distribution of a statistic, usually the mean return. In the case of multiple comparisons, the proposed methods for hypothesis testing involve adjusting p-values by a suitable factor. The p-value represents the probability of achieving profitability as extreme as what the trading system shows, assuming it is unprofitable. For example, if the p-value is equal to 0.01, it means that there is one chance in 100 of obtaining the observed profitability, assuming that the null hypothesis of zero profitability is true.

The actual null hypothesis is that the system is either random and non-intelligent or has zero profitability, given the results obtained from the data samples used. If market conditions remain the same, the results will remain the same, and a statistically significant edge will persist. However, if market conditions change, then the performance results will differ, and as a consequence, the sampling distribution will have a different mean and variance. If the sampling distribution parameters change substantially due to changing market conditions, then the edge may no longer be significant. For example, in the presence of adverse market conditions, such as those developed through the financial crisis of 2008, an edge may lose its significance, and this failure actually impacted algos that were profitable before that specific event. Therefore, the use of hypothesis testing implies the notion of large samples to guarantee stability, but this is not often the case when it is applied. In addition, even in the case that a large sample is available, naïve quants employing hypothesis testing do not often consider the impact of data mining. When market conditions change substantially from those in the in-sample and out-of-sample, the system may fail regardless of a low p-value, even when adjusted for multiple comparisons.

Hypothesis testing can help reject unprofitable ideas, but it can also reject potentially profitable ones. It can only support the null hypothesis that an idea is unprofitable, given that conclusions may rely on potentially limited samples. For example, a trend-following system that performs well in both the in-sample and out-of-sample tests, which consist of long price trends with minor corrections, will not perform well during forward trading in a prolonged period of sideways market action. This system may show high significance and a low p-value in the out-of-sample but then generate large losses in the forward sample where there is no trend. Market wizards of the 1980s understood these market realities, but the introduction of mathematical jargon by academia has caused confusion with terms such as p-values, t-statistics, multiple comparisons, bootstrapping, and false discovery rates. In reality, the crucial point is that all these tests fail when there is a significant change in market conditions. We cannot elevate trading system development to the status of an academic subject, as it is inherently an art. If trading system development was only a mathematical problem, then the math giants of the 19th century would have already solved it, and there would be nothing new to say about it.

Getting fooled by hypothesis testing during trading system development is very common among Level III naïve quants that embrace statistics more than common sense but lack an in-depth understanding of the factors that render them inapplicable. Fortunately, several practical tests can be performed to maximize the probability that a trading system will stay profitable, as we shall see later in this chapter. However, relying solely on statistics will lead to significant disappointment.

Fooled by validation tests

Data mining from random data can result in trading systems that are profitable out-of-sample but do not possess any predictive ability. For example, consider the equity curve in Figure 6-4 that was generated by tossing a coin with a payout equal to +1 for heads and -1 for tails. The in-sample test encompasses approximately the first 630 trades, while the out-of-sample test serves as the validation for the remaining trades. The lesson here is that if many equity curves are generated by mining the data, the probability of finding one that passes the validation test is close to 1. Therefore, out-of-sample tests are mostly useless for validating data mining results, except for a single unbiased strategy. However, most naïve quants use out-of-sample validation tests that not only deprive the in-sample of important market conditions but are also useless as confirmatory tests due to the exploratory nature of the process.

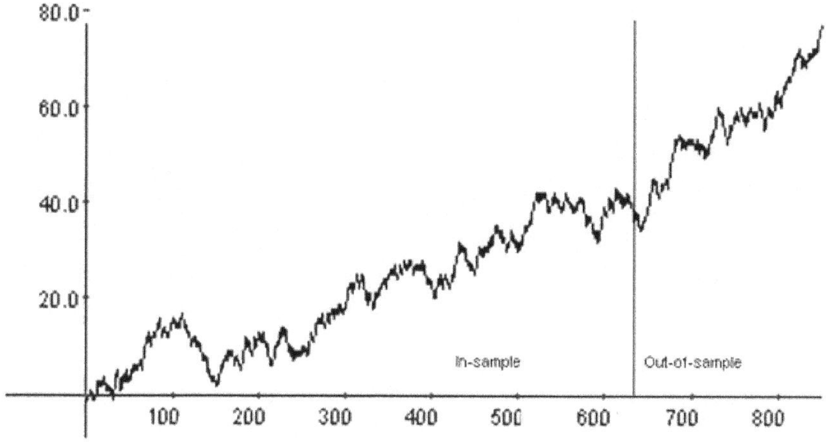

Figure 6-4. An equity curve generated by tossing a fair coin

Even when analysis (back-testing a single strategy) or synthesis (data mining) validates with data from several other markets, the probability of finding a spurious system that validates across all markets approaches 1 as the number of iterations or multiple comparisons becomes enormous. The same is true with the method that has been promoted recently as a way of determining the best parameters to use in a system, known as *walk-forward analysis* or *walk-forward optimization.* This method *in*volves dividing the available data into multiple in-sample and out-of-sample periods, optimizing in the former and walking forward in the latter. Thus, this method involves not one in-sample backtest followed by an out-of-sample validation test but several in-sample backtests, each followed by out-of-sample tests. The claim is that this is how traders use systems in real life: by re-optimizing their parameters and then using the new parameter set forward. In the context of the two methods for discovering edges already discussed, analysis and synthesis, walk-forward optimization involves an added number of iterations at the backtesting level, and it barely reduces the data-mining bias introduced by multiple comparisons. This validation test may be valuable when testing a single strategy only once on unique data; however, if a strategy is rejected and a new or modified one is tested, walk-forward optimization contributes to a process that suffers from data-mining bias, regardless of how the data is divided into multiple in-samples and subsequent out-of-samples. Like simple backtesting, walk-forward optimization can be used to support the idea that a system's poor past performance predicts poor real-world trading results, but it cannot support the idea that the system will perform well in the future.

More importantly, walk-forward optimization is primarily used for determining the best parameters to use in the next out-of-sample period (forward sample), and this method assumes that all samples are representative and drawn from the same population. However, determining the best parameters to use is not the fundamental problem of trading system development. It is an important issue but a secondary problem, and it is desirable to have as few parameters as possible in the model to avoid overfitting and its contribution to data-mining bias. A more difficult problem arises from the fact that the historical data used may generate trade samples that are not representative of the population. Then, in actual trading, conditions arise that were not present during the analysis. Because of this, walk-forward analysis might be fun for Level III quants and a nice feature of trading programs for marketing purposes, but it does not really help solve the main problem with trading systems that are created by backtesting. Repeating this process with the same historical data leads to an increase in data-mining bias.

Fooled by Monte Carlo Simulations

Technical traders frequently use Monte Carlo simulations to assess the robustness of systems developed through analysis or synthesis, even as part of the validation stage. These simulations are also used to determine capitalization requirements. Monte Carlo simulation usually involves changing the optimized system parameters, the entry and exit parameters, and even adding noise to the data to obtain distributions of some key statistics. These then yield confidence intervals for the system's performance and, especially, its maximum equity drawdown, which is a key parameter for figuring out how much capital is needed. However, we find that parameter variations strongly influence the robustness of overfitted systems, particularly those generated by neural networks and genetic algorithms. Therefore, Monte Carlo tests of optimized and overfitted systems tend to be optimistic, and this is another reason that they have not helped Level III quants discover edges. In addition, the use of Monte Carlo simulation suffers from the same problem as hypothesis testing. This issue arises because the calculated confidence intervals are based on limited samples of trades that may not be representative of the population. One other problem of Monte Carlo tests is that when they become part of an iterative process of discovering trading systems, either through analysis or synthesis, data-mining bias is still present, and a spurious system can be found when the number of strategies tested becomes large. Monte Carlo analysis is ineffective, especially when testing billions or even trillions of systems to obtain a list of the best performers, as shown in Figure 6-3.

Basic Monte Carlo Method

Given a vector of n trade results (P/L):

$$T[0] = \{T1, T2, T3, ..., Tn\}$$

Then k new vectors may be generated by reshuffling them. The new k+1 vectors of trade results and corresponding equity curves can be used to assess the potential of the system, its risk, drawdown, etc. The rationale behind this method of analysis is that T[0] represents just a particular order of trades, and naturally, the order could be different. The reshuffling of results is employed to arrive at different possibilities. The main assumption here is that all outcomes in T[0] are independent in the same way that fair coin tosses are independent. If the independence condition is violated, then this particular method of assessing risk does not apply and may produce misleading results.

Monte Carlo simulations may generate misleading results when the following conditions are true:

1. The systems are overfitted and/or have a high win rate
2. There is forced long-short symmetry in trade generation
3. The systems do trend-following
4. The systems take trades that depend on the outcome of other trades
5. The system logic uses equity curve feedback
6. The system dynamics depend on the position-size method

7. The trade sample is very large

Cases 2, 4, 5, and 6 above directly violate the independence assumption, while case 3 indirectly, but significantly, does so.

All validation schemes and robustness tests lose their effectiveness when the data-mining bias is large, something that occurs when reusing historical data to test many strategies. In the next section, we will discuss ways of minimizing the data-mining bias so that the chances of finding robust systems with an edge increase. We will achieve that by minimizing each component of data-mining bias separately.

Expert quant analysis

An expert quant, who is also called a Level IV technical trader in Chapter One of this book, knows that backtesting has its limits and that using it over and over with old data increases data-mining bias and the chance of finding false correlations. Expert quants accept backtesting as an indispensable tool for developing trading systems but use various rules, guidelines, and procedures to minimize its pitfalls while keeping the adverse effects of data-mining bias to a minimum. This task is often complicated and time-consuming, but it is what allows for separating statistical flukes from actual trading edges, and, as a result, the specifics are often kept proprietary and constitute a higher-level edge or a *trading meta-edge*. This sums up the significant difference between expert quants and quants who utilize backtesting programs in a naive manner.

In this section, some specific rules, procedures, and guidelines are offered that could allow a trading system developer to transition from Level III to Level IV. Based on 30 years of experience in developing trading systems, the author of this book believes that these may not constitute a formal or complete method for arriving at the final goal, which is the discovery of a trading edge, but they nevertheless offer a starting point. This book does not claim that a unique, universal formal method exists. Rather, the reader ought to scrutinize the efficacy of methods touted as solutions to this issue. Such methods are often the result of a lack of experience with actual trading and system development and, at times, reflect naïve attempts to apply simple concepts from statistics where they have limited effectiveness. This section presents the two key components of the expert quant methodology in more detail.

- Minimizing data-mining bias
- Applying effective validation

Note that some may wrongly assume that data-mining bias can be eliminated or even quantified. This bias is inherent in the process of developing trading systems via the use of backtesting in a repetitive fashion, manual or automatic. It is a qualitative aspect with several quantitative effects. Millions of technical traders around the world have used data mining, and many still do. Magazine articles, blog posts, and academic papers have attempted to improve a trading system someone else has published in the past. Any subsequent attempt to improve data-mined systems increases the bias due to the reuse of the data they were developed on. Furthermore, when a trader conceives an idea to test, it is highly possible that it was already data-mined in the past by someone else and then used or even published in some form. Therefore, generating original ideas for testing or implementing a data-mining process capable of identifying unique ideas is crucial.

Minimizing the impact of data-mining bias

Recall from Figures 6-2 and 6-3 that three main processes contribute to data-mining bias:

- Optimization and curve-fitting
- Model selection
- Data snooping

Below, we consider ways of minimizing the contribution of each process that contributes to data-mining bias.

Optimization and curve-fitting

In mathematics, curve fitting is the process of finding a curve that best fits a collection of data points in the sense that some objective function subject to constraints is maximized (or minimized). For example, *least squares* is a curve-fitting method that minimizes the sum of squared residuals. A residual is a difference between a fitted value and an actual value. Thus, the objective function to minimize when using this method is the sum of the squared residuals. Optimality can only be defined relative to an objective, and curve-fitting is essentially the result of optimization.

There has been some confusion in the trading literature about the notion of curve fitting as it applies to trading system development. This is possible because of an effort to generalize. A trading system is a process that generates a sequence of entry and exit signals. Usually, the algorithm, or model, of a trading system includes a set of variables, referred to as the *system parameters*. One of the objectives of trading system development is to select the values of these parameters so that the system performs best under actual market conditions. It is common practice to set these parameters by back-testing the system on historical data so that some objective function, usually referred to as a *metric*, is maximized (or minimized). For example, one can set the parameters so that the net profit is maximized, the maximum drawdown is minimized, or even some linear or non-linear function of these two performance parameters or any other performance parameters is maximized or minimized.

Basically, when backtesting is used to change system parameters, the timing of the signals is changed so that they fit past data in a way that maximizes an objective function. This differs from traditional curve-fitting because it determines the best sequence of entry signals that, in conjunction with the exit signals, maximizes some objective, rather than merely trying to identify a curve that best fits the historical data. This process is much more involved and complicated than simple curve-fitting because it includes the selection of entry and exit signals that maximize an objective function. It is a highly nonlinear optimization problem rather than just a curve-fitting problem. As already mentioned, curve-fitting usually involves optimization, but the latter is a process with a much broader scope and includes many more possibilities.

As an example, let us consider a simple moving average crossover system that generates long entry signals when SMA(n1) > SMA(n2) and short entry signals when SMA(n1) < SMA(n2), where n1 and n2 are the periods and n2 >

n1, as shown in Pseudocode 6-2. This is a stop-and-reverse system, i.e., when an opposite signal is generated, the previous position is closed and reversed. This system cannot be used in practice unless the values of n1 and n2 are selected. One could select the values via optimization of performance after backtesting the system on historical data.

N=integer(equity/close) //calculate number of shares

If MA(n1) crosses above MA(n2) then Buy N shares at the close //buy signal

If MA(n1) crosses below MA(n1) then Short N shares at the close //short signal

Pseudo code 6-2. A moving average crossover system with two free parameters

Let us suppose that on January 1, 2013, the trading system developer thinks that {n1=10, n2=35} are acceptable values for the moving average crossover system for trading SPY ETF. He then backtests the system with these initial values on SPY ETF data for 2013 (Note that the data sample is small but this is an example to illustrate the concept.) The resulting equity curve is shown in Figure 6-5.

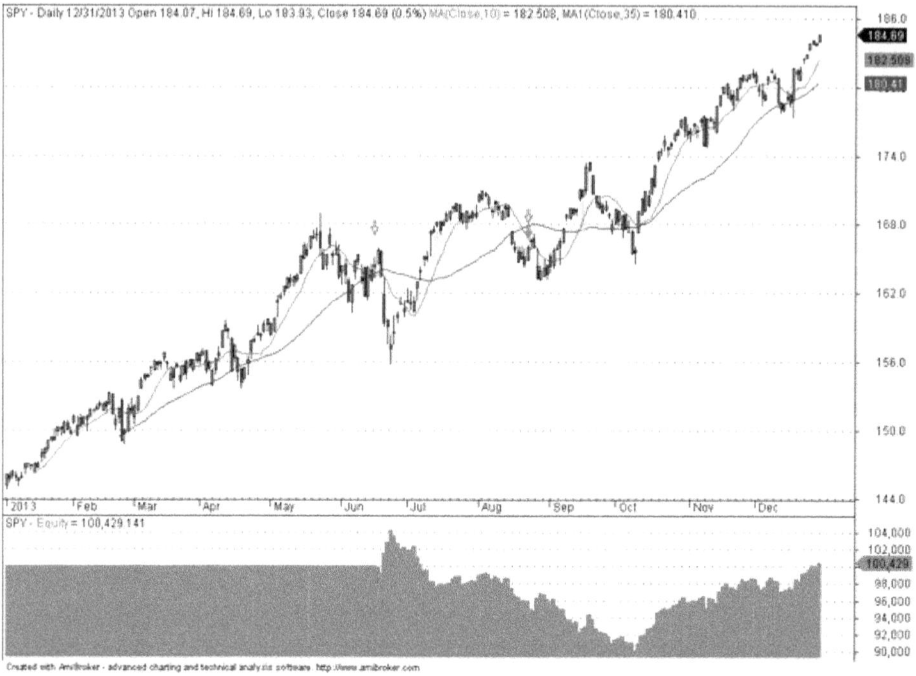

Figure 6-5. Backtest results for the system in Pseudocode 6-2 with n1 = 10 and n2 = 35 during 2013

The net profit of the system with a $0.01 commission per share is shown on the detailed trade report in Figure 6.6, and it is equal to $442.77. The initial capital is $100K. Four trades were generated, with the last one being an open long and the only profitable one. Note that trade is generated only when the 10-day moving average crosses above or below the 35-day moving average, and thus there is no trade for the first half of the year in this example, as shown in Figure 6-5 with a flat equity curve. CAR is 0.44%, and the maximum drawdown is -13.78%.

Next, the system developer decides to determine the optimum values of n1 and n2 that maximize the net profit. He uses a genetic optimization algorithm that comes with his backtesting program to find out that the values n1 = 5 and n2 = 15 generate better results, as shown in Figures 6-7 and 6-8.

Ticker	Trade	Date	Price	Ex. date	Ex. Price	% chg	Profit	% Profit	Shares	Cum. Profit	# bars	Profit/bar
SPY	Short	6/17/2013	164.29	7/15/2013	167.97	2.24%	-2,249.60	-2.25%	608	-2,249.60	20	-112.48
SPY	Long	7/15/2013	167.97	8/22/2013	164.9	-1.83%	-1,801.47	-1.84%	583	-4,051.07	29	-62.12
SPY	Short	8/22/2013	164.9	9/17/2013	170.46	3.37%	-3,236.40	-3.38%	580	-7,287.47	18	-179.80
SPY	Open Long	9/17/2013	170.46	12/31/2013	184.69	8.35%	7,730.24	8.34%	544	442.77	75	103.07

(4 rows) Profit = 442.77 (0.44%), CAR = 0.45%, MaxSysDD = -14391.15 (-13.79%), CAR/MDD = 0.03, # winners = 1 (25.00%), # losers = 3 (75.00%)

Figure 6-6. Trades-by-trade backtest results for the system in Pseudocode 6-2 with n1 = 10 and n2 = 35 Created with Amibroker – advanced charting and technical analysis software: www.amibroker.com

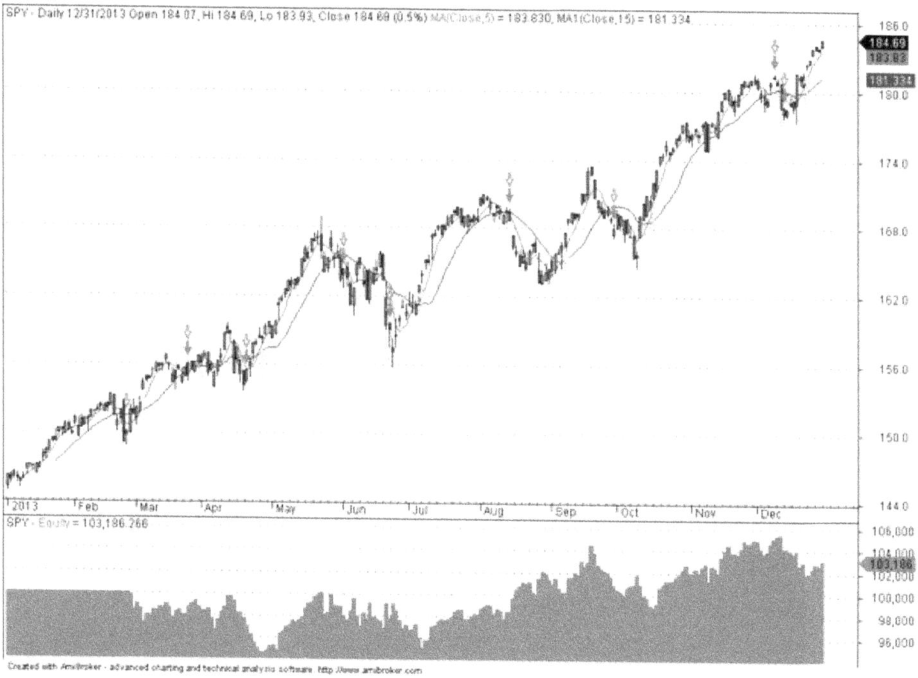

Figure 6-7. Backtest results for the system in Pseudo code 6-2 with n1 = 5 and n2 = 15 in 2013

The total net profit of the system with the optimum parameters and with a $0.01 commission per share traded is shown in the detailed trade report in Figure 6-8, and it has increased to $2,267. In this case, 18 trades were generated, with the last one being an open long. Note that trade is generated only when the 5-day moving average crosses above or below the 15-day moving average, and thus there is no trade for the first two months, as shown in Figure 6-7 with a flat equity curve. CAR is 3.27%, and the maximum drawdown decreased to -5.47%.

Ticker	Trade	Date	Price	Ex. date	Ex. Price	% chg	Profit	% Profit	Shares	Cum. Profit	# bars	Profit/bar
SPY	Short	2/26/2013	149.72	3/5/2013	153.66	2.63%	-2,641.32	-2.64%	667	-2,641.32	6	-440.22
SPY	Long	3/5/2013	153.66	3/25/2013	156.01	1.53%	1,481.80	1.52%	636	-1,159.44	15	98.79
SPY	Short	3/25/2013	156.01	4/1/2013	156.59	0.37%	-378.60	-0.38%	631	-1,538.04	5	-75.72
SPY	Long	4/1/2013	156.59	4/19/2013	154.5	-1.33%	-1,325.08	-1.35%	628	-2,863.12	15	-88.34
SPY	Short	4/19/2013	154.5	4/26/2013	158.33	2.48%	-2,413.95	-2.49%	627	-5,277.07	6	-402.32
SPY	Long	4/26/2013	158.33	6/3/2013	163.83	3.47%	3,271.56	3.46%	597	-2,005.51	26	125.83
SPY	Short	6/3/2013	163.83	6/20/2013	161.86	-1.20%	1,162.20	1.19%	596	-843.31	14	83.01
SPY	Long	6/20/2013	161.86	6/21/2013	159.64	-1.37%	-1,357.44	-1.38%	606	-2,200.75	2	-678.72
SPY	Short	6/21/2013	159.64	7/8/2013	163.86	2.64%	-2,590.64	-2.66%	611	-4,791.39	11	-235.51
SPY	Long	7/8/2013	163.86	8/14/2013	169.53	3.46%	3,299.60	3.45%	584	-1,491.79	28	117.84
SPY	Short	8/14/2013	169.53	9/9/2013	166.45	-1.82%	1,777.86	1.80%	581	286.07	18	98.77
SPY	Long	9/9/2013	166.45	9/30/2013	167.48	0.62%	609.03	0.61%	603	895.10	16	38.06
SPY	Short	9/30/2013	167.48	10/16/2013	170.72	1.93%	-1,978.82	-1.95%	607	-1,083.72	13	-152.22
SPY	Long	10/16/2013	170.72	12/9/2013	181.47	6.30%	6,255.59	6.29%	583	5,171.87	38	164.62
SPY	Short	12/9/2013	181.47	12/11/2013	180.82	-0.36%	363.51	0.35%	577	5,535.38	3	121.17
SPY	Long	12/11/2013	180.82	12/12/2013	178.64	-1.21%	-1,282.60	-1.22%	583	4,252.78	2	-641.30
SPY	Short	12/12/2013	178.64	12/23/2013	182.45	2.13%	-2,232.89	-2.14%	583	2,019.89	8	-279.11
SPY	Open Long	12/23/2013	182.45	12/31/2013	184.69	1.23%	1,247.64	1.22%	562	3,267.53	7	178.23

(18 rows) Profit = 3267.53 (3.27%), CAR = 3.29%, MaxSysDD = -5478.40 (-5.47%), CAR/MDD = 0.60, # winners = 9 (50.00%), # losers = 9 (50.00%)

Figure 6-8. Trade-by-trade backtest results for the system in Pseudocode 6-2 with n1 = 5 and n2 = 15. Created with Amibroker – advanced charting and technical analysis software: www.amibroker.com

It may be seen from the above simple example that optimization (and curve-fitting) amounts essentially to determining the best parameters that allow the selection of a system that fulfills certain objectives over the backtest period. This process introduces bias because the selected system and its associated parameters may not indicate a true advantage; instead, they may only represent survival due to chance. Consequently, when market conditions change, the system is likely unable to perform as expected and will fail. This is the case with this particular example, as backtesting the system with data for 2012 results in a failure with a CAR of -17.60%, as shown in Figure 6-9. Thus, if the trader is lucky and the same conditions as in 2013 continue during 2014, the system will generate profit, but this system lacks the ability to adapt to changing market conditions. Note that had the system been optimized using data from 2012, the best parameters would be n1 = 10 and n2 = 40, with 6 trades generated, a 100% win rate, and a CAR of 12.17%. However, these parameters would have resulted in negative performance in 2013, yielding a CAR of -0.27%. This example shows that the results of sequential optimization methods, such as walk-forward optimization, depend on the path a system follows and are not inherently more robust.

Figure 6-9. Backtest results for the system in Pseudo code 6-1 with n1 = 5 and n2 = 15 in 2012

The simple moving average crossover example, which uses limited samples for illustration purposes, allows us to derive the following conclusions about the impact of optimization and curve-fitting:

- Sample size varies as parameters change
- The timing of entries and possibly exits varies

The result of the above two effects is the introduction of selection bias in the development of trading systems. Next, we classify trading systems based on how optimization and curve-fitting affect them for the purpose of reducing bias.

Classification of trading systems

Type I trading systems

Adjusting the parameters of Type I systems affects the timing of both the entry and exit signals. An example of a Type I trading system is a simple moving average crossover system, such as the one in Pseudocode 6-1. In this case, optimization and curve-fitting result in different sequences of entry and exit signals, and selecting one that performs best increases data-mining bias. These systems have the highest probability of failure in forward trading because selection ignores variations that have failed or performed poorly.

Type II trading systems

Adjusting the parameters of Type II systems only affects the timing of their entry signals. In this case, optimization and curve-fitting result in collections of entry and exit signals that differ only in their entry parts. A final selection usually introduces less bias as compared to Type I systems. Example: Enter long if SMA(n1) > SMA(n2) and exit long at P1 or P2, where P1 and P2 are fixed price levels. Note that Type II systems are rarely used in practice.

Type III trading systems

Adjusting the parameters of Type III systems only affects the timing of the exit signals. In this case, optimization and curve-fitting result in sequences of entry and exit signals that differ only in their exit parts. For example, enter a long position if today's close is greater than the close from two days ago, and exit the long position either at the entry price plus X points or at the entry price minus Y points, where X represents the profit target and Y represents the stop-loss parameters to optimize.

In general, systems that include lagging indicators of price are Type I. Type II systems are not common, especially in trending markets such as equities. Type III systems include a broad class of systems based on price patterns of open, high, low, and close. When you only use Type-III systems, curve-fitting and optimization have the least impact because the trade sample does not change and selection bias is kept to a minimum since only the profit target and stop-loss values are optimized. The impact of the optimization on the exit part can be minimized if, during the development of the trading system, sufficiently small values are used that avoid the fitting of the exits to the data and only allow establishing if a system has market timing ability. The traded market influences the actual magnitudes of exit values, which should vary for intraday and position trading systems. For example, for position and swing systems based on daily data, profit-target and stop-loss values in the range of 0.5%–3% may be used in some equities and ETFs. Then, after a system is developed that can successfully time the market, different exits can be used to increase the profit potential, such as trailing stops, for example.

Use of exits that fit market data, such as trailing stops, should be avoided during the development phase of the trading system because the objective should be to discover an edge that can time price action properly, not to curve-fit some algo to past data. This is a mistake that a lot of Level III quants make, especially those who use off-the-shelf programs that use neural networks, genetic algorithms, or permutation methods to identify trading systems. Traders who believe that market entries are unimportant as long as they can ride trends are also mistaken. By using curve-fitting on historical data, these technical analysts have fallen for randomness and selection bias. No matter when one enters the market during a strong uptrend, if they exit before the top, they will realize a profit. However, a system with random entries that tries to ride a trend through the use of a trailing stop in a sideways market usually fails. Since one cannot know when a sideways market will occur or how long it will last, relying on random entries and trailing stops is often the result of wishful thinking. If a trading system lacks an edge in timing entries and exits, it is inevitable that it will fail. An exception to this empirical fact is when trading a biased market, usually an up-trending market, as discussed in Chapter Four and illustrated in Figure 4-16. However, in such rare cases, beating the buy-and-hold return with random trading is challenging.

The use of a genetic programming engine by a Level III quant along with an assortment of indicators and some exit rules, including trailing stops, average true range, moving average crossovers, etc., is a certain path to failure. The data-mining bias is so large that the best systems obtained have a probability close to 1 of being flukes. This chance can go down if you use indicators with no parameters or only look at one type of similar indicator, like moving averages, in a system that has two free parameters at most. Even when indicators with no parameters are used, for example, price patterns, the use of exits that can fit the system signals to the data should be avoided. Figure 6-10 shows the equity curve of a system for trading SPY developed on data from January 1, 2003, to 12/29/2006 using a program that was based on genetic programming. The code of the best-performing system is shown as Pseudocode 6-3. The system generates an entry at the open of the next day when the low of six days ago is larger than the open of 18 days ago. A 10% trailing stop and a stop-loss of 2% based on the entry price are used for exits. Figure 6-10 displays the equity performance of the aforementioned system during the specified period.

N=integer(equity/close) //calculate number of shares

If the low of 6 days ago is greater than the open of 18 days ago then

Buy N shares at the close //buy signal

Exit if 10% trailing stop or 2% stop-loss

Pseudo code 6-3. A trading system discovered by a genetic programming engine

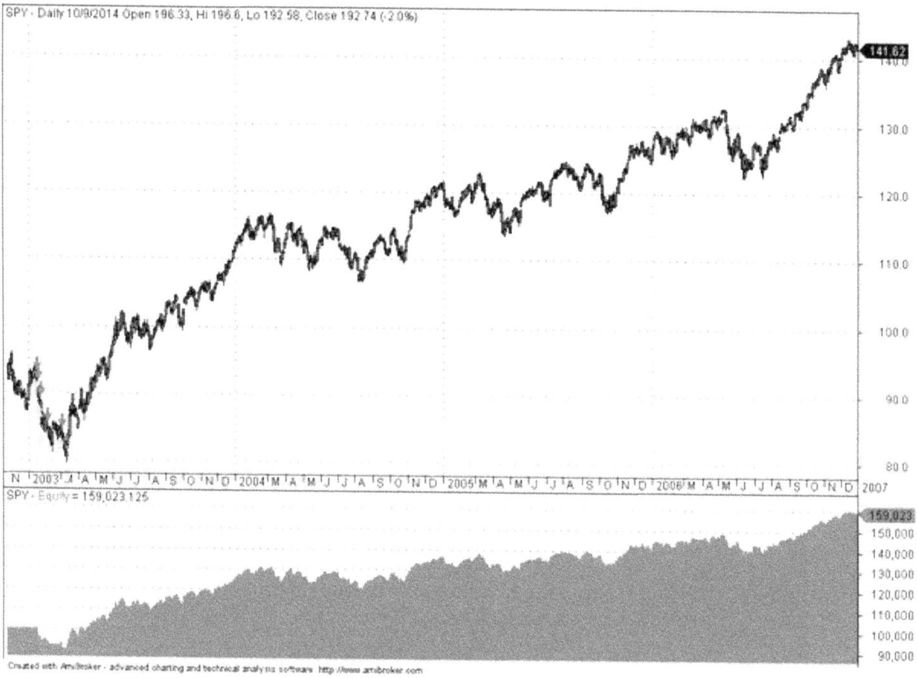

Figure 6-10. Equity curve of the system in Pseudocode 6-3 in the period 01/02/2003 to 12/29/2006

The net return of the system in Pseudo Code 6-3 is 50% for a starting capital of $100K and a $0.01 commission per share traded. The CAR is 12.32%, and the maximum drawdown is -10.33%. The system is fitted to the data because the market is on an uptrend, and the trailing stop facilitates exactly that, while the stop-loss is only hit five times at the beginning of 2003. After February of the same year, there is only one long position that stays open until the end of the backtesting period. However, when the system is tested on data from 01/02/2008 to 12/31/2008, it fails because market conditions change. The maximum drawdown increases to -38%, the net return is -30.5%, and the CAR is -16.6%. An expert quant could have suspected the deterioration in the performance of a system just by looking at its code because it appears random. However, Level III quants frequently fall for quick trading system discovery schemes without realizing the impact data-mining bias has on the outcomes. In this case, the combination of curve-fitting through the use of a trailing stop and the selection of the best-performing model produced a fluke that could not cope with changing market conditions. Relentless data-fishing and data-snooping often uncover similar or even worse systems.

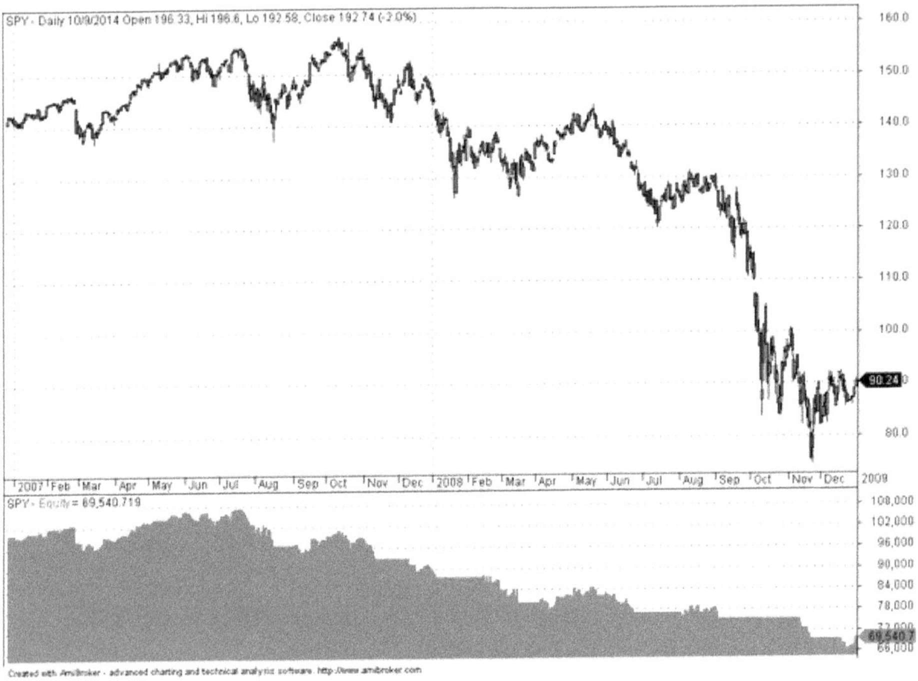

Figure 6-11. Equity curve of the system in Pseudocode 6-3 in the period 01/03/2007 to 12/31/2008

The following measures could result in lower data-mining bias due to optimization and curve-fitting:

- If possible, use only Type III systems or systems with a maximum of two parameters
- During development, avoid using exit logic that facilitates curve-fitting
- Backtest the system after introducing a sufficiently small profit target and stop-loss
- Perform an analysis after introducing randomness in the entry logic

When traders use Type III systems, they do not have to optimize the entry part, and the order of the entries stays the same. However, the exit part may have parameters that can be curve-fitted to the data. During development, avoid using exit rules that curve-fit historical data. Different exits may be added to a system, but only after it is determined that it has an edge. Removing the exit logic and testing a system with a small profit target and stop-loss may, in some cases, indicate whether the entry part does its job in determining proper market timing. Finally, adding the right amount of randomness to the entry logic lets you rank the system and test the null hypothesis that it does not have any intelligence on the given data sample.

Example 1: Moving average crossover system

Optimization of the free parameters of the moving average crossover system in Pseudocode 6-2 was performed on SPY ETF data from inception to 7/23/2014. Based on the objective of maximum net profit, the resulting best values for the moving average periods were n1 = 25 and n2 = 295.

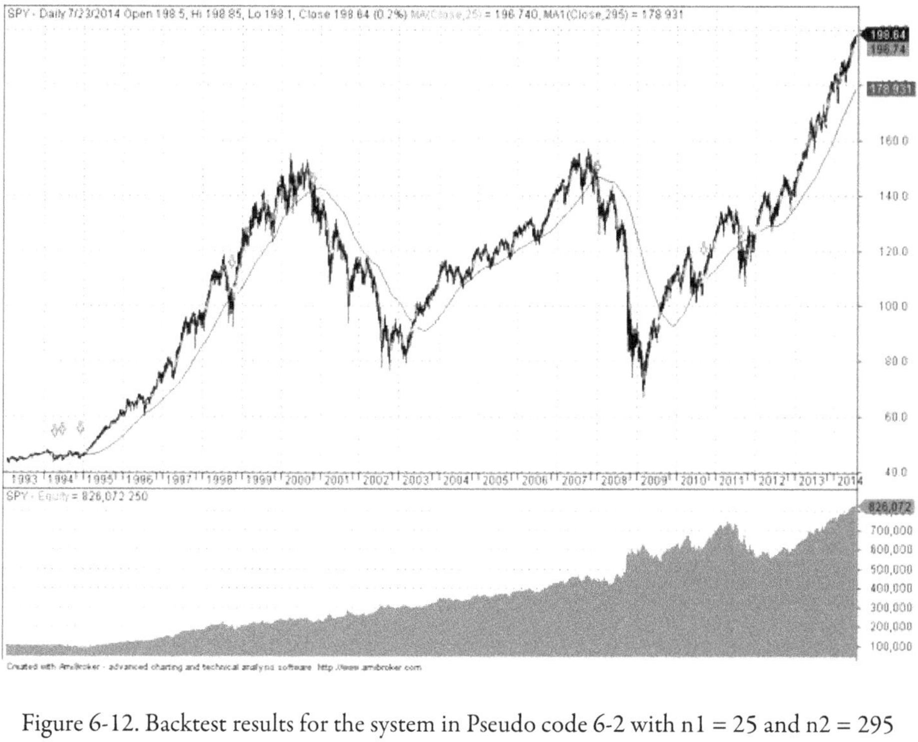

Figure 6-12. Backtest results for the system in Pseudo code 6-2 with n1 = 25 and n2 = 295

Figure 6-12 displays the equity performance with the optimum values, while Figure 6-13 displays the trade-by-trade report. The starting equity was $100K, commissions were $0.01 per share, and the available equity was fully invested.

Ticker	Trade	Date	Price	Ex. date	Ex. Price	% chg	Profit	% Profit	Shares	Cum. Profit	# bars	Profit/bar
SPY	Short	4/18/1994	44.64	6/22/1994	45.22	1.30%	-1,344.00	-1.34%	2,240	-1,344.00	46	-29.22
SPY	Long	6/22/1994	45.22	6/24/1994	44.78	-0.97%	-1,006.48	-1.02%	2,188	-2,350.48	3	-335.49
SPY	Short	6/24/1994	44.78	8/25/1994	47.09	5.16%	-5,105.03	-5.20%	2,191	-7,455.51	44	-116.02
SPY	Long	8/25/1994	47.09	12/6/1994	45.44	-3.50%	-3,276.54	-3.55%	1,962	-10,732.05	72	-45.51
SPY	Short	12/6/1994	45.44	1/24/1995	46.67	2.71%	-2,463.75	-2.75%	1,971	-13,195.80	34	-72.46
SPY	Long	1/24/1995	46.67	9/30/1998	103.5	121.77%	105,609.79	121.73%	1,859	92,413.99	932	113.32
SPY	Short	9/30/1998	103.5	11/2/1998	110.81	7.06%	-13,809.72	-7.08%	1,884	78,604.27	24	-575.40
SPY	Long	11/2/1998	110.81	10/19/2000	136.84	23.49%	42,266.25	23.47%	1,625	120,870.52	497	85.04
SPY	Short	10/19/2000	136.84	5/29/2003	95.88	-29.93%	64,808.02	29.92%	1,583	185,678.54	652	99.40
SPY	Long	5/29/2003	95.88	1/10/2008	139.68	45.68%	130,595.74	45.66%	2,983	316,274.28	1,164	112.20
SPY	Short	1/10/2008	139.68	8/19/2009	98.31	-29.62%	123,801.90	29.60%	2,994	440,076.18	406	304.93
SPY	Long	8/19/2009	98.31	9/9/2010	111.65	13.57%	72,847.08	13.55%	5,469	512,923.26	267	272.84
SPY	Short	9/9/2010	111.65	9/23/2010	112.49	0.75%	-4,668.08	-0.77%	5,428	508,255.18	11	-424.37
SPY	Long	9/23/2010	112.49	8/24/2011	116.19	3.29%	19,732.16	3.27%	5,362	527,987.34	233	84.69
SPY	Short	8/24/2011	116.19	1/23/2012	131.51	13.19%	-83,081.44	-13.20%	5,416	444,905.90	104	-798.86
SPY	Open Long	1/23/2012	131.51	7/23/2014	198.64	51.05%	276,828.75	51.03%	4,125	721,734.65	630	439.41

(16 rows) Profit = 721734.65 (721.73%), CAR = 10.30%, MaxSysDD = -205757.07 (-27.94%), CAR/MDD = 0.37, # winners = 8 (50.00%), # losers = 8 (50.00%)

Figure 6-13. Trade-by-trade backtest results for the system in Pseudocode 6-2 with n1 = 25 and n2 = 295. Created with Amibroker – advanced charting and technical analysis software: www.amibroker.com

The optimized system has a CAR equal to 10.30%, a 50% win rate, and a maximum drawdown of about -28%, as shown in Figures 6–13. Next, a small profit target and a stop-loss of 2% are applied to each entry signal to assess whether the entry signals demonstrate market timing ability or if they are essentially random, with the actual effectiveness relying on the exit signals. Figure 6-14 displays the resulting equity performance.

Figure 6-14. Backtest results for the system in Pseudo code 6-2 with n1 = 25 and n2=295 and 2% profit target and stop-loss

Ticker	Trade	Date	Price	Ex. date	Ex. Price	% chg	Profit	% Profit	Shares	Cum. Profit	# bars	Profit/bar
SPY	Short (max loss)	4/18/1994	44.64	5/2/1994	45.54	2.02%	-2,060.80	-2.06%	2,240	-2,060.80	10	-206.08
SPY	Long	6/22/1994	45.22	6/24/1994	44.78	-0.97%	-995.90	-1.02%	2,165	-3,056.70	3	-331.97
SPY	Short (max loss)	6/24/1994	44.78	7/29/1994	45.78	2.23%	-2,218.50	-2.28%	2,175	-5,275.20	25	-88.74
SPY	Long (max loss)	8/25/1994	47.09	9/21/1994	46.14	-2.02%	-1,950.67	-2.06%	2,011	-7,225.87	19	-102.67
SPY	Short (max loss)	12/6/1994	45.44	12/27/1994	46.35	2.00%	-1,898.13	-2.05%	2,041	-9,124.00	15	-126.54
SPY	Long (profit)	1/24/1995	46.67	2/3/1995	47.67	2.14%	1,908.06	2.10%	1,947	-7,215.94	9	212.01
SPY	Short (profit)	9/30/1998	103.5	9/30/1998	101.43	-2.00%	1,836.80	1.98%	896	-5,379.14	1	1,836.80
SPY	Long (profit)	11/2/1998	110.81	11/4/1998	113.03	2.00%	1,876.60	1.99%	853	-3,502.54	3	625.53
SPY	Short (max loss)	10/19/2000	136.84	10/20/2000	139.58	2.00%	-1,945.80	-2.02%	706	-5,448.34	2	-972.90
SPY	Long (profit)	5/29/2003	95.88	6/2/2003	97.8	2.00%	1,873.40	1.98%	906	-3,574.94	3	624.47
SPY	Short (max loss)	1/10/2008	139.68	1/10/2008	142.48	2.00%	-1,945.80	-2.02%	690	-5,520.74	1	-1,945.80
SPY	Long (profit)	8/19/2009	98.31	8/19/2009	100.28	2.00%	1,873.95	1.98%	961	-3,646.79	1	1,873.95
SPY	Short (max loss)	9/9/2010	111.65	9/20/2010	113.89	2.01%	-1,948.12	-2.02%	662	-5,594.91	8	-243.51
SPY	Long (profit)	9/23/2010	112.49	9/24/2010	114.74	2.00%	1,870.97	1.98%	839	-3,723.94	2	935.49
SPY	Short (max loss)	8/24/2011	116.19	8/25/2011	118.74	2.19%	-2,127.96	-2.21%	828	-5,851.90	2	-1,063.98
SPY	Long (profit)	1/23/2012	131.51	2/3/2012	134.15	2.01%	1,873.30	1.99%	715	-3,978.60	10	187.33

(16 rows) Profit = -3978.60 (-3.98%), CAR = -0.19%, MaxSysDD = -9840.80 (-9.77%), CAR/MDD = -0.02, # winners = 7 (43.75%), # losers = 9 (56.25%)

Figure 6-15. Trade-by-trade backtest results for the system in Pseudocode 6-2 with n1 = 25 and n2 = 295 with a 2% profit target and stop-loss. Created with Amibroker – advanced charting and technical analysis software: www.amibroker.com

A trade-by-trade report of the results in Figure 6-14 shows the same entries but different exits due to the applied profit target and stop-loss. Performance is now negative with a CAR of -0.19%, a win rate of 43.75%, and a smaller drawdown of -9.77% due to the small stop-loss, as shown in Figure 6-15. These results offer an indication that the optimized system relies on its exits to perform well, while its entries do not offer any market timing ability. Although relying on the exits is not a disadvantage in principle and is desirable, sole reliance on them opens the system to potential troubles when market conditions change. This phenomenon was already demonstrated with an example in Figures 6-10 and 6-11, where a trailing stop was used. Essentially, in that case, the optimized system entered the market randomly, hoping that the reversal exit signal would be far enough from entry and that profit would be generated. This technique is no different from the type of random trading used by Level I chartists, where entries are mostly random. A trading system with a random entry behaves similarly to a naïve chartist who hopes that the exit price will be higher than the entry price, although trading is in reality random. This strategy is equivalent to "buy (or short) and hope."

A randomization study involves making the system entry logic random while maintaining the same exits. Note that this is just one possible form of randomization. The pseudo-code for this purpose is given in Pseudo Code 6-4. This process involves tossing a coin: if the outcome is heads and the fast average is above the slow average, a long position is opened after closing any open short position; if the outcome is tails and the fast-moving average is below the slow average, a short position is opened after closing any open long position. The exits remain the same, i.e., long positions are exited if the fast-moving average crosses below the slow, and the opposite holds in the case of short positions.

N=integer(equity/entry price) //calculate number of share

If MA(25) > MA(295) AND Heads then Buy N shares at the close //buy signal

If MA(25) < MA(295) AND Tails then Short N shares at the close //short signal

Exit long if MA(25) < MA(295)

Exit short if MA(25) > MA(295)

Pseudo code 6-4. Code for randomization study of a moving average crossover system

The system in Pseudo code 6-4 was backtested 10,000 times to obtain a frequency distribution of the resulting CAR values, as shown in Figure 6-16. The distribution is close to normal, with a mean of 10.11% and a standard deviation of 0.221%. The kurtosis is low and slightly negative, and the skewness is also small and negative. As it turns out, after ranking the original system, 19.22% of the random entry systems have a higher value than 10.30%, which is the value of the original system's CAR. Significance at the 5% level would require a CAR of 10.46%, or 16 basis points more than what was obtained during the original backtest.

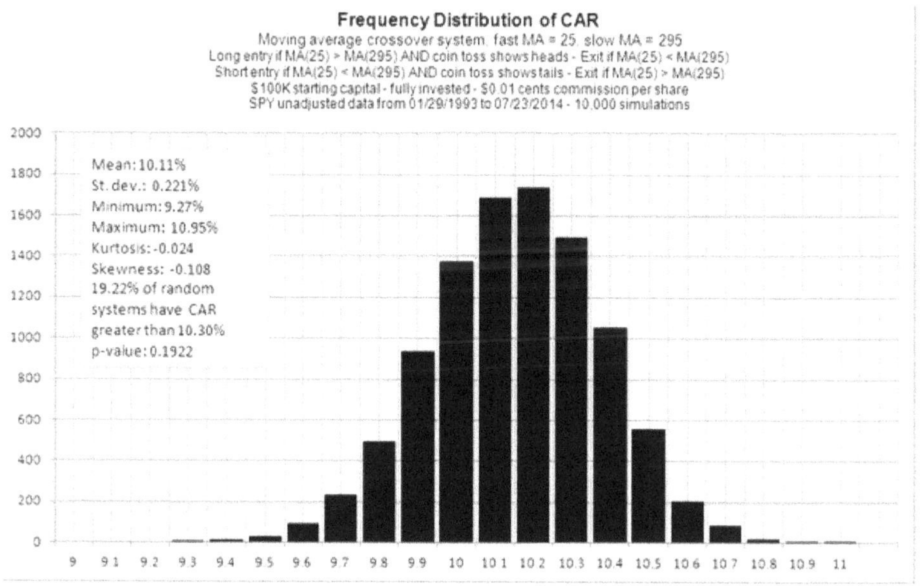

Figure 6-16. Randomization study results for the system in Pseudocode 6-2 with n1 = 25 and n2 = 295

Although the difference in values for significance appears small in this example that is used to illustrate the method, it translates to roughly $27,500 of additional profit in the backtest period. This analysis demonstrates that the exit part of this system performs the actual work, while the entry part does not add any intelligence. If market conditions change in the future, the performance of this system may deteriorate because it possesses no intelligence in timing price action but instead relies solely on its exit logic. Conditions that could cause deterioration could include a protracted period of sideways market activity with high volatility. In that case, the exit logic would be too slow to capture returns, and the drawdown could become excessively large.

For example, a market condition similar to those encountered in XLF from January 1, 2000, to December 31, 2002, would result in a negative performance with excessive drawdown. We can see the backtest results of the moving average crossover system in Pseudocode 6-2 for n1 = 25 and n2 = 295 when it was used on XLF data in Figure 6-17. In this case, the entry part of the system is not intelligent enough to avoid the whipsaw market that began in 2001, and drawdown accumulates due to consecutive losers.

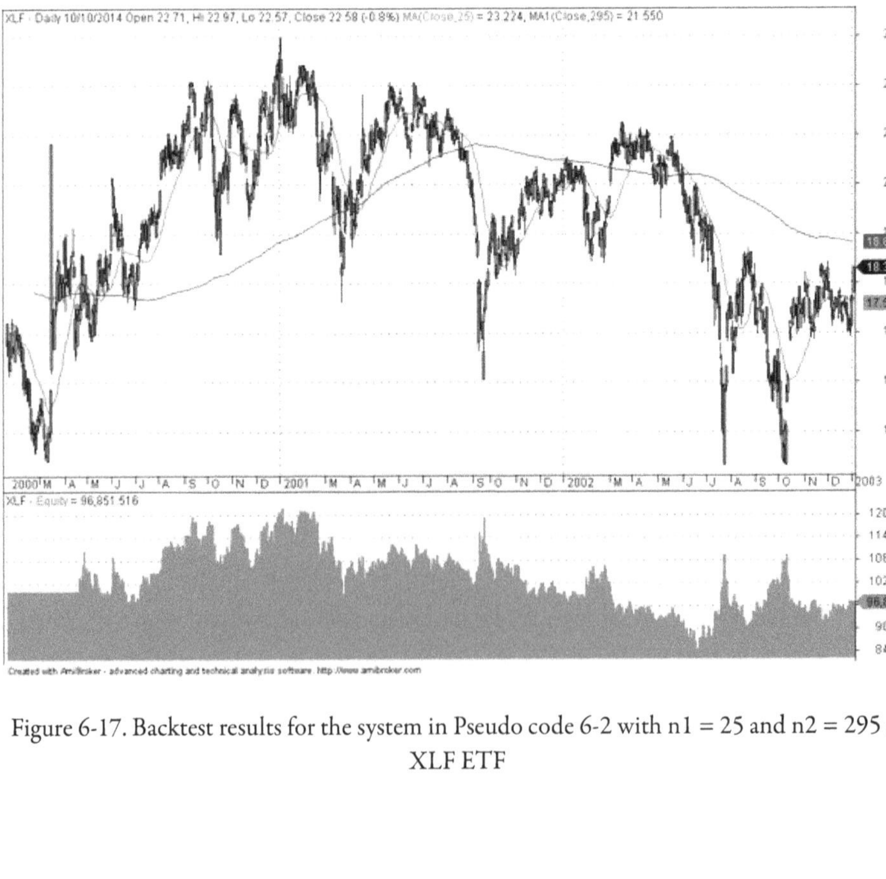

Figure 6-17. Backtest results for the system in Pseudo code 6-2 with n1 = 25 and n2 = 295 in XLF ETF

The conclusion from this example is that the original moving average crossover system was curve-fitted, and the tests that were performed allowed us to determine that this system lacks intelligence, as was expected. We used this simple example to demonstrate a methodology for identifying whether a system underwent curve-fitting during the design phase.

Example 2: The RSI(2) system

In recent years, books, magazines, and blog posts have featured several variations of a trading system based on the RSI indicator. The basic rule of the system involves going long when the RSI of two days, denoted as RSI(2), drops below a certain value, supposedly indicating an oversold condition, and exiting when the same indicator enters the overbought territory. In Chapter Four, it was shown that the RSI is essentially a strength indicator, as its name implies, and not an overbought or oversold indicator because this assessment relies on the gambler's fallacy. Note that this seemingly "simple" system, as it has been described, already involves four parameters: n1, the RSI period for the long entry; n2, the period for the long exit; the overbought level OB; and the oversold level OS, as shown in Pseudocode 6-5.

N=integer(equity/entry price) //calculate number of shares

If RSI(n1) < OS then Buy N shares at the close //buy signal

Exit if RSI(n2) > OB

Pseudo code 6-5. A trading system based on the RSI indicator

The rules of trading system development presented in this section indicate that having four parameters is already too many for reducing the impact of curve-fitting on data mining bias. Optimizing this system further increases the data-mining bias due to curve-fitting. But let us suppose that the recommended parameter values are as follows: n1 = 2, n2 = 2, OS = 10, and OB = 90. These values could have been the result of some optimization in the past based on some unknown objective function. A backtest of this system on unadjusted SPY ETF data from 01/29/1993 to 07/23/2014, with a starting capital of $100K, fully invested equity at each position, and 0.01 cents per share commission, yielded the equity curve shown in Figure 6-18. The equity performance of this system nearly matches that of buy and hold with a CAR of 7.16%; the maximum drawdown is equal to -38.84%, the win rate is 77.91%, the profit factor is equal to 1.88, and the Sharpe ratio is 1.05. A total of 172 trades were generated, and the net return is 342%. These performance parameters may impress a naïve quant, but an expert quant will attempt to debunk this system for three reasons: (a) it involves too many parameters, (b) its payoff ratio (average win to average loss) is only 0.53, which is considered low, and (c) it operates effectively in markets with a strong upward bias during mean-reversion phases, as will be explained in more detail below.

Figure 6-18. Backtest results of the system in Pseudo code 6-5 with n1 = 2, n2 = 2, OS = 10, and OB = 90 in SPY ETF

As the first step in our effort to debunk this system, let us remove the exit logic and introduce a small profit target and stop-loss of 2%. Figure 6-19 displays the resulting equity performance.

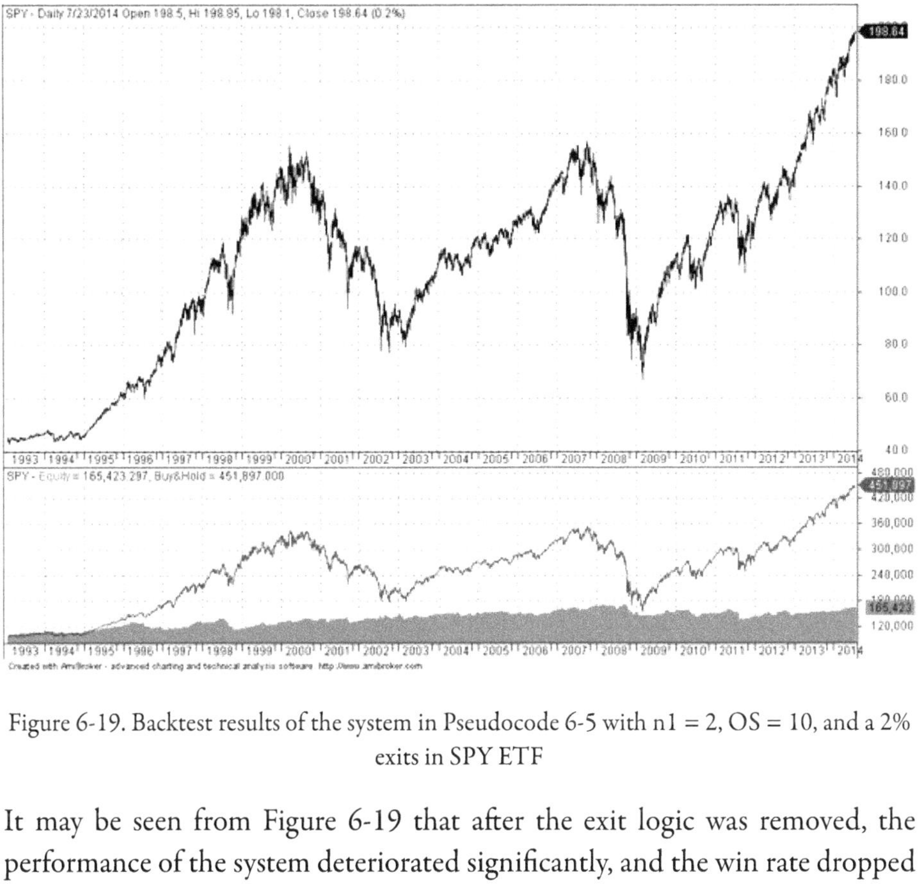

Figure 6-19. Backtest results of the system in Pseudocode 6-5 with n1 = 2, OS = 10, and a 2% exits in SPY ETF

It may be seen from Figure 6-19 that after the exit logic was removed, the performance of the system deteriorated significantly, and the win rate dropped to 54.63. Still, the performance is positive with a CAR of 2.37% due to the longer-term upward bias of SPY ETF. The small profit factor of 1.15 indicates that the results may not be better than random.

We next perform a random simulation in the same SPY data with a biased coin that generates heads (long signals) 75% of the time. When tails show up, the positions are exited. Thus, long positions stay in the market for some time, comparable to the average bars in trades from the backtest in Figure 6-19, which are equal to about 15 days. The frequency distribution of 20,000 such simulations with the same initial capital, fully invested equity at each position, and the same commission rate is shown in Figure 6-10. The RSI(2) system's test return of 342% outperforms only 75.69% of the random systems, resulting in a p-value of 0.2430. Therefore, based on the results of this simulation, the evidence supports the null hypothesis that this system lacks intelligence. Keep in mind that the simulation in Figure 6-20 shows that the RSI(2) system needs to generate a net return of at least 385.82% before it can be considered significant at the 5% level.

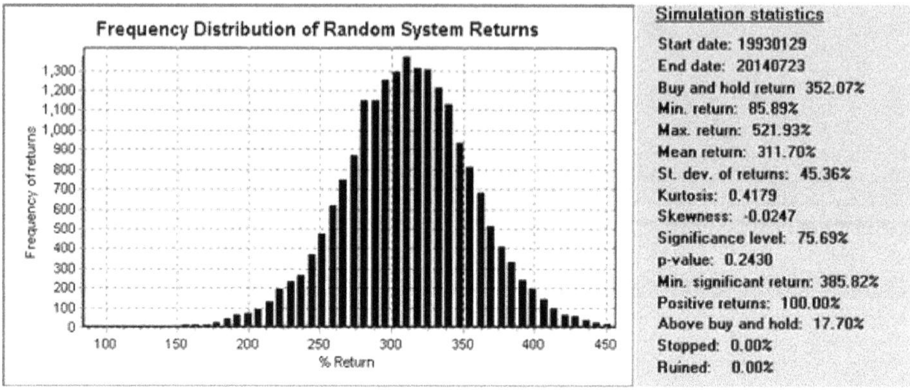

Figure 6-20. Randomization study results of a coin toss system for trading SPY ETF with p{heads} = 0.75. Generated by DLPAL software. www.priceactionlab.com

Besides the four parameters that can lead to overfitting, this naive version of the RSI(2) system aims to capture short-term trends as the indicator's strength rises from its low points. However, in a strongly uptrending market such as the SPY ETF, all random position systems profit, as shown in Figure 6-20, with a minimum return of 86.69% and a maximum return of 521.93%. Furthermore, about 18% of the random systems manage to make more than the buy-and-hold return. A trader, who tosses a biased coin, enters long positions when heads appear, and exits them when tails appear would have slightly less than a 1 in 5 chance of making more than 352% and outperforming the buy-and-hold strategy. Furthermore, it is evident to an expert Level IV quant that a system such as the RSI(2) could fail during downtrends, as shown in Figure 6-21 when it is applied to GLD ETF data.

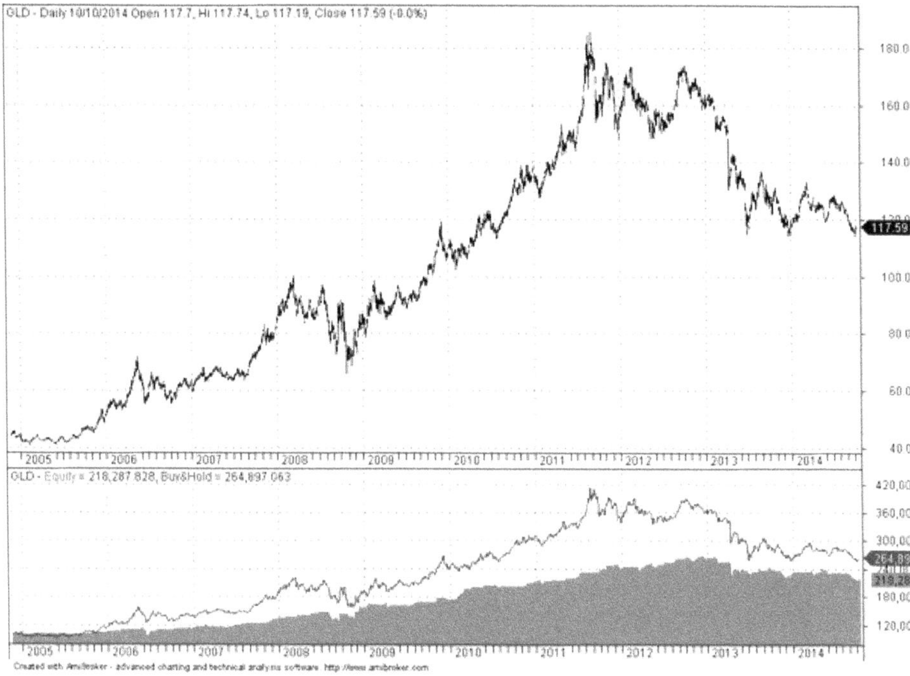

Figure 6-21. Backtest results of the system in Pseudo code 6-5 with n1 = 2, n2 = 2, OS = 10, and OB = 90 in the GLD ETF

It may be seen in Figure 6-21 that the RSI(2) system profits during the uptrend in the GLD ETF, but when a downtrend starts after 2013, its performance deteriorates. This should be expected because, during downtrends, rebound rallies fizzle fast. However, instead of tossing this system away, naïve quants have tried to improve it by adding all sorts of filters and thus more parameters that facilitate more curve-fitting, leading to more data-mining bias. One proposed variation included adding an extra condition to the entry logic to check for an uptrend in prices, thereby avoiding downtrends; this condition is represented as C > MA(200). Additionally, the exit logic was modified to include C < MA(5) to manage quick reversals. However, as it may be seen from Figure 6-22, after repeating the backtest of Figure 6-21 with these two rules that add two more parameters to the system for a total of six parameters, the performance in GLD has not improved significantly in the period since the start of 2012.

Figure 6-22. Backtest results of the system in Pseudo code 6-5 with n1 = 2, n2 = 2, OS = 10, and OB = 90, along with extra filter added in GLD ETF

Although the RSI(2) system with the added filter manages to avoid a disastrous trade during the downtrend in 2013, it nevertheless suffers losses due to the sideways price action during 2014. The filters work when the downtrend is smooth, but not when the averages turn flat. Thus, the filters that were added in hindsight helped little when market conditions changed and there was a prolonged whipsaw. Furthermore, using the same filters without optimizing the RSI period reduces the CAR to 4.86% from 7.16% in the SPY ETF case. In general, when many parameters are already involved and filters are added, the result is a random system with a high probability of failure. Additionally, optimizing the parameters increases the probability of a random result to nearly 1, a consequence of high data-mining bias.

The two rules presented in this section—(1) considering systems with a maximum of two parameters and (2) avoiding the use of exit rules that curve-fit equity performance to data during development—can help reduce data-mining bias caused by optimization and curve-fitting. The two proposed tests, which involve replacing the exit logic with a small profit target and stop-loss, followed by a backtest and conducting a randomization study to rank performance, can help an expert quant evaluate the potential of trading systems developed either manually or through automated data mining.

Remember, the inability of the two suggested methods to support the null hypothesis does not necessarily imply that the alternative is viable. This is because the test data sample may not represent the entire population. The aim of a trading system developer should be to try to demonstrate support for the null hypothesis that the trading system does not have an edge because true edges are exceptionally difficult to identify and the probability that a trading system is random is always high. While most authors focus on techniques that try to confirm an edge, this book aims at educating traders that it is easy to be fooled by technical analysis into thinking that an edge has been discovered. A system can be so intelligently optimized that it passes all tests and appears to possess an edge, i.e., it may show timing ability when a small profit target and a stop loss are applied, and it may also rank at a high significance level during randomization studies. Therefore, it is important to always remember that tests are used to reject systems. If a system cannot be rejected, it doesn't necessarily indicate that it has an edge. Gaining an understanding of these concepts is the first step towards becoming an expert quant. An expert quant should diligently search for reasons to reject a system and work towards achieving this objective.

Next, we discuss how the bias due to system selection can be minimized, and we introduce additional tests for supporting the null hypothesis of no profitability.

Selection of systems

In the previous section, we discussed in some detail and with a few examples how optimization and curve-fitting increase data-mining bias. Specific rules were suggested for minimizing the bias and testing the null hypothesis that a trading system possesses no edge. In this section, we will discuss the impact of selection on the data-mining bias. Trading system selection, via a manual or automated process for developing trading systems, introduces data-mining bias because selecting a model based on some performance criteria, even when they are calculated out-of-sample, ignores many other models that did not perform as well.

Figures 6-2 and 6-3 indicate that selection is involved in two stages of the process: after backtesting and optimizing with the in-sample data and after backtesting with the out-of-sample data. If the trading system development process in Figure 6-2 is used repeatedly to test new strategies, then it becomes equivalent to the automated one in Figure 6-3. One difference between the two processes is the method of generating hypotheses for testing: in the manual process, a human conceives them through a complex cognitive process, while in the automated process, an algorithm generates them; in the simplest case, this algorithm uses permutations, and in the most complex case, it employs an evolutionary algorithm. Essentially, both processes try to achieve the same thing and discover an edge. The automated process creates a list of the best systems that fulfill some performance criteria, while the manual process generates a similar list but over a longer period of time.

Another difference between the automated and manual processes of discovering trading systems is that the former can test millions, billions, or even trillions of strategies in a short period, but note that in both cases, the act of selecting a final system to trade increases the data-mining bias because a large number of systems are excluded. The key point to understand is that although the selection is desirable and even unavoidable, any selected trading system, evaluated on historical data, may have survived due to luck alone and may lack an edge. This is the reason that selection introduces bias.

After selecting a system, one must test it to determine if it possesses an edge. The final decision can't be based solely on out-of-sample backtesting, as multiple comparisons can skew the results. In other words, performing repeated data-fishing may lead to the discovery of a random system that successfully passes the out-of-sample validation test. In the case of automated trading system development via the use of neural networks, evolutionary algorithms, or permutations, it is easier to see why, after testing a large number of alternative hypotheses, one or even several can be found that pass the out-of-sample validation test. That may not be evident to those who try to discover systems manually, but it is a similar process, and in this case, only the speed by which data-mining bias is increased is different. Data-snooping bias, which often occurs in manual development—where a new strategy is created after knowing the results of backtesting other out-of-sample strategies—limits any benefits that could arise from the slower increase of data-mining bias.

Following the aforementioned introduction, it may appear rational to do away with out-of-sample testing and instead utilize the existing data history to develop trading systems, either manually or automatically. This approach enables the exploration of a wider range of market conditions during backtesting, potentially reducing the number of random systems. However, selection must take place based on some criteria, and the final system, or systems, must be validated on some other data sample. Comparable markets might be able to supply this new data sample. To develop a system for trading the QQQ ETF, researchers could test the final choice of strategies on a sufficiently large number of similar securities that were selected in advance, rather than after development started. The securities group should comprise price series that not only reflect a diverse range of market conditions but also maintain low correlation. In the case of the QQQ ETF, the comparable securities group could include, for example, SPY, IWM, DIA, TLT, GLD, DBC, XLE, XLF, and EEM. However, this is where most naïve quants make a mistake: they consider the combined portfolio performance to decide whether the selected system has an edge. Outperformance in only a few securities could positively skew the results. The analysis of long-term trend-following systems, tested on a portfolio of securities or futures contracts, often commits this error. A better criterion is the number of failures. If the system fails in over 10% of the portfolio's securities or contracts, it may mean that the system had no edge in past market conditions. Since the same conditions can repeat in any market, the system will fail in the future with a high probability.

The following may contribute to minimizing data-mining bias due to selection:

- Limiting the number of tested strategies by limiting the number of rules
- Using all of the available histories to develop systems (no out-of-sample testing)

- Backtesting the final system on a group of comparable securities
- Setting a performance threshold and selecting all systems that rank above it

The first example below shows how the test using comparable securities can expose a system that was fitted intelligently and, as a result, passed the curve-fitting test. The second example concerns a system that a computer created. It demonstrates how using a performance threshold in conjunction with a test on comparable securities can help reduce selection bias.

Example 1: The z-score system

Variations of a trading system based on the z-score became popular about 10 years ago. The z-score measures the number of standard deviations the price is away from the mean price. A contrarian system can use the z-score to generate buy and sell signals in anticipation of reversion when the price diverges from its short-term mean. A variation of this system and performance results for the SPY ETF were published in November 2010 on the website of a popular trading platform (Ref. 8). The technical analyst conducting the study reported that the system did not curve-fit and successfully passed tests using data from comparable securities. It was unclear if the comparable securities were chosen after the results were known, as no out-of-sample testing was used. But the main point of this example is to show how hard it is to reject a well-fitted system.

The code of the z-score system is shown in Pseudocode 6-6. The average price is first calculated via the use of an exponential moving average with period n1. The standard deviation is calculated using the same period, n1. Then, the z-score is calculated using the average price and the standard deviation. The next step involves the calculation of the average z-score using an exponential moving average with period n1. Finally, the n2-day momentum of the average z-score is calculated. A buy signal is generated at the next open if the momentum is negative, and a sell short signal is generated at the next open if it is positive. This model is a long/short system that is always in the market, with short positions exiting long positions and *vice versa*. Position size is determined based on fixed initial capital.

N= (initial capital/entry price)

avgp= exponential average of price in n1 days

s= standard deviation of price in n1 days

z-score=(price-avgp)/s

avgz-score= exponential moving average of z-score in n1 days

momentum=avgz-score of today-avgz-score of n2 days ago

Buy N shares if momentum < 0

Short N shares if momentum >0

Pseudo code 6-6. The z-score system

The z-score system in Pseudo Code 6-6 has 3 parameters: the period for calculating the average price and standard deviation, the period for calculating the average z-score, and the momentum period. The three parameters were reduced to two by equating the first two, n1 and n2. The variation of this system presented in Ref. 8 had n1 set to 10 and n2 set to 5.

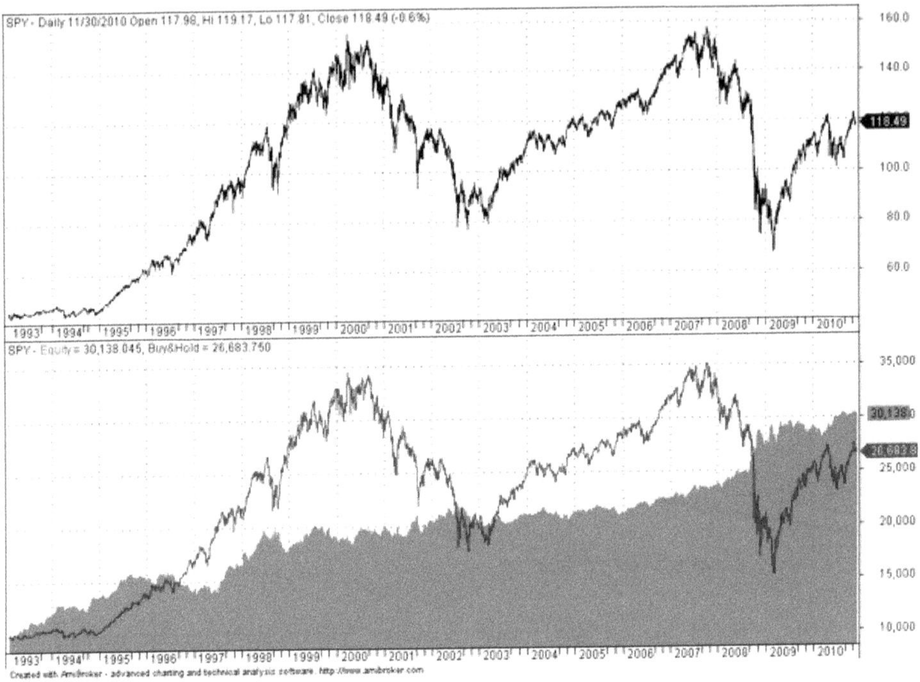

Figure 6-23. Equity performance of the z-score system from 02/02/1993 to 11/30/2010

Figure 6-23 displays the equity performance of the z-score system as calculated using SPY ETF data from the same time period as in the cited reference, i.e., from 02/02/1993 to 11/30/2010. No commission was included. The system generated 646 trades with the following values for the performance parameters:

Net return: 201.33%

CAR: 6.38%

Win rate: 64.20%

Payoff ratio: 0.78

Sharpe ratio: 0.65

Profit factor: 1.40

The net return is higher than the buy-and-hold return of 169.66% during the test period. The equity curve is relatively smooth, but the low Sharpe and payoff ratios immediately raise some questions about the robustness of this system. As argued previously, the primary goal of a trading system developer should be to try to debunk a system and prove that it has no edge. Since the maximum data history for the SPY ETF was fully utilized during the testing of this system, we will not conduct tests on out-of-sample data; instead, we will use other tests that may lead to rejection. In the first test, we set a small profit target and a stop-loss of 1.5%. The resulting equity curve after backtesting the system with this change is shown in Figure 6-24 and shows performance degradation but still a positive net return over the testing period. Specifically, the net return is about 22%, the CAR is 1.09%, and the win rate is 52.40%.

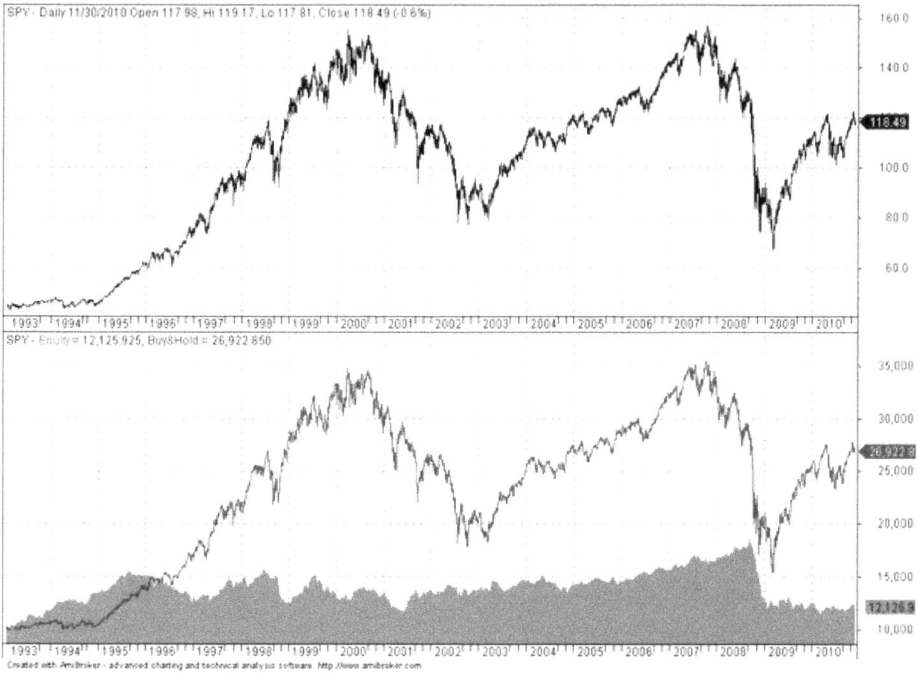

Figure 6-24. Equity performance of the z-score system in SPY ETF from 02/02/1993 to 11/30/2010 with a 1.5% profit target and stop-loss

After the first test, the win rate dropped to 52.40%, suggesting that this system is fitted to the data, but performance is still positive. The next step involves ranking the performance of this system after simulating a large number of random systems that use the same rule for position size determination. The logic that generates the random systems is based on tossing a fair coin at the end of each day. If heads show up, any open short position is exited and a long position is established, which in turn is closed and reversed to a short position when tails show up.

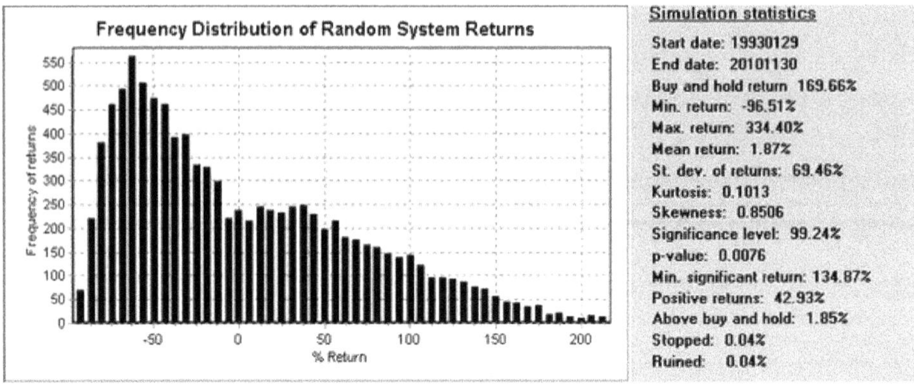

Figure 6-25. Randomization study results for the system in Pseudocode 6-5 with n1 = 10 and n2 = 5. Generated by DLPAL software. www.priceactionlab.com

Figure 6-25 displays the results of the randomization study. It may be seen that the minimum return for significance over the test period from 01/29/1993 to 11/30/2010 is 134.87%, and the z-score system with a return of 201.38% ranks better than 99.24% of the random system. According to these results, there is evidence supporting the null hypothesis that the z-score system is not intelligent or random. However, one requirement for the rejection of the null hypothesis in trading system development is that the data sample used is representative of the population. As shown below, this system lacks an edge because this requirement is unmet.

We have been unable so far to reject the z-score system based on simple tests, and we must go one step further and perform tests on comparable securities. The equity performance from a backtest of the z-score system on GLD ETF data from its start on November 18, 2004, to November 30, 2010, is shown in Figure 6-26. The results reveal a consistently losing system with a net return of approximately -48%, a CAR of -10.24%, and a win rate of 56.70%.

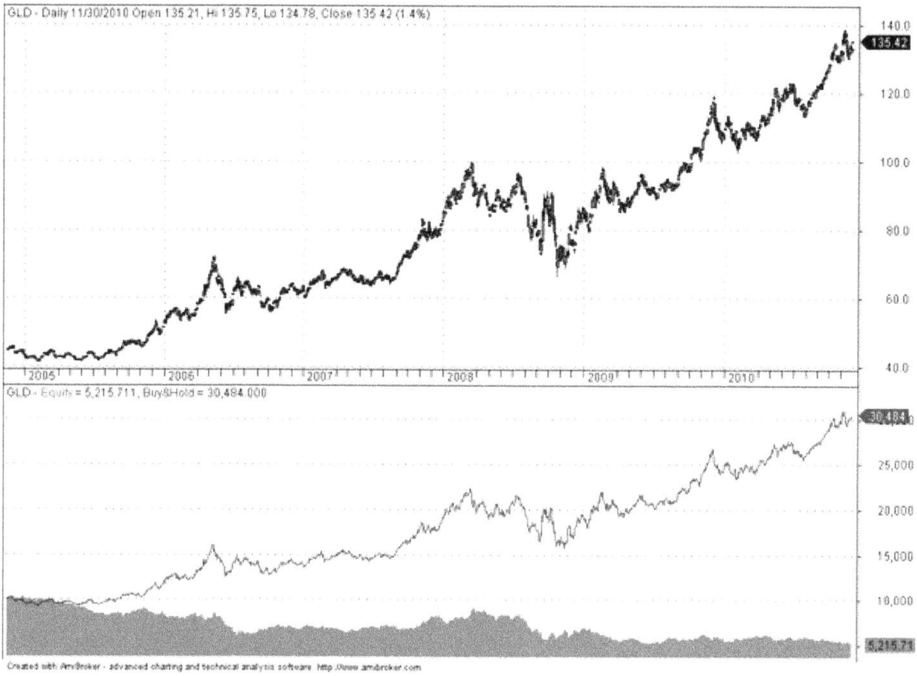

Figure 6-26. Equity performance of the z-score system in GLD from 11/18/2004 to 11/30/2010

The z-score system consistently generated losses when tested on DBC data from February 5, 2006 (when it was first created) to November 30, 2010, as shown in Figure 6-27. The net return is -56.58%, the CAR is -15.90%, and the win rate is 52.67%.

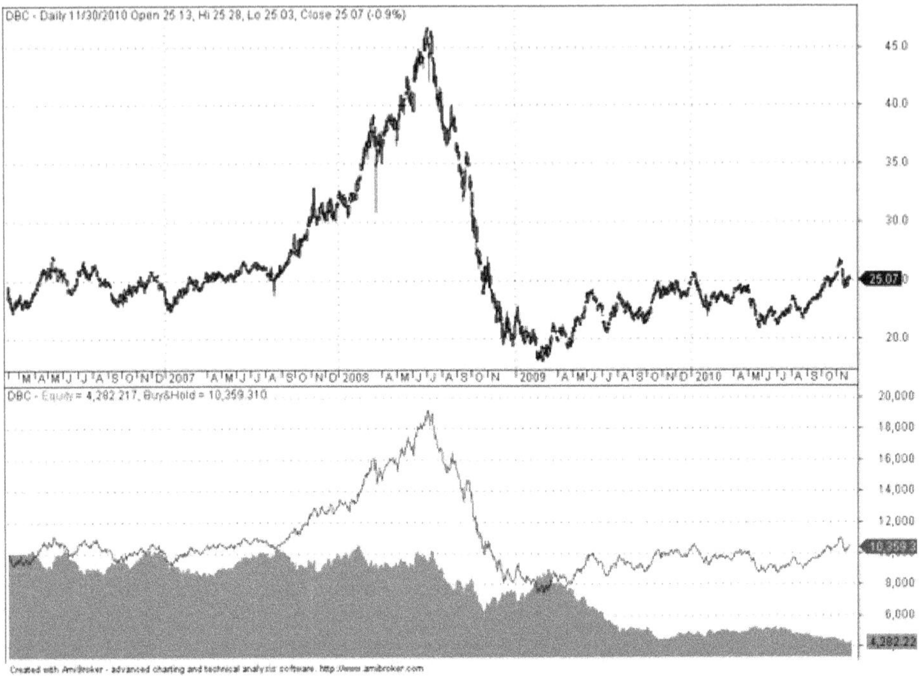

Figure 6-27. Equity performance of the z-score system in DBC from 02/06/2004 to 11/30/2010

Therefore, we have succeeded in rejecting the z-score system after applying tests on comparable securities. It appears that the system had previously undergone intelligent optimization, or it might have come from a data-mining program that used descriptive statistics as its input. The system was tested on data from other securities, but only those with acceptable results were considered, something that increased the data-mining bias because the results were skewed by a few securities that performed well. The deeper reasons that the system has no edge are unimportant now, and system developers should focus on rejection instead of trying to understand why systems fail, as that can be distracting. The z-score system does not perform well during smooth or steep trends. Reference 8 also acknowledged this issue, a credit to the system developer. However, in our opinion, the mistake was the selection of a portfolio where this system performed well. Developers should always look for conditions where a system does not perform well. Such conditions occurred in the SPY ETF after 2013, and the trading system underperformed the buy-and-hold return by a wide margin, as shown in Figure 6-28. Buy and hold for the SPY ETF (dividends not included) in the period from January 3, 2013, to October 17, 2014, was about 29%, but the z-score system gained only 9.57%. In that period, the minimum significant return based on a randomization study was 24.3%, somewhat less than the buy-and-hold return, and a 9.57% return was better than only 75% of the random system, a result that provides support to the null hypothesis that the z-score system does not possess any intelligence.

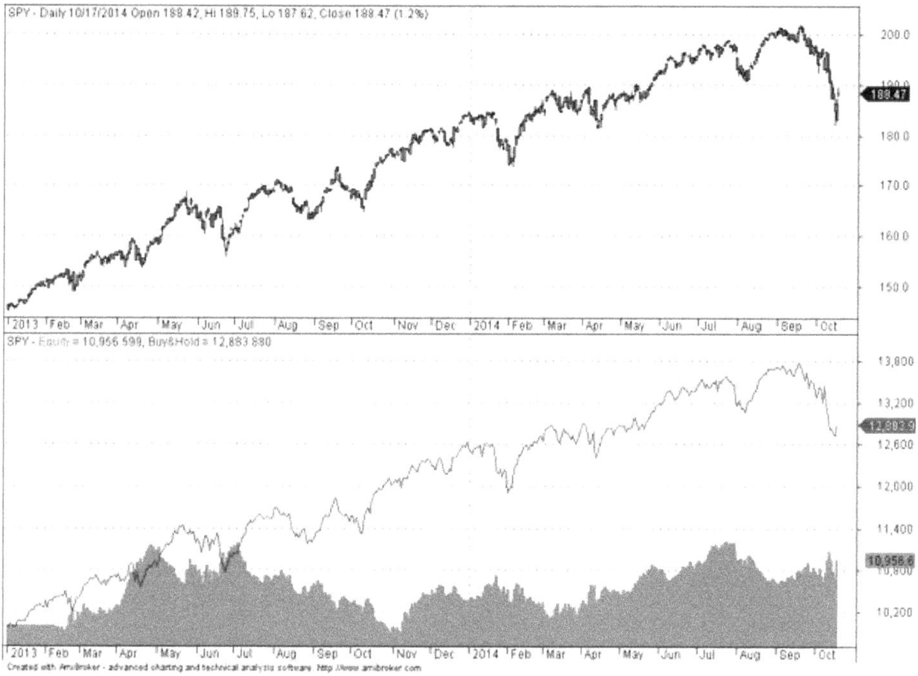

Figure 6-28. Equity performance of the z-score system in SPY ETF from 01/02/2013 to 10/17/2014

In this example, we considered a trading system that was backtested manually, although it may represent a strategy that was not initially conceived by a human developer but was the outcome of an automated data-mining process. If you use an automated process, you can lower selection bias by setting a performance threshold based on a metric like the profit factor, the compound annual return, or even a mix of metrics. Then, you can pick all the results that rank above the threshold and treat them as a single system. The next example shows how this additional rule fits with the other three rules mentioned earlier.

Example 2: A machine-designed trading system

This example involves a trading system that was machine-designed by a software program called Deep Learning Price Action Lab (DLPAL). DLPAL finds strategies based on the open, high, low, and close of a price series. These strategies are of Type III because they have no parameters in their entry logic. After the strategies are found, only the exit logic parameters (profit target and stop-loss) can be changed. Each strategy is essentially a complete trading system, but many of these can be combined to develop a final trading system.

The machine design used SPY ETF data from 01/29/1193 to 12/31/2012 and was set to discover strategies based only on daily bar closings. DLPAL is capable of finding strategies made up of 2 to 9 bars. The metrics chosen for the selection threshold were the win rate, the profit factor, the number of trades, and the number of consecutive losers of each strategy discovered. Table 6-2 summarizes the parameters of the machine design process.

Security	SPY ETF
Timeframe	Daily
Data range	01/29/1993-12/31/2012
Minimum win rate	66%
Minimum profit factor	1.5
Minimum number of trades	20
Maximum consecutive losers	8
Profit target	2.5%
Stop-loss	2.5%
Trade entry on	Open

Table 6-2. Parameters for SPY ETF trading system data-mining

DLPAL found 109 different strategies that met the requirements—89 long strategies and 20 short strategies. The results are shown in Figure 6-29, with the strategies ranked by highest win rate.

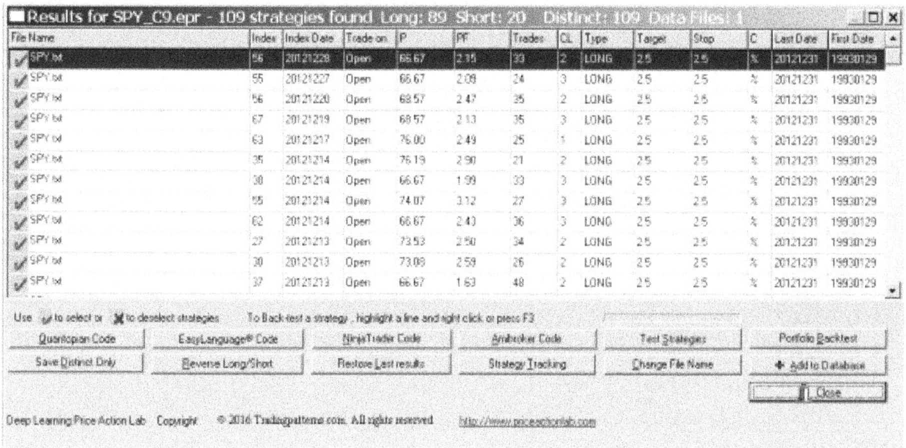

Figure 6-29. Results of a data-mining process for SPY ETF price patterns with parameters in Table 6-2. Generated by DLPAL software. www.priceactionlab.com

Each line in the results of Figure 6-29 corresponds to a strategy that satisfies the performance parameters in Table 6-2. The program internally uses the Index and Index Date to classify strategies. Trade on is the entry point, in this case, the open of the next bar. P is the success rate of the strategy, PF is the profit factor, Trades is the number of historical trades, CL is the maximum number of consecutive losers, Type is LONG for long and SHORT for short strategies, Target is the profit target, Stop is the stop-loss, and C indicates whether it is % or points for the exits; in this case, it is %. Last Date and First Date are the last and first dates in the historical data file, respectively.

To reduce the bias, we select all strategies in the results based on the defined threshold, and we use them to develop a system that takes long and short positions in SPY with a 2.5% profit target and stop-loss. Reverse signals cause an exit from any open position, and no multiple positions are allowed. The starting capital is set at $100,000, and positions are sized based on a constant dollar amount equal to the starting capital divided by the entry price. Note that when the system equity is fully invested, the risk per trade of this system is 2.5%, which is equal to the stop-loss of 2.5%. Table 6-3 shows the compound annual return (CAR) of the final system for each of the 10 ETFs, with data from inception to 12/31/2012.

ETF	CAR (%)
SPY	8.86
QQQ	3.98
IWM	3.53
DIA	4.22
EEM	5.99
GLD	4.97
TLT	4.25
XLF	4.09
XLE	5.55
DBC	0.64

Table 6-3. CAR performance of a machine-designed system.

It may be seen from Table 6-3 that the SPY ETF system based on the 109 strategies discovered by a data-mining program was also profitable in the other nine major ETFs. The tests on the nine comparable securities yield a mean CAR value of 4.6% and a standard deviation of 1.53%, indicating small variability. Excluding the low but still positive result for DBC, the mean is 5.04% and the standard deviation is 1.63%. These results allow us to conclude that the system passes the comparable securities test.

In this example, we first limited the number of strategies by considering only price patterns, and we also restricted the system to Type III. Then we used all of the available data (at the time the system was developed). We also selected all strategies above a predefined threshold and then performed a test on comparable securities to validate the results. The system passed all tests, but that does not guarantee future profitability because untested market conditions may develop. However, the probability of failure was minimized.

Next, a forward test was done from January 2, 2013, to June 30, 2014. Using the same position sizing method, the SPY ETF system that had been data-mined from January 29, 1993, to December 31, 2012, showed a net return of 25.66% during this time. The buy-and-hold return of SPY ETF during the same period was 34%. As shown in Figure 6-30, based on a randomization study, the return of the system was better than 97.53% of that of random systems, resulting in a p-value of 0.0248. As a result, the null hypothesis that the system is random was rejected. However, as mentioned already several times, rejecting the null hypothesis does not imply that an edge will be maintained in the future, as market conditions may change from those encountered in all tests.

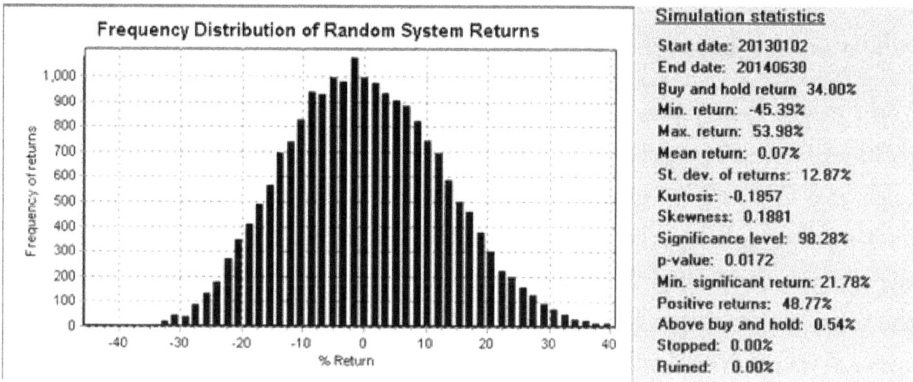

Figure 6-30. Randomization study results for a test return of 25.66% in SPY ETF. Generated by DLPAL software. www.priceactionlab.com

In this section, we discuss ways to reduce selection bias during both manual and automated trading system development. In the next section, we deal with data snooping and its impact on the data-mining bias.

Data snooping bias

In trading system development, data snooping bias arises when, after an out-of-sample test, the process of system discovery is repeated, as indicated in Figures 6-2 and 6-3. When this is done, the out-of-sample becomes part of the in-sample used to develop the system. Data-mining bias is increased due to data snooping, and the chances of discovering a random trading system that performs well in the out-of-sample increase. Trading system developers that use backtesting repeatedly to test many ideas with out-of-sample data have small chances of discovering an edge as time goes by because data mining becomes enormous. The following two rules may reduce the impact of data snooping in the case of manual development:

- Perform backtests only when there is a promising idea
- Eliminate out-of-sample testing and validate with data from comparable securities

Most naïve quants continuously backtest ideas, thinking that this increases their chances of finding an edge when in fact the chances decrease as time goes by, and at some point, they discover a fluke that passes all out-of-sample and validation tests but then fails in actual trading.

You can get rid of data snooping bias when you use automated data mining to identify trading systems, as long as any out-of-sample tests are only done once and the process is not started over. However, the majority of users of data mining software are likely to either restart the process after changing the metrics they want to maximize or minimize or even set an option that the software developer may offer to automatically use out-of-sample results to cause a restart. Needless to say, when data snooping is present in an automated process such as the one shown in Figure 6-3, the chances of finding an edge before finding a fluke are zero for all practical purposes. There is no need for formal mathematical proof; just consider the fact that there are millions or even billions of flukes and only a small number of edges. If one backtests hundreds of millions of trading strategies, then the chances that a fluke will be overfitted to the data are high, especially when such strategies employ several indicators with optimized parameters. Therefore, eliminating out-of-sample tests and using all available history as the in-sample effectively eliminates data-snooping bias. Instead of out-of-sample validation, backtests on comparable securities could be used to reduce the selection bias that comes with data mining.

The notion that the extensive use of backtesting lowers the chances of finding a profitable edge may sound counterintuitive to some, but it is what expert quants already know that separates them from naïve quants doing random tests and constantly discovering spurious correlations. Backtesting is a science, but it is also an art. Successful traders who use backtesting are like artists who create a work of art from a canvas (data) and some media (rules). Trying more often does not make them better artists unless they have a solid idea. Trying to paint every day can only result in worthless work. One must wait for the right moment to use the canvas with the right media. Only then are the chances of success higher.

Myths about data-mining bias

At the highest level, data-mining bias results from testing multiple hypotheses on historical data. As the number of tested hypotheses increases, so do the chances of accepting a random rule as genuine. Data-mining bias has a hugely adverse effect on the quality of the data-mining process. The myths this book exposes are the result of naïve efforts to deal with a qualitative feature of a process from a quantitative perspective.

Myth No. 1: Data-mining bias can be measured

Data-mining bias cannot be effectively measured because it refers to the quality of a process and not to some specific parameter. Any definitions of data-mining bias that attribute to it a specific measure are the result of unjustified attempts to quantify a non-quantifiable notion. For example, some quants attempt to measure this bias by generating random data and then applying data mining to them. They hope that by repeating this process many times and by getting a distribution of some metric based on the random results, they will be able to correct the original results from the actual data and compensate for the data-mining bias. However, such methods essentially rank the performance of an algorithm with respect to the performance of a large number of algorithms mined on random data and nothing more than that. There is no justification for the claim that something that ranks high will perform better in actual trading. For example, if the original algorithm found by data mining was overfitted with historical data, then it still has low chances of performing well if market conditions change, regardless of whether or not it had a better rank when compared to algos obtained from random data.

Myth No. 2: Out-of-sample testing can deal with data-mining bias

Out-of-sample tests are part of an overall algo-development process that is plagued by data-mining bias. If many hypotheses are tested on historical data, then some of them will pass out-of-sample tests by chance alone. Therefore, out-of-sample testing does not suffice to guarantee that an algo is not random. In addition, it is false to call out-of-sample testing a "cross-validation" method. This type of testing is only a validation method that cannot eliminate the data-mining bias in the presence of multiple hypothesis testing. Note that "cross-validation" methods are in general hard or impossible to use in manual development or machine learning due to the nature of the process and the data used.

Myth No. 3: Forward testing can deal with data-mining bias

When machine learning software vendors are confronted by customers who have used out-of-sample testing without success, they recommend forward testing. However, forward testing is just another form of out-of-sample testing, and it is essentially its continuation. If one tests many hypotheses, then there is a high probability of finding a random one that passes all tests in both the out-of-sample and forward sample. As the number of hypotheses increases, this probability tends to 1, i.e., finding a random algo that passes all tests is a certain event.

Myth No. 4: Monte Carlo Analysis can deal with data-mining bias

Some trading system developers use Monte Carlo analysis to determine the effect of parameter variations on performance. If the algo is robust enough when subjected to such variations, then it is perceived as genuine. However, Monte Carlo analysis becomes part of the data-mining process as soon as it is applied. Even if Monte Carlo analysis is performed on unseen data, when a large number of hypotheses are tested, there is a high probability of finding one that passes all out-of-sample, forward sample, and Monte Carlo analysis tests. The probability becomes 1 as time passes and the same data are reused. Any machine learning process, when used repeatedly and extensively, will generate algos that are random but pass all tests, even Monte Carlo analysis. In addition, note that this type of analysis has many flaws and applies only to a small subset of possible strategies, as already discussed earlier in this chapter.

Myth No. 5: If you do not use data-mining, then there is no data-mining bias

The only difference between thinking of a hypothesis and having a computer generate it is the processing speed. Data-mining bias is always present as long as the hypothesis is tested on historical data. Unless one can think of a truly unique hypothesis that no one else has, chances are it was already data-mined by a computer. Researchers started applying machine learning to the markets in the mid-1980s, and since then they have mined data relentlessly. One of the most naïve things one could do nowadays is to try to combine some indicators with exit rules using a machine learning algorithm, hoping to discover gold. Although some results may work for some time, inherently they are random because, when one adjusts for the multiple comparisons, the results are not significant.

Pitfalls of validation methods

Because it is easy to overfit strategies on historical data during development and fall prey to randomness, strategy development validation is necessary in trading. Although the best validation method is actual performance, it is an expensive method, and most developers would like to assess potential before employing strategies. In most cases, the developer attempts to modify a failed strategy after a failed validation test or conceive a new one. This leads to the dangerous practice of reusing data until a strategy that passes some validation tests is developed. There are some misconceptions about multiple comparisons, data-mining bias, and p-hacking, mostly as a result of the way academics with strong mathematical backgrounds but little trading experience have presented these topics.

High statistical significance, which academics often favor, does not equate to a good strategy; in fact, the majority of trading strategies developed using this flawed method fail at some point in real trading, with some failing immediately. In other words, strategies that exhibit high statistical significance can fail, and they frequently do so due to changes in market conditions, which are referred to as regime changes. Therefore, statistical significance is not a panacea, as purported in some academic publications, and developers should be aware of this and the fact that market regime changes also play an important role.

1. Out-of-sample tests

This is the most popular and also the most abused validation method. Briefly, out-of-sample tests require setting aside a portion of the data to be used in testing the strategy after it is developed and obtaining an unbiased estimate of future performance. However, out-of-sample tests

- reduce the power of tests due to a smaller sample
- results are biased if the strategy is developed via multiple comparisons

In other words, out-of-sample tests are useful in the case of unique hypotheses only. The use of out-of-sample tests for strategies developed via data mining shows a lack of understanding of the process. In this case, the test can be used to reject strategies but not to accept any. In this sense, the test is still useful, but trading strategy developers know that good performance in out-of-samples for strategies developed via multiple comparisons is, in most cases, a random result.

A few methods have been proposed for correcting out-of-sample significance in the presence of multiple comparison bias, but in almost all real cases, the result is a non-significant strategy. However, as we show in Ref. 1 with two examples that correspond to two major market regimes, highly significant strategies, even after corrections for bias are applied, can also fail due to changing markets. Therefore, out-of-sample tests are unbiased estimates of future performance only if future returns are distributed in an identical way as the past returns. In other words, non-stationarity may invalidate any results of out-of-sample testing.

Out-of-sample tests apply only to unique hypotheses and assume stationarity. In this case, they are useful, but if these conditions are not met, they can be quite misleading.

2. Robustness tests and Stochastic Modeling

Due to the high Type-II error (false rejection) of other validation methods, practitioners have long resorted to robustness tests. Robustness tests fall under the more general subject of stochastic modeling.

Robustness tests usually involve small variations in parameters and in the entry and exit logic of a trading strategy. The objective is to determine whether the resulting distribution of some performance metric, usually the mean return or maximum drawdown, has a low variance. If the variance is high, then it is assumed that the strategy is not robust. Different metrics can be used along with different methods for evaluating robustness. Briefly, robustness tests, in reality, determine how well a strategy is overfitted and, in most cases, indicate the opposite of what is desired, i.e., high robustness may be an indication of an excessive fit to historical data. For this reason, it is appropriate to apply robustness tests on an out-of-sample, but as a result, the power of the test is low. More importantly, any robustness tests and stochastic modeling, in general, are subject to data-snooping bias if used repeatedly with the same data. The probability that a random strategy passes all tests, even the out-of-sample, increases as the number of hypotheses increases. However, for unique hypotheses, the practical tests can reveal certain properties that are useful but vary on a case-to-case basis.

Robustness tests and stochastic modeling in general can assess overfitting conditions, but Type-I error (false discoveries) is high, especially in the case of multiple comparisons, even when applied to an out-of-sample.

3. Portfolio backtests

The main idea of this method is to avoid out-of-sample tests and the use of the whole price history in developing trading strategies. By using a sufficiently high number of price series in a portfolio, the power of a test for significance increases. A simple statistical hypothesis test may be used in this case based on the T-stat as follows:

$$\text{T-stat} = \text{Sharpe} \times \sqrt{\text{number of years}}$$

The null hypothesis is that the strategy returns are drawn from a distribution with a zero mean. If the null hypothesis is rejected, then there is a low probability of obtaining the strategy's performance, given that the null hypothesis is true.

Portfolio backtests, as well as tests on comparable securities, suffer from at least two problems: the first is that these tests are too strict, and the Type-II error (missed discoveries) is high. The other, and maybe more serious, problem is that strategies usually fail when market conditions change, despite their high significance. Statistical hypothesis testing has limited application in trading strategy development, despite offering grounds for publishing academic papers. In general, the logic of the strategy and the process used to derive it are more important than any statistical test. Statistics cannot uncover hidden value if there is none. Note that it is easy to cheat portfolio backtests by selecting the securities to use post hoc. Some trading strategy developers frequently do this, typically out of ignorance. The securities to be used in the portfolio must be selected beforehand. Then, if the test fails, the strategy must be rejected. Any effort to improve the strategy and repeat the tests will introduce data-snooping bias and p-hacking.

Portfolio tests and tests on comparable securities are useful under certain conditions, given that they are not abused with p-hacking as a goal.

4. Monte Carlo simulation

Monte Carlo simulation is part of stochastic modeling, but we list it here separately because of its popularity. These tests are the least robust and effective in trading strategy development and should be avoided, except in cases where the strategies fulfill certain requirements, as discussed earlier in this chapter. Monte Carlo simulations are especially inapplicable in the case of data-mined strategies and multiple comparisons. If these simulations are used with data-mined strategies, it is a strong indication that the developer lacks experience. Overfitted strategies usually generate good Monte Carlo results. When this method is used in a loop of multiple comparisons, it loses its significance completely.

Use Monte Carlo tests only when it is appropriate to do so. In general, the choice of validation method depends on the nature of the strategy, and the application and interpretation of results are more of an art than a science. Most validation tests are done by practitioners, but also academics suffer from either multiple comparison bias or fail under changing market conditions. The nature of markets is such that there is no robust test to assess strategy robustness. This is what makes trading strategy development very difficult but also an interesting and challenging task.

Quant discretionary trading

Mechanical trading systems became popular in the 1990s because traders thought that by removing emotions from trading, the chances of success were higher. But not all emotions are negative, especially if they are based on experience and knowledge of market microstructure and dynamics. A well-known issue in trading system development is data-mining bias, which cannot be easily fixed. More and more traders are also realizing that removing emotions also removes human intelligence and a deeper understanding of price action that is hard or impossible to express mathematically. For these reasons, there is a return to the basics, specifically discretionary trading, but this time within a quantitative framework. Mechanical systems still dominate the high- and medium-frequency spectrums, but for position and swing trading, quantitative discretionary trading is gaining ground. Below is a list of the main advantages and disadvantages of quantitative discretionary trading.

Advantages of quant discretionary trading

- It does not remove human intelligence from trading
- It does not tie traders to specific markets
- It forces constant personal improvement by studying price action
- It offers more flexibility in managing risk
- It adjusts to changing market conditions
- No data-snooping is possible since there is no out-of-sample data

Disadvantages of quant discretionary trading

- The sample size is usually small
- Data-mining bias is still present
- No out-of-sample validation is possible
- Time-consuming task that must be well organized

Example of quant discretionary trading

This example shows how the disadvantages listed above are being dealt with. DLPAL software was used for the identification of price patterns in daily data.

Figure 6-31 shows the output of the scan function of the program after the close of Monday, February 2, 2015. Unadjusted daily data since inception was used with the program to scan 12 popular ETFs.

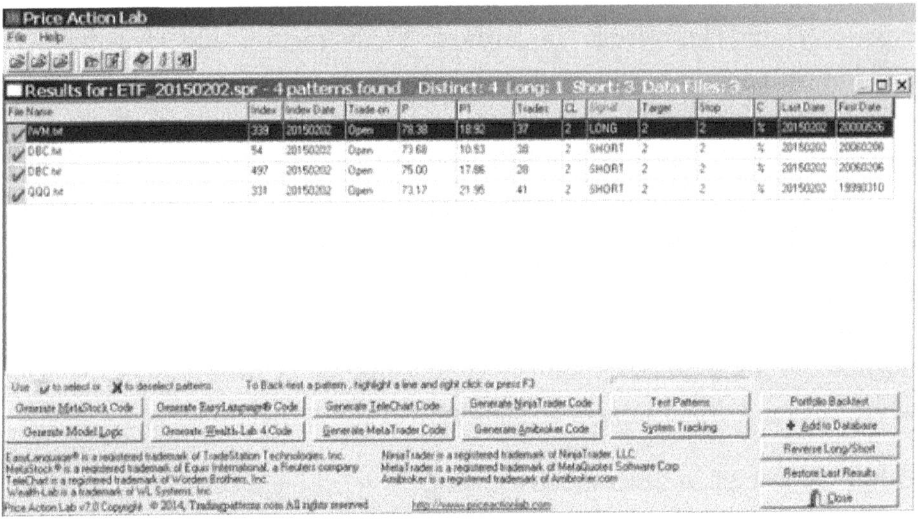

Figure 6-31. Results of a scan of a group of ETFs as of the close of February 2, 2015. Generated by DLPAL software. www.priceactionlab.com

In Figure 6-31, each line corresponds to an exact price pattern found in the data. P is the win rate, Trades is the number of historical trades, CL is the maximum number of consecutive losers, and Target and Stop are the values of the profit target and stop-loss. C indicates the type of target and stop-loss; in this case, it is a percentage added to the entry price that is shown under Trade On as the open of the next bar.

Patterns in three ETFs were found: one long pattern in IWM, two short patterns in DBC, and one short pattern in QQQ. However, when data mining for patterns occurs, the following problems arise:

- Data samples are usually small
- Patterns may be fitted to the data
- Data-mining bias may be large

One must address the above three issues before using the results. Unfortunately, most naïve Level III quants that use pattern scanners do not deal with such issues.

<u>Evaluating the significance of patterns</u>

The first step in the evaluation involves increasing the sample size. Normally, hundreds, or even thousands, of trades are required to determine the statistical significance of trading signals. This is partly because the small trade samples may not be representative of the actual population. For example, 30 trades in 1-minute data do not represent a significant sample, and thousands of trades are required instead. To increase the sample size, we may perform a backtest of the patterns using data from a large group of comparable securities. The idea is that if a pattern is significant, then the significance should be reflected in the results of portfolio backtests. In this example, the S&P 500 component stocks were used with data since 01/2000, and the results are shown in Figure 6-32.

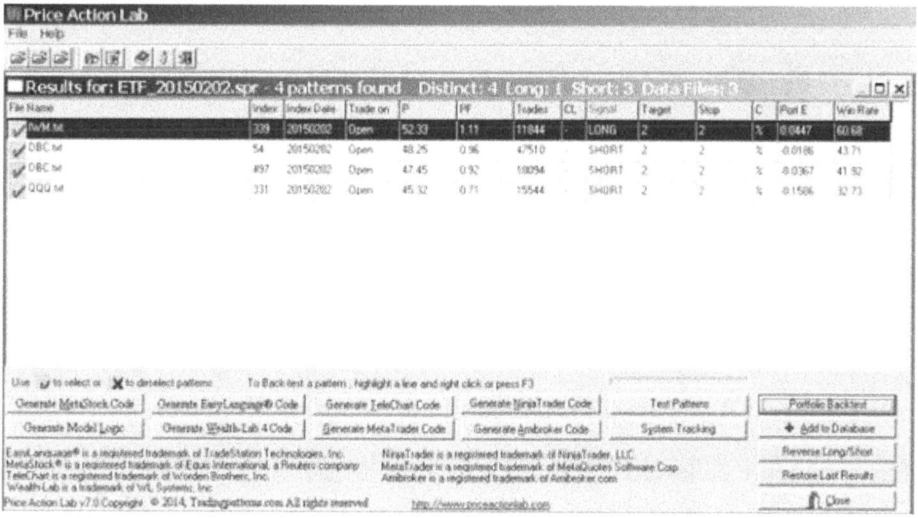

Figure 6-32. Results of a portfolio backtest applied to the results of an ETF scan as of the close of February 2, 2015. Generated by DLPAL software. www.priceactionlab.com

The Last and First Date columns in the original results shown in Figure 6-31 were replaced in Figure 6-32 by the portfolio expectation and success rate (the number of profitable tickers out of the 500), and the P1 column was replaced by the portfolio profit factor, i.e., the ratio of the sum of winners to the sum of losers. It may be seen from Figure 6-32 that the pattern in IWM was profitable in 60.68% of the stocks, and the profit factor is 1.11, while the number of trades increased to 11,844. The results for the other patterns show negative expectation and a profit factor of less than 1.

The long signal in IWM hit its profit target of 2% on February 5, 2015, three days after it was identified, as shown in Figure 6-33.

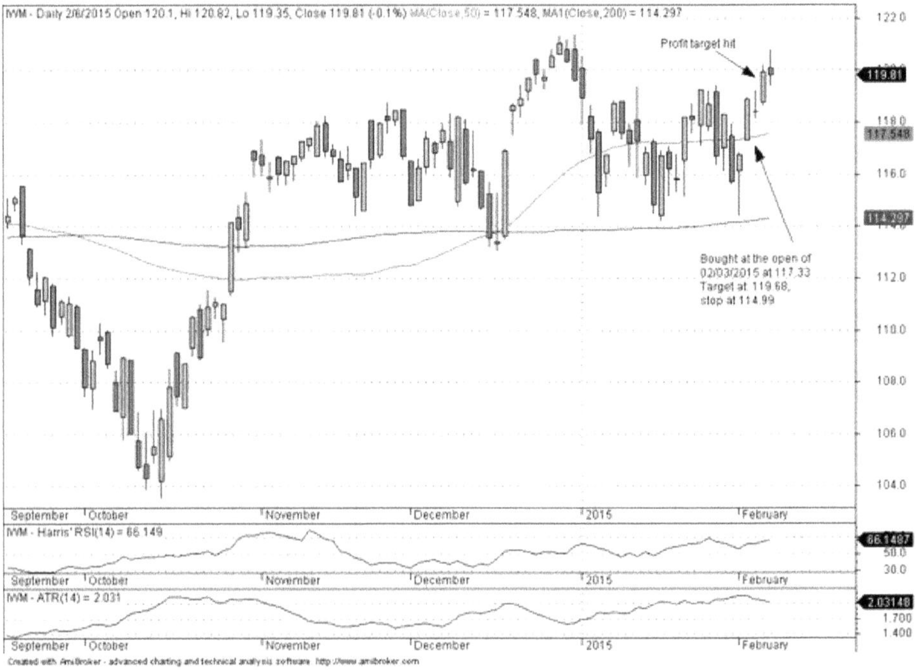

Figure 6-33. A pattern in IWM identified by Level IV quant discretionary analysis

The procedure followed in this example for identifying and testing trading patterns is just one of several possibilities. It involves algorithmic and deterministic data mining, i.e., the same data and parameter settings always produce the same results. Reproducibility is important; otherwise, there is no testing that can be done that conforms to scientific standards.

Fooled by momentum strategies

There are two basic momentum strategies: trend-following and relative strength.

Trend-following, which is also called absolute or time-series momentum, tries to get high risk-adjusted returns by predicting market moves and limiting losses. In the stock market, high drawdowns occurred after the dot-com bubble burst and the financial crisis. The strategies use simple models, such as the long-only 50/200 moving average crossover or price breakout systems.

Relative strength and momentum Investors benefit from price crashes and the premiums created by panicked investors who sell at the bottom. Fundamentally, these strategies buy outperforming securities and sell, or even short, underperforming securities. The strategies also use trivial models, such as the rate of price change.

The historical profitability of momentum strategies is the result of hindsight and data mining. Allocation in stocks, funds, or ETFs based on momentum naturally affects overbought or oversold levels and the decisions of value investors, something that is not reflected in backtests. With these strategies, we are not dealing with trading a few contracts or shares but with substantial investments from funds, and the dynamics of the relevant markets are affected as a result. Often, momentum strategies entail the ranking of securities based on past returns, followed by the purchase of top performers and the sale or shorting of the worst performers. Published studies on momentum strategies are usually based on lookback periods that were optimized through backtests. Therefore, there is data mining involved, and the selection of a certain look-back period ignores other such periods that did not produce good results.

Momentum strategies are popular because they are supposed to generate excess alpha at lower risk as compared to buy-and-hold and passive allocations. However, as in the case with traditional trading systems, momentum represents just another method that must be tested for significance and, more importantly, for intelligence in capturing alpha.

One cannot simply appeal to academic studies that demonstrate the momentum anomaly effect in stock markets and then claim that there is a general method for transforming this effect into excess alpha. All trading hypotheses must be analyzed on a case-by-case basis. Part of the analysis could involve testing the following hypothesis regarding backtested and real performance:

H0: The method does not possess any intelligence.

H1: The method possesses intelligence.

By "possessing intelligence," it is meant here that a system was not curve-fitted on past data or was lucky in actual trading but that its returns were due to its ability to adjust to changing market conditions.

If the analysis is carefully performed, it will usually show that momentum-based strategies have no intelligence because of the selection of the best-performing securities in the past and the optimum look-back periods for calculating the ranking score. In addition, long-term backtests of such strategies involve results that were positively impacted by the tech bubble market of the 1990s. It can be shown that after the 1990s, these strategies did not generate excess alpha [Ref. 11].

Mean reversion took the place of sustainable momentum in the U.S. stock market in the late 1990s. This is illustrated in the S&P 500 daily chart shown in Figure 6-34 by the Momersion indicator. This indicator measures momentum and mean reversion over a period of 250 daily bars. It is an oscillator that is calculated as follows:

$$\text{Momersion}(n) = 100 \times \text{Mc}/(\text{Mc}+\text{MRc}) \quad (6.1)$$

where Mc is a count of momentum and MRc is a count of mean reversion, calculated as shown in Pseudocode 6-7.

Mc = 0

MRc = 0

For i = 1 to n=250 do

{

If r(i) × r(i-1) > 0 then increment(Mc)

If r(i) × r(i-1) < 0 then increment(MRc)

}

Momersion(n) = 100 × Mc/(Mc+MRc)

Pseudo Code 6-7: Calculating the Momersion indicator

In Pseudo code 6-7, r(k) is the kth arithmetic return and it is calculated as follows:

$$r(k) = [close(k)/close(k-1)] - 1 \quad (6.2)$$

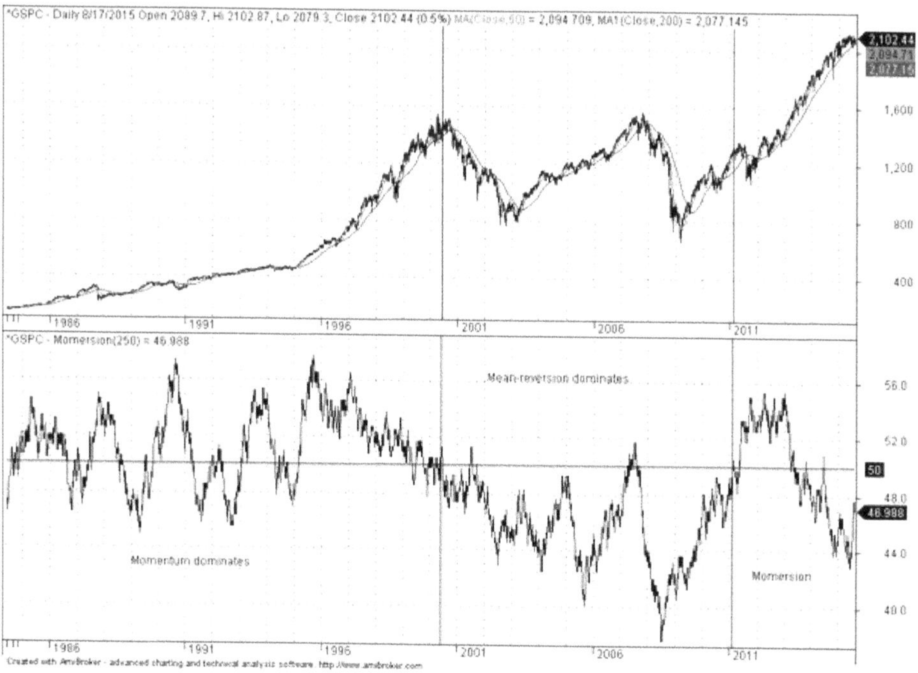

Figure 6-34. Momersion indicator applied to daily S&P 500 index data

It may be seen from Figure 6-34 that during the 1990s, momentum dominated, but after the 2000 top and the dot-com bubble burst, mean reversion dominated until 2011. This is shown by the Momersion indicator staying below the 50% line after 2000. After 2011, the S&P 500 is in a state of "Momersion," i.e., a period where price action alternates between momentum and mean reversion.

Putting it all together

The chances of finding an edge via backtesting with historical data may be maximized when the following rules are followed:

Rule 1: Backtesting should be used only when there is a promising idea

The frequent backtesting of random ideas contributes to an increase in data-mining bias and facilitates data snooping. Traders should backtest only when there is something worth the dangers involved from a large data-mining bias.

Rule 2: Backtest trading strategies that involve only a few parameters or preferably none at all

The more parameters the model has, the easier it is to overfit it to the data, and the more selections are available that can facilitate data-fishing, increasing data-mining bias.

Rule 3: Limit the number of strategies considered by limiting the number of basic rules they employ

This may not be a problem with infrequent manual backtesting, but with data-mining software, thousands, millions, or even billions of entry and exit rules can be combined to produce a final result. The chances of finding a true edge are inversely proportional to the number of rules involved. If automated data mining is employed, quants must try to limit the number of tested rules. Remember that the objective is to find an edge, not a function that fits the data.

Rule 4: Avoid, during the initial development, the use of exit rules that naturally curve-fit to the data

If exit rules are used that naturally fit the data, such as a trailing stop, for example, then the entries may play no important role. If the same conditions as in the backtest do not repeat in the future, the system may fail. The entries need to have market timing ability. Exits that maximize profit potential can be employed after the final result is obtained and validated.

Rule 5: Use all of the available data to develop systems to increase the range of market conditions

Unless backtesting will only be done once for a given market, then there is no point in using out-of-sample validation. Each time a new or modified strategy is backtested after an out-of-sample test, data-mining bias increases due to data snooping. Using all the data in backtests exposes a system to more market conditions during the development phase. Afterward, Rule 6 may be applied.

Rule 6: Backtest a promising result on a group of comparable securities selected in advance

It is important to have a standard group of securities that reflect a wide variety of market conditions and correlations for validation. Data-mining bias is increased when only looking at securities where a system works after it has been developed and ignoring many others where it fails. This is because survivors are chosen.

Rule 7: In the case of automated data mining, accept all systems above a set performance threshold

Selecting the best-performing system out of a large number of systems introduces selection bias, which in turn increases data-mining bias. All systems above a certain threshold that is set in advance must be selected and treated as a single system to minimize data-mining bias due to selection.

Rule 8: Test the null hypothesis on a forward sample

This test is confirmatory and should be made on a forward sample where the system is tested either on paper or in real trading. It can indicate whether the system has an edge in the tested sample. It usually involves ranking the performance of the system against a large number of random systems with similar characteristics and operating within similar timeframes.

Note that even if all the above rules are applied, the final result may fail in actual trading because of a major change in market conditions due to a regime where positive performance is not possible. Unfortunately, there is no guarantee in trading that an edge will stay robust, and an expert quant must work constantly towards discovering new edges that will replace old ones when performance starts deviating from desired levels. This fact about trading systems has discouraged many to the point that they have started seeking alternatives to technical analysis. Chapter Eight briefly mentions some of these alternatives and the issues associated with their use.

CHAPTER SEVEN

Position Size Determination

Authors without any actual trading experience have in the past duped retail traders into considering position determination strategies that have high risks. While trading wizards kept recommending small fixed-fractional position sizes, i.e., risking only a small percentage of the available capital on every trade, in the order of 1% to 2%, some authors promoted elaborate methods for determining position size, possibly to gain authority and publicity. These optimal methods rely on knowledge of some key parameters, such as the win rate and average win-to-average loss ratio. In addition, these methods often assume that the key parameters stay constant or within certain bounds. However, in reality, trading system parameters are never constant, and their values may vary widely. For example, the win rate of a trading system can stay above or below its longer-term average when the system initially starts trading. Let us assume that the longer-term average is 55%, but during initial trading, the win rate increases to 85% due to a good streak of winners. Most optimal methods for position size determination will overestimate risk when the adjustment from a higher to a lower win rate begins, and that could result in large losses and possibly ruin. Since traders can hardly predict how key performance metrics of a trading system will change over time, this book warns against using methods for finding the best position size because they might trick traders into taking on more risk than they should. Instead, this book focuses on practical methods for sizing positions, which have demonstrated their effectiveness through experience.

The questions surrounding the use of a stop-loss become more intriguing. Some argue that a stop-loss negatively affects profitability, and therefore, one should steer clear of it. Such claims target the retail trader crowd, which usually risks small amounts in terms of trading capital. The lack of stop-loss is inconceivable in professional trading. If they want a chance to succeed, traders who have fallen for false claims about the use of technical analysis in retail trading must comprehend how professionals trade. Therefore, if a system does not incorporate a stop-loss by design, one must implement a risk control method by some other means to reduce the risk of ruin. Otherwise, trading without a stop-loss is indistinguishable from gambling. In this chapter, we shall discuss a method of including a stop-loss in every system in the event that the system logic does not allow it because of an adverse effect on dynamics and profitability.

Basic types of trading systems

There are two basic types of systems that traders use:

- Systems that use stop-loss
- Systems that do not use stop-loss

The stop-loss can be expressed in dollars, ticks, points, pips, or as a percentage of the entry price. The determination of position size is, in principle, easier when a stop-loss is used since the approximate exit price is known in advance in most cases. In the case of a percent stop-loss, the entry price may not be known in advance, and a position size determination must be made based on an estimated entry price.

An example of a system that incorporates a well-defined stop-loss was given in Example 6.2 of Chapter 6. That was a machine-designed trading system based on price patterns with a 2.5% profit target and stop-loss. Both the profit target and stop-loss levels were calculated based on the entry price.

Position size determination often involves an approximation because the exact entry price is not known in advance. For example, if the trade entry occurs at the opening of the next bar, that price level is not known exactly. Only in cases where the trade entry involves a stop order, i.e., buy or sell on a stop, can the position size be determined with higher accuracy, although in fast markets there is slippage because when a stop level is hit, the order is usually executed at market unless a limit order is also used. Therefore, there is already a lot of uncertainty to start with when determining position size.

There are a number of systems that do not have a clear stop-loss. These include stop and reverse logic systems, like the long-short 50-200 moving average crossover system in Pseudo Code 6-2; long- or short-only systems that exit based on an indicator signal, like the RSI(2) system in Pseudo Code 6-5; and some systems that exit based on time. In this case, position size determination is not possible in a straightforward manner, and different methods must be used to control risk.

Systems with a stop-loss

Definitions

C is the current bankroll

P is the entry price

Rc is the risk percent (based on current bankroll)

Rs is the stop-loss percent

SLp is the stop-loss in points (absolute value)

Note that Rs is given by:

$$Rs = 100 \times SLp/P \quad (7.1)$$

Equation 7.1 means that if we know the stop-loss in points, we can determine the stop-loss percent by dividing it by the entry price and multiplying the result by 100. This calculation is inexact for most trading systems except for those that initiate positions using a stop order, in which case there will be just slippage. For example, for systems that enter trades at the open price of the next day, P cannot be known in advance and can only be estimated. In reality, the actual open price may not deviate much from estimates that are offered before the market opens under normal conditions, but there will be variations during fast markets. In general, calculating position size involves some approximations and must be treated as an inexact procedure.

We next define the *risk ratio (RR)*. This is the ratio of the risk percent based on available capital per position to the stop-loss percent:

$$RR = Rc/Rs \quad (7.2)$$

The following formula determines the position size N:

$$N = C \times RR/P = (C \times Rc)/(P \times Rs) \quad (7.3)$$

In this formula, N represents the number of shares (rounded to an integer value), C denotes the available capital, RR indicates the risk ratio, and P signifies the entry price.

For example, if Rc is equal to 2%, i.e., 2% is risked on each trade based on the current bankroll, and the percent stop-loss Rs is also 2%, then RR = 1. In this case, the position size is equal to the available capital divided by the entry price.

The risk ratio (RR) denotes the fraction of equity allocated to a trade. If RR = 1, then the full equity is utilized. If RR $<$ 1, then equity is underutilized, and if RR $>$ 1, then the number of shares calculated by Equation 7.3 must be reduced to that allowed by the available equity. According to this position sizing method, also known as *fixed fractional*, the optimum risk ratio RR is 1, in the sense of fully utilized equity, and this occurs when the risk percent Rc based on available capital is equal to the stop-loss percent Rs. Usually, it is recommended that Rc be 2% or even lower to minimize the risk of ruin.

<u>Example: Stock trading</u>

Account equity: $100,000

Risk percent: 2%

Stop-loss: 4 points

From Equation 7.1, we obtain:

$$Rs = 100 \times SLp/P = 100 \times 4/P = 400/P \quad (7.4)$$

After substituting the result from Equation 7.4 into Equation 7.3, we obtain the following:

$$N = C \times RR/P = (C\times Rc)/(P\times Rs) = (\$100{,}000 \times 2)/(P \times 400/P) \quad (7.5)$$

The entry price cancels out as expected, and the result is as follows:

$$N = \$100{,}000 \times 2/400 = 500 \text{ shares}$$

The maximum number of shares that are allowed is equal to \$100,000/P, where P is the price of the security. Instead of using the result of Equation 7.5, the position size should be the maximum number of shares permitted if the price is higher than 200.

Example: E-mini futures

Account equity: \$100,000

Risk percent: 2%

Stop-loss: 20 points

From Equation 7.1, we obtain:

$$Rs = 100 \times SLp/P = 100 \times 20 \times 50/P = 100{,}000/P \quad (7.6)$$

Note that to calculate the stop value in dollars, we had to multiply the number of points by the E-mini futures contract's big point value of 50 (Note that the big point value for stocks is 1.) After substituting the value of Rs from Equation 7.6 into Equation 7.3, we obtain the following:

$$N = C \times RR/P = (C\times Rc)/(P\times Rs) = (\$100{,}000 \times 2)/(P \times 100{,}000/P) \quad (7.7)$$

The entry price cancels out as expected, and the result is

$$N = (\$100{,}000 \times 2)/(100{,}000) = 2 \text{ futures contracts}$$

If the account lacks enough equity to pay for the calculated number of contracts' initial margin, the results must be adjusted. The results must also be changed to account for any limits that apply if the amount of equity given per contract is higher than a minimum value established by analysis. For instance, after determining the position size, it is necessary to take into account the minimum initial capital per contract for a specific system and market, which is $30,000 in this case. If the available equity is $90,000 and the calculated number of contracts is 4, then the position size must be reduced to 3 contracts (90,000/30,000).

Fooled by optimal methods

Some trading book authors have proposed methods for determining optimal position size that are supposed to increase profitability by accelerating equity growth even at a geometric rate. The authors and their methods are often detached from reality, possibly because of a lack of actual trading experience. Applying methods for determining optimal position size necessitates the knowledge of certain performance parameters of the trading system in advance and their stability. In reality, none of the system parameters stay the same for long periods of time. This means that optimal methods may overestimate the size of a position, and when there is a streak of losers, the drawdown that is generated can be too high. Some of the proponents of optimal methods for position size determination have claimed that equity can never be reduced to zero since a fraction of available equity is always risked. However, these arguments ignore a simple arithmetic fact: if the loss is 50%, for example, a 100% gain is required to recover it. If the loss is 80%, a 400% gain is required to recover lost capital. Unless one assumes excessive risk through leverage, which can lead to ruin, the markets typically prevent such gains in a short period. Thus, there is no free lunch with optimal methods. This technique includes the well-known but ambiguous Kelly fraction method.

The Kelly formula was based on the work of John Kelly of Bell Laboratories in the 1950s on the subject of the telephone transmission signal-to-noise ratio. The following is the version of the original Kelly formula that traders frequently use:

$$K\% = W - [(1-W)/R] \quad (7.8)$$

In this formula, K% represents the percentage of capital to risk per trade, while W denotes the win fraction and R indicates the ratio of the average win to the average loss.

To use the Kelly formula to determine the best position size, you need to know the actual values of a trading system's performance parameters, specifically W and R. Therefore, new trading systems usually cannot provide the exact values for the two parameters needed in the Kelly formula to find the best position size ahead of time. But even systems used in real trading for a long time may not have stable parameters. This phenomenon is especially true in the case of trend-following systems, where the average win-to-average loss ratio R is a random variable because it depends on the magnitude of unknown future trends and price volatility. Because of this, regular checks on the system's performance parameters are required when using advanced methods, like the Kelly formula, to determine the best position size. Such monitoring is required to ensure that the parameters maintain some minimum values. Let us look at a specific example in the case of a stock trading system:

Trading capital: $100,000

Win fraction: 0.65

Ratio of average win to average loss: 1.25

To determine the optimal position size according to the Kelly formula, first we use Equation 7-8 to calculate K%, the optimal bet size:

$$K\% = 0.65 – (1 - 0.65)/1.25 = 0.37 \text{ or } 37\%$$

If the stop loss is 5% and the entry price is $85, then the number of shares according to the optimal betting strategy of the Kelly formula can be found by applying Equation 7.3:

$$\text{Number of shares } N = (0.37 \times \$100{,}000)/(0.05 \times \$85) = 8{,}705 \text{ shares}$$

If the stock drops 5%, then the loss will be equal to 8,705 × 85 × 0.05 = $36,996.25, close to the allowable bet size due to the rounding of the number of shares.

The first problem with the above calculation of position size is that the number of shares it yields cannot be purchased with the available capital of $100,000 because 8,705 shares × $85 per share = $739,925. In this particular case, only

$100,000/$85 = 1,176 shares can be purchased if no margin is available. Instead of the 37% risk level that the Kelly formula predicted, the actual risk is 5%. However, if the system has no stop-loss, then the risk percent would be 37%. In that case, let us suppose that the next trade is a loser and equity is reduced to $100,000 minus $37,000 = $63,000. The win rate will also drop due to the new loser. Let us assume that it becomes 60%. The new K% for the next trade is calculated using Equation 7.8:

$$K\% = 0.60 - (1 - 0.60)/1.25 = 0.28, \text{ or } 28\%$$

Let us now assume that the next trade is also a loser. As a result, the equity is reduced to $45,360. After the second consecutive loss, the account is down over 50%, and a gain of more than 100% is required to recover the losses. If there are more losing trades, the drawdown will increase to a level where recovery will be impossible for all practical purposes. It should be obvious that this type of "optimal" trading is indistinguishable from gambling. Promises of high returns deceive anyone using this or similar methods for determining optimal position size, and they fall prey to hype made by individuals who are either careless speculators or lack actual trading experience. Even K% fractions, for example, what is known as half-Kelly or any other fraction, could result in excessive risks.

Systems without stop-loss

During the 1980s and 1990s, trading systems without a stop-loss gained popularity because locals in pits would chase stops even in liquid markets. I remember a situation from the mid-1990s during a visit to a friend's office to help him backtest some strategies. He was a CTA and managed client accounts. I arrived just before the release of the unemployment report because I also had open positions and I needed to watch the market. My friend was long 10 T-bond futures contracts from a few days before with a stop-loss set half a point, or 16/32s, below the entry price. The position had an open gain of about 4 ticks. As soon as the numbers were released, prices plunged straight down by 20 ticks and hit the stop-loss; afterward, once the stop was triggered, prices surged back to their previous level and remained relatively stable for the rest of the day. That was a $5,000 loss in just a few seconds. I asked my friend why he did not use a "mental stop." He told me that a mental stop could cultivate a loss of discipline and diversion from the rules of the trading system. I had to agree with that. Using mental stops is only for well-experienced traders who operate almost mechanically. However, letting the market know about the stop was also not a beneficial idea.

To avoid locals chasing their stops, traders during the 1990s turned to systems that did not incorporate a stop-loss. However, there was a new problem that had to do with controlling risk because position size could not be easily determined. Speculative funds and CTAs found a relatively simple solution, according to which the customer was offered a choice of how much of a total loss was tolerable before terminating trading. The average response to this question was 20%. Then, the trader would invest 80% of the capital in T-Bills and leverage the remaining 20% in actual trading. This scheme provided a solution to the challenge of implementing stop-loss strategies during periods of high T-bill yields, but it also led to reckless practices, as some funds took excessive leverage to generate profits, believing that the customer's cumulative stop-loss would be honored. Often, the set-aside cash for trading ran out within a few weeks.

Traders and funds that do not use a stop-loss strategy currently employ a similar strategy. Usually, the trader sets a threshold that corresponds to a cumulative stop-loss, let's say 20%. For example, if the invested amount is $100,000, only $20,000 is used for trading, and the remaining $80,000 is invested in T-Bills. Then, the manager leverages the trading capital of $20,000 accordingly, which is usually determined by backtesting. To get the high leverage required, traders often make use of futures and/or forex products. The availability of high leverage is one reason that most systems do not use stop-loss trade derivatives or currencies.

Needless to say, the type of trading just described involves high risks, and in the low-probability case of an extreme (tail) event, there can be a total loss. Although some quants use the continuous version of optimal Kelly, also known as Kelly leverage, for determining the leverage factor, this method is quite ambiguous. This is because financial price series are non-stationary, and the mean and variance are not constant.

The Kelly leverage *f* is equal to the excess return (m-r) divided by the variance of returns, as follows:

$$f = (m\text{-}r)/s^2 \quad (7.9)$$

where r is the risk-free rate. Note that *f* is equal to the Sharpe ratio divided by the standard deviation.

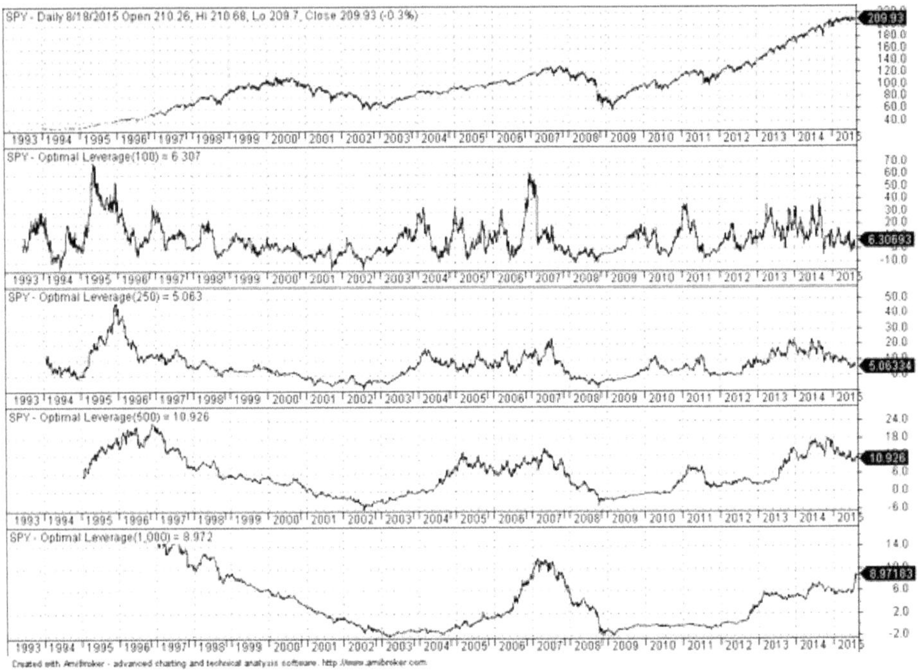

Figure 7-1. Optimal Kelly leverage for daily SPY ETF data and various periods

Figure 7-1 reveals that the period considered determines the optimal Kelly leverage (with r set to 0) in SPY EF. As of the close of August 18, 2015, and for a 100-day period, the Kelly leverage value was 6.3. For a 1,000-day period, the value was about 9. These wide variations make the use of the hypothetical optimal leverage ratio impractical. Another problem is that the parameters of the ratio become parameters of the trading system, thus increasing the danger of curve-fitting and data-mining bias. However, the most serious problem is that, often, the calculated values are unrealistic and lead to excessive leverage. Therefore, this book recommends against traders using such ambiguous methods. Claims of quantitative solutions that are unrealistic, except for simplistic casino games with fixed rules and payouts, are outright rejected as naïve. When traders hear the term "optimal position size," they should, in most cases, run fast because they are probably dealing either with a reckless speculator or with someone who has no experience with the markets and no understanding of the probability of ruin.

CHAPTER EIGHT
Alternatives to Technical Analysis and Conclusion

No matter how long or how diligently they try, some traders will fail because success necessitates being aware of the traps of technical analysis. There is always a small element of luck, even if we do not like to admit it. The development of trading systems to trade the markets profitably, using price series and backtesting, is a complex process that is not for everyone. The same is true about expert chart analysis. There are a few alternatives for individuals who either do not succeed in becoming expert chartists or quants. The alternatives include news trading and algos based on patterns from data-mining social media messages. There are also some esoteric methods, including the use of astrology and techniques based on precognition, i.e., predicting the immediate future. The alternatives are difficult to implement, and any success with them also requires discovering an edge. The author of this book has no proof that these methods work and does not endorse them. They are mentioned because some traders use them, and the lack of information about them could be considered somewhat positive. The information presented in this chapter is introductory because effectively employing such methods requires substantial research and analysis that is beyond the scope of this book.

Trading the news

Financial news is the primary driver of price action. A secondary driver is technical price action, i.e., when price moves because of key technical levels, such as, for example, overbought or oversold conditions or support or resistance levels. Economic reports affect price action in all major markets, such as equities, fixed income, and forex. For example, company earnings reports and corporate announcements can cause significant swings in equity prices, and weather reports can affect commodities.

Trading the news profitably involves a complex process of forecasting price direction and volatility that must be based on a solid understanding of valuations, economics, investor psychology, and risk and money management. The trader must know when news is already discounted and by how much to properly forecast direction. If there is a surprise in an economic report, for example, about the GDP or employment, the market may fluctuate for several minutes or even hours before finding a direction. Proper risk and money management are required for success, and without them, large losses and even ruin are possible.

Figure 8-1. A 7.1% drop in IBM on October 20, 2014, due to a negative earnings report

Figure 8-1 shows an example of a negative reaction to IBM's stock due to an earnings report released after the market closed on October 23, 2014. The next day, the stock fell 7.1% on a closing basis, from $182.05 to $169.10. A news trader could have profited from this move by anticipating the negative earnings report and shorting the stock a few days before the drop. However, executing such a trade can be challenging.

News trading is the oldest method and was extensively used before personal computers became available. Reliable information sources were used to determine entry and exit points. Nowadays, automated news trading is used at the institutional level mainly because of the high cost associated with subscribing to several reliable news sources and developing the algorithms for news analysis. The cost for retail traders is high for effective real-time news trading at the quant level. There are software products that scan the Internet for news reports about companies, but for news trading to be effective, it requires a rapid reaction nowadays. Therefore, it is highly questionable whether some edge can be found by searching news stories, as it takes time for search engine robots to index the relevant information. Part of the edge in automated news trading relies on the speed of receiving news and executing the trades. In manual news trading, the edge relies on the ability to anticipate the news and the right price reaction. For most retail traders, trading the news is a zero-sum game before commissions due to random price action, and it becomes a negative-sum game after accounting for commissions.

Social media sentiment and trends

This is an intriguing method that became possible due to the sheer volume of messages exchanged on social media daily. Trading on this information requires data-mining messages for patterns and implementing algorithms for monitoring social media feeds to calculate indicators that reflect sentiment and trends. In theory, traders can identify profitable patterns in the data. People also believe that sentiment and trends can impact stock valuations. However, no conclusive proof of such an effect has been presented. A hedge fund that exclusively traded based on Twitter sentiment closed a year after its launch, reportedly with a small profit. The rationale for launching such a hedge fund was based on a paper by Bollen et al. [Ref. 9] that concluded that Twitter sentiment could be used to predict the daily up-and-down changes in the Dow Jones Industrial Average with 87.6% accuracy. However, the referenced paper does not fully clarify the methods used to address data-mining bias, despite performing some form of validation.

The analysis of billions of text messages can result in spurious correlations that are challenging to detect. A notoriously spurious correlation emerged in 2011 when it was found that when a famous actress was in the news, a company with the same name would exhibit erratic price action behavior. While similar spurious correlations are rare, they may become more frequent as the volume of messages increases. This phenomenon is related to the data-mining bias that arises from the continuous use of historical data, as discussed in Chapter Six. For the results to be significant, they have to be validated in some way. For example, analysis finds that when it rains in New York, the price of stock XYZ falls. Validating this result requires going beyond text messages and getting access to weather data to backtest an event-driven algorithm on historical XYZ data. Due to the problem of multiple comparisons and data mining bias, such a process will generate many spurious correlations. Due to the sheer number of uncorrelated strategies that can arise from text messages, data mining for patterns may produce bias levels significantly larger than those generated by the technical indicators process outlined in Chapter Six, Figure 6-3. Therefore, after correcting for multiple comparisons, the statistical significance of any results obtained from data mining text messages is effectively 0. One can still find genuine correlations in social media messages, but statistical significance is an issue.

Social media bots and the possibility of using them to spread rumors on social media platforms are a problem when developing mood indicators. There have been instances of "pump and dump" schemes using social networks, leading to legal prosecution. This outcome is not relevant to those who used the sentiment indicators to trade. Despite that, the data mining of social media messages is considered a hot research area, and there is probably some potential here, but only for those who will be able to identify an edge. A true edge based on social media messages is probably rarer than trading with traditional technical analysis due to the need to develop and apply suitable noise filters. Concentrating on a few very liquid stocks, ETFs, currency pairs, or commodities may be a better way of applying social network data mining. Still, a challenging task is finding a robust algorithm that can offer predictions with returns above transaction costs. There is too much noise in social media; the amount of data is huge, and the trend indicators offered by the platforms are public and thus may offer no edge.

The VanEck Social Media ETF (BUZZ) inception day was March 4, 2021. The maximum drawdown was 56.9% on December 28, 2022.

Figure 8-2. As of November 17, 2023, the BUZZ ETF was down 40% from all-time highs and down 30% from inception

Finally, keep in mind that technical analysts produce a sizable portion of the daily messages on social media about the market. Thus, technical analysis indirectly affects any sentiment indicators. In addition, most of the authors of the messages are either Level I or Level III technical analysts (naïve chartists or naïve quants) that are trying to learn in the process of posting messages. Therefore, any sentiment indicators should be properly compensated for this fact. If sentiment ranges from 0 to 100, with values above 70 generating a buy signal when a value of 75 is calculated, a favorable fraction of that may be due to naïve technical analysis. Although the noise may cancel out in the longer term, in the short term it can cause a streak of consecutive losers, similar to those obtained when tossing a coin. Developing noise filters is a challenging task, yet it provides a significant advantage in data-mining social media text messages and social media analytics overall.

Esoteric trading methods

This book refers to these techniques as esoteric because they are difficult to categorize within a scientific framework and only a small number of people use them. They include trading based on astrology, the training of trader animals, and precognition. Trading based on the use of astrology is the oldest method of all. There are also several books written on this subject. Even some finance professionals have been involved with such methods. On July 7, 2010, the Royal Bank of Scotland published a paper under the title "Sheer Lunacy Staring at the Heavens." The paper claimed statistically significant profits from the study of the correlation between the moon phases and the behavior of the financial markets. The author of this book did some analysis trying to replicate the results for SPY ETF trading and found out that the apparent outperformance was during bear markets because these strategies were out of the market for almost 50% of the time. Therefore, the study revealed a spurious correlation. One cannot conclude the usefulness of astrology in trading based on just one study. There is a possibility that complex and significant astrological patterns exist that forecast price action. However, when one tries to discover such patterns using historical data, there is the danger of spurious correlations due to data-mining bias. The bias is even higher than when using only price data because of the addition of astrological data. There may be a signal hidden in the noise, but discovering a consistent, longer-term edge based on astrology, if it exists at all, is probably much more difficult than trying to achieve the same using automated data mining with historical data. The idea that astrological events affect prices is as unproven as the scientific notion of causality. Causality can only be supported in some counter-factual sense, i.e., with statements of the form

If the light switch is not turned on, then the room will stay dark

The above statement attempts to support a causal connection between the flipping of a switch and the light turning on in a room. However, the light can turn on due to other random effects, such as mutual induction of current in the electrical wires caused by electromagnetic waves from a passing car's transmitter. In that case, there is light in the room without any apparent cause. Any loose causality between particular astrological aspects and market prices is most likely contaminated by noise, which is similar to market noise but is a dominant effect. Consequently, the signal-to-noise ratio remains extremely low, and it cannot offer excess returns above buy-and-hold strategies. In other words, there may be an astrological aspect during a certain period that normally correlates with market rallies, but disappointing fundamental news may counter its effect and cause a reversal. Therefore, for those who would like to mine astrological data for patterns, fundamental news information should also be used. Such analysis is evidently a complex process, but it is manageable today because relevant databases and computer power are available.

Market participants anticipate moves in securities. The market is an anticipatory system. In advanced system theory, there is a weird class of systems that are called *anticipatory*. The output of such systems at time t depends on the future values of their input at (t+T). Thus, these systems anticipate their future input and act accordingly at present. Similarly, some market participants may be correctly anticipating or forecasting the price movement of some securities. Given a large number of market participants, it is likely that a small subset will correctly anticipate important unscheduled events and profit from options based solely on probability, rather than precognition. Thus, the occasionally unexplained rise in option volume before unscheduled news announcements may be attributed to random events rather than to some market participants experiencing precognition. However, precognition for very short intervals of time, such as a few seconds in advance, cannot be discarded as unscientific because it is compatible with certain aspects of quantum mechanics and relativity theory. However, elaborating further on this subject is beyond the scope of this book.

Conclusion

Trading and quant analysis are not for everyone. Even if one can master all the tricks, failure is still possible because of a change in market conditions that renders all validation tests useless. However, as long as conditions do not change dramatically and proper validation is performed on candidates for an edge, returns that exceed the risk-free return, or even buy-and-hold performance, are possible. Trading markets that exhibit an inherent longer-term bias is one way of applying a positive filter to the results. Based on randomization analysis from Chapter Four, a lot of random, long-only SPY traders can make money because the market is biased toward the long term. Adding a small edge to this bias makes consistent long-term profit from such markets quite possible.

High-frequency trading was not included in this chapter due to the costly infrastructure needed to implement it and the potential for future legislation to restrict it. It is doubtful whether high-frequency trading will disappear now that fast-algo traders have taken over market-making. Retail traders may use high-frequency trading services offered by some brokers, but success will depend on commission costs, slippage, and spread. In daily or even weekly timeframes, retail traders have a better chance of finding an edge that is unaffected by high-frequency activity.

One of the most important messages of this book is that the continuous use of backtesting with random ideas increases data-mining bias and the probability of finding spurious correlations. Backtesting should be used only when there is an idea with potential. Automated discovery of trading systems increases data-mining bias to even higher levels in a short period, and such methods should be used with caution. Even if we reduce curve-fitting by selecting parameter-less rules as the input, the bias in selecting survivors remains high. As argued in Chapter Six and demonstrated via an example, we can reduce the bias by selecting all results above a certain threshold.

Position size and initial capital determination are basic notions, but traders can be fooled by "optimal schemes" promising geometric growth of equity. These optimal schemes incorporate numerous unrealistic assumptions. In all markets, including forex, this author recommends avoiding leverage completely and limiting it to no more than 2x. The use of leverage is the primary cause of trader failures, especially for the undercapitalized group.

The simplest and most robust method of determining proper position size is based on the use of a small stop-loss in the order of 1% to 2% of available equity. If a stop-loss is not used, as is the case with some stop-and-reverse and mean-reversion strategies, then the trader must determine how much initial capital is willing to lose and then fully invest that in every position after applying leverage, but not more than 2x. Alternatively, a hypothetical stop loss could be determined based on simulation and then used to determine position size.

There are some alternatives to technical analysis, but there are still issues of data mining bias, such as in the case of social media analytics or when trying to find patterns based on astrological data. If Level IV quantitative analysis can't find an edge, other methods will be even less likely to. Dealing directly with price action seems to offer better chances for success in discovering a market edge.

Finally, chart analysis based on classical patterns and indicators lacks a logical foundation. The automated scanning of hundreds or even thousands of charts for patterns is a vicious data-mining operation that lacks validation and cannot offer significant results. Unless one is an expert with price action and has spent many years watching the tape, these methods of trading are not recommended. Traders need edges in the form of well-defined algos that are free of subjectivity. As the "collective data-mining bias" from searching for such algos increases, finding consistently profitable ones becomes harder. Users of simple methods for trend-following and momentum investing will possibly face a hostile market in the future. The claim that "simple methods work" is a result of the notorious cognitive bias of the *availability cascade*. As more traders adopt these "simple" methods, the probability that they will stop working increases fast. To succeed and profit from others' losses, traders must think creatively, disregard the advice of experts, and seek unconventional yet robust algorithms that other market participants are unlikely to discover. Only then do traders escape the second "singularity" that is about to take place. The first "singularity" in the markets occurred when backtesting tools became publicly available. Due to that, 95% of the technical analysis known at the time stopped working. The next "singularity" is taking place nowadays because of social media. The trading and investing methods that are distributed on social media will stop working in the near future, and in the process, the market dynamics will change to accommodate that. Not everyone can profit using publicly available methods.

I appreciate you taking the time to read this book, and I hope all your endeavors bring you success.

Michael Harris

September 2015 - October 2025

REFERENCES

1. Papoulis, A. Probability, Random Variables, and Stochastic Processes, 1965. McGraw-Hill
2. Campbell R. H, Yan, L., "Evaluating Trading Strategies", http://papers.ssrn.com/sol3/papers.cfm?abstract_id=2474755
3. Harris, M., Profitability and Systematic Trading: A Quantitative Approach to Profitability, Risk, and Money Management, Michael Harris, 2008, Wiley & Sons. Out of print.
4. Technical Analysis of Stock Trends, R. Edwards, J. McGee (1948)
5. Encyclopedia of Chart Patterns, Thomas N. Bulkowski, 2005, Wiley.
6. Investopedia, Relative Strength Index, http://www.investopedia.com/terms/r/rsi.asp
7. Harris, M., "Price Pattern Autopilot", Active Trader Magazine, September 2002, p. 70.
8. Contrarian Z-score. Tradestation Education.
9. Bollen, J., Huina, M. and Zeng, X., "Twitter Mood Predicts the Stock Market," http://arxiv.org/abs/1010.3003
10. Aronson, D., Evidence-Based Technical Analysis: Applying the Scientific Method and Statistical Inference to Trading Signals", 2007, Wiley.
11. Soosung, H, Rubesam, A., "The Disappearance of Momentum"., http://ssrn.com/abstract=968176
12. Harris, M. "Limitations of Quantitative Claims About Trading Strategy Evaluation", https://ssrn.com/abstract=2810170

About the Author

Michael Harris started trading stocks, commodities, and currency futures 30 years ago. Michael is the author of the Price Action Lab Blog website. Michael also develops and sells trading strategies and software designed to empower traders and market professionals.

Michael was a pioneer in developing software for identifying price action anomalies 25 years ago. In the past 10 years, he has worked on the development of DLPAL LS, which is a software program that can identify short-term anomalies in market data for use with rule-based and machine-learning models. Michael has also developed several new technical indicators for the analysis of price action and identification of market regimes, such as the Momersion indicator.

Michael has worked in the past for several financial firms, where he developed a program for optimizing bond portfolios and strategies for trading commodities and equities. He has also worked as a long-short equity and ETF trader for a hedge fund.

In 1999, Michael published his first book, "Short-Term Trading with Price Patterns." He published his books "Stock Trading Techniques with Price Patterns" in 2000 and "Profitability and Systematic Trading" in 2008, respectively. In 2015, he published his most recent book, "Fooled by Technical Analysis: The Perils of Charting, Backtesting, and Data-Mining Bias." He has also published many articles as an invited author.

Michael holds two master's degrees, one in mechanical engineering with an emphasis in control systems and optimization and another in operations research with an emphasis in forecasting and financial engineering.

Read more at https://www.priceactionlab.com/Blog/.

About the Publisher

Read more at https://www.priceactionlab.com/Blog/.

www.ingramcontent.com/pod-product-compliance
Ingram Content Group UK Ltd.
Pitfield, Milton Keynes, MK11 3LW, UK
UKHW020125290926
15471UKWH00003B/286

9 798232 430917